Brittany

Brittany made to measure

Brittany à la carte

Brittany in detail

Northern Brittany

Brittany made to measure

THE CLIMATE
As you may imagine from its proximity to the UK, the weather in Brittany
suffers from the same sort of unpredictability as its neighbour. However, it
does receive its fair share of sun and the temperature in the summer months
reaches an average of 24/25°C in July and August. June and September, when
the beaches are less crowded, can be delightful months, but whenever you go,
you should be prepared for the odd burst of rain. The coast in particular can
be very windy, although this does create ideal conditions for mariners.

A long weekend on
Belle-Île

Y ou will never forget this weekend because the island really deserves a much longer visit. The houses have brightly painted shutters, and the flora is almost Mediterranean – mimosa, palms and fig trees. The boat will leave you at Belle-Île's main town, Le Palais, but it is best to travel up to the little port of Sauzon (pp. 264–7). If you choose to stay in a hotel, book a room at the Phare, which overlooks the pier, as it would be hard to find a more romantic and picturesque setting. If possible, arrive on Friday evening so that you have two full days in which to explore the island. The best way to get around this little paradise is by bicycle so that you can reach the white, sandy beaches and the wild, wave-lashed coasts. Some of the most impressive and important landmarks to visit are the Grotte de l'Apothicairerie and the Needles of Port-Coton, both on the west coast looking out towards the open sea. After visiting the Grand Phare (lighthouse) and Goulphar cove, a lovely little natural port, continue to the Grand-Village. Beyond it the coastline is dotted with tiny coves, each with its own secluded beach, which are never overcrowded. At the other end of the island the village of Locmaria is a good place to stop for a rest, and Grands-Sables beach, on the north coast, is the perfect place to relax and soak up some sun. There will be just enough time to have an ice-cream and buy a few souvenirs at Le Palais before taking the boat back to the mainland.

A long weekend on the
Rhuys peninsula

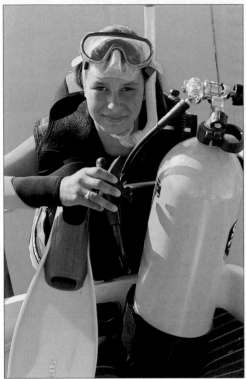

there are many activities on offer to the energetic, including scuba-diving, sailboarding and sand-yachting. The Grand Mont headland and Port-Navalo, at the tip of the peninsula, mark the place where the Atlantic Ocean meets the gulf of Morbihan. There are magnificent views of the bay of Quiberon and the islands of Houat and Hoëdic, and on some days you can even see as far as Belle-

The Rhuys peninsula is really worth seeing for its contrasting, windswept landscape, vast beaches, footpaths and several interesting buildings (pp. 262–3) including the old tide-mills, many of which have been converted into second homes. There is also the splendid Suscinio fortress, the favourite residence of the dukes of Brittany, and the Château de Kerlévenan, with its surprising Italianate architecture. The Saint-Gildas-de-Rhuys cliffs are wonderful for bracing walks. The ancient salt marshes on the gulf side of

the peninsula are popular with fishermen, who work from the shore and catch shellfish when the tides are high (pp. 40–41). You can even have a go yourself. The Rhuys peninsula is an important oyster-farming area, and fresh oysters are to be had everywhere. You can visit the oyster-beds, courtesy of the Association L'Ostréane (p. 263). The greatest attractions on the peninsula are, however, the extensive beaches of Beg Lan, Landrézac and Penvins on the Atlantic side, where

Île. A few miles from here you will find that there are two immaculately preserved tumuli at Tumiac and Petit Mont.

A weekend
in Guérande
and La Baule

This weekend break is like a journey back in time, from Guérande (pp. 284–5), the stronghold of the dukes of Brittany in the Middle Ages, to La Baule (pp. 286–7), a seaside resort founded in the late 19th C., which is extremely popular in summer. The little town of Guérande is protected by 11 round towers. It was, and still is, important for its salt pans. There are organised trips and guided tours to the salt pans (see p. 285). You can also cycle or drive around the salt marshes that surround the town. Local salt production had fallen into disfavour, but it regained its former importance in the mid-1970s. If you want to taste this 'white gold' you can buy it from small roadside stalls or sample it in local dishes (pp. 86–9). The best quality of sea salt is called *fleur de sel* (flower of the salt), fine crystals gathered from the surface of the water. The Brière National Park, further inland (p. 288–9), is a marshland nature reserve populated by migrating birds, otters and coypus. There are trips by water in a type of punt called a *chaland* (p. 289). Stroll around the marshes and reed-beds, or visit some of the charming little villages with thatched cottages such as Kerhinet (p. 289), also famed for its crafts, and Saint-Lyphard, which has a fine church with a steeple. Try to keep the next day for the beaches at Le Pouliguen, La Baule and Pornichet (pp. 286–7). You can go horseback riding in the morning, trotting or galloping along the beaches, or sunbathe when the weather is fine. If you have time, visit the *Espadon*, the former nuclear submarine at Saint-Nazaire (p. 290).

A weekend
in Nantes

or go boating on the river Erdre, whose banks are lined with châteaux and manor houses. After a day in town, visit one of the vineyards of Vallet or La Haie-Foussierè and sample some Muscadet. A trip to the vineyards will also take you to Clisson (p. 300–301), with its delightful Italianate architecture. A few local dishes will add to your enjoyment of the weekend. Try pike with white butter sauce, Loire shad with sorrel stuffing, or duck with Muscadet sauce. Follow it with pastries or cakes, such as *gâteau nantais*, a sponge cake flavoured with ground almonds and rum, *fouace*, a sweet bread originally baked on the hearth and said to be one of the oldest of French foods, or *rigolettes nantaises*, delicious candies filled with crystallised fruit paste.

T ry a weekend in Nantes, the historic capital of the dukes of Brittany, where the river Loire meets the Erdre and the Sèvre, about 30 miles (50 km) from the Atlantic Ocean. Strolling in the old town (p. 296), you will discover a rich historic and artistic past in its medieval streets. There are numerous museums (p. 297–8) one of the best of which, the Musée des Beaux-Arts, founded after the Revolution, contains superb examples of fine art. The Musée Jules-Verne and the Planetarium are well worth a visit, unless you would rather go window-shopping in the elegant Pommeraye arcade. The town

of Nantes made a great deal of money out of commercial shipping as you can see from the mansions built by the wealthy shipowners on the Île Feydeau. Water lovers can go canoeing on the Canal de la Martinière, near the river Loire, spend a day sailing in the Loire estuary to the seaside resort of Saint-Brévin,

A week in the
gulf of Morbihan

Take a good look. The numerous narrow channels surrounding the huge number of islands and islets, underwater plant colonies, quicksands, swamps and ancient salt marshes, make the gulf of Morbihan one of the most beautiful parts of Brittany. Vannes, the capital of the *département* (p. 258–61), is a convenient place to stay and from which to tour the area. *Morbihan* means 'small sea' in Breton, and as the gulf is protected from the prevailing winds it is a real paradise for boat trips. There are several possible options. You can rent a small motorboat and visit the islands at your own pace, but beware of the currents, which can be rather strong! Or you might prefer to let yourself be taken through the maze of islets on board a *sinagot*, a traditional sailing boat with square, brick-red sails. You could also go sailing with a local skipper, or you can even plan your own made-to-measure trip, thanks to the numerous boats that regularly ply between the various islands (p. 256). You really should visit the Île aux Moines, the biggest island in the gulf, and very wealthy. The Île d'Arz is less showy, but just as captivating. A coastal path allows you to walk right around the island, and

there are views of the gulf and the different landscapes – coves, beaches and meadows sloping down to the sea. Another day trip to the islands will take you to Gavrinis and the impressive cairn, which dates from the first human presence in the

gulf. This is an excellent place for viewing wildlife, from fish to many species of birds. The best place to birdwatch is southeast of Vannes, in the Séné marshes. There is an international bird sanctuary (organised tours with commentary, see p. 257). If you have time, take a plane or helicopter ride. The gulf of Morbihan is just as worth seeing from the air as from the ground.

A week by canal
from Redon to Josselin

Watching the sunrise on the Île aux Pies (Magpie Island) (p. 277), as mist rises on the canal, is a magical and unforgettable experience. There will be many other wonderful moments on this trip, but back to basics! Before setting out on your journey, make a point of visiting the charming old city of Redon (pp. 278–9). The Musée de la Batellerie, the canal museum, will tell you about the history of the canal. The Redon region is famous for the marshes that surround the city, which, with its abbey, dominates the area. One of the largest rock-climbing sites of the region is to be found here. You can stop at Saint-Vincent-sur-Oust and stroll around the marshes of Glénac, or you may prefer to visit Saint-Martin-sur-Oust and walk along the tow-path or take one of the various tours of the marshes and hills.

Near the Île aux Pies take a detour by following the river Aff up to the village of La Gacilly (p. 279), with its attractive houses, pretty flower gardens and window-boxes. Back on the canal you can sail leisurely through a wonderful world of local flora and fauna and see the chateaux, towns and villages of Brittany from a unique viewpoint. Start with Malestroit, the 'Pearl of the Oust' (p. 272). The village of Roc- Saint-André is perched on rocky slopes. Tie up for the night beneath the towers of the castle at Josselin (p. 270). Dine at one of its crêperies and sample a *galette de blé noir*, a buckwheat pancake filled with a variety of cooked meats, a delicious local speciality. Josselin's roots stretch back over one thousand years. It is worth taking time to stroll through its narrow streets lined with 15th-, 16th- and 17th-C. houses, chapels and ruined priories.

A week on the
Quiberon peninsula

You really need to spend some time here to do full justice to the region (pp. 246–7). In addition to the lovely beaches, mild climate and open-air cafés there are many other things to see and do, not least of which being the puzzle of the stone alignments at Carnac (pp. 248–9), as well as by the Stone Age sites of Locmariaquer (pp. 250–51). In addition to its spa and treatment centre, Quiberon is an unspoilt, family-oriented seaside resort, and is popular with water-sports enthusiasts. The Penthièvre beach offers one of the best windsurfing and surfboarding environments in Brittany, and at low tide a large stretch of sand is exposed, which with a stiff wind is ideal for sand-yachting. Portivy is a pleasant little port, south of which is the beginning of the Côte Sauvage (the wild coast), which is exposed to strong winds and

surf. There is a clifftop footpath that hugs the coastline. The cliffs have huge, natural formations cut out of them, with picturesque names such as Trou du Souffleur (blow hole) and Arche de Port-Blanc (arch of the white port). The huge rollers are perfect for experienced surfers, but beginners should be wary of the strong currents. The Conguel headland is at the tip of the peninsula, where you can see the ancient kilns that were used for drying seaweed, evidence of one of the unusual

traditions of the region. If you go north you will see Saint-Pierre-Quiberon, where the École Nationale de Voile (National Sailing School) is situated, and there is a good view of Quiberon bay. From here, at low tide, you can walk back along the coast to Carnac, a distance of about 2 miles (3 km). To the west, past Plouharnel bay, near the Erdeven dunes, a naturist resort, you reach the river Étel. The best time to visit this part of the peninsula is during the Fête du Thon (tuna festival), an exciting event which is usually held in August.

Ten days in Perros-Guirec
and on the Pink Granite Coast

During your stay you will have the chance to enjoy long walks that will delight all nature-lovers. Water-sports enthusiasts won't be disappointed either, because there are plenty of opportunities for sailing and surfing. The best way to explore the coastline is on foot. The Pink Granite Coast (Côte de Granit Rose) begins at Perros-Guirec (pp. 144–5) and extends for 6 miles (10 km). Although pink granite predominates, there is an incredible variety of rocky landscapes. The Trestraou beach is linked by the Perros-Guirec Chemin des Douaniers (customs officers' path) to Ploumanac'h, which is famous for its towers of granite rock. Keep walking along this footpath as it hugs the coast revealing some extraordinary rock formations, shaped by millions of years of erosion. The jumble of granite blocks at Squewel is an amazing sight. You might want to go canoeing in the bay between Trégastel and Ploumanac'h, under the guidance of an instructor, to enjoy a different view of the scenery (p. 147). Enjoy a

sightseeing tour of the nature reserve of the Sept-Îles (seven islands), of which only the

Île aux Moines is accessible, or visit the Ile-Grande (pp. 144–5), from whose bird sanctuary you will be able to observe a unique array of puffins, gannets, guillemots and even little penguins. A path there will take you right round the island, and after your hike you can have a rest on the beaches of Trégastel, Pleumeur-Bodou or Trébeurden. Go to see the imposing menhir of Saint-Uzec at Pleumeur-Bodou or the Telecommunications Museum, which traces the history of communication from the telegraph to the early days of the exploration of space.

Ten days at
Cap Sizun

There could scarcely be a more invigorating trip! This wild and rocky region looks like it is at the world's end, where the sky, sea and rocks combine, but here you will find a multitude of things to do. Nature lovers can enjoy the unique experience of birdwatching in a truly wild place. You can also take boat trips in order to watch the hundreds of species of birds that live on the massive cliffs at Britanny's 'land's end', or you may wish to explore the Pointe de Raz (pp. 212–13). If you are lucky, you will witness the flight of small multicoloured birds which perform a kind of aerial ballet in order to catch the updraughts of warm air. Audierne Bay is another beauty spot (pp. 216–17) with its stretches of fine sand and huge breakers. If you would like to learn the finer points of surfboarding, go south to the Pointe de la Torche (p. 217), where you will be able to learn surfing under the aegis of the Fédération Française de Surf, which organises lessons. Alternatively, you might be tempted by sand-yachting or speed-sailing. Along this coast, which runs from Bigouden to the Cap Sizun, you will find lovely little

Left: (from top to bottom) the Trégastel coast; a street in the Ile-aux-Moines; the beach at Trébeurden

harbours. On the eastern side of the cape there is the famous port of Douarnenez (p. 215), which has a rich maritime tradition. If you are interested in the lives of the local fishermen, you should go to a fish auction. But don't forget to set your alarm clock as the auctions start extremely early in the morning! The medieval village of Locronan (pp. 218–19), with its many crafts shops, is also worth a visit. The same applies to the Île-de-Sein (p. 210–11). This island, which has 350 hardy inhabitants who have always made a living from fishing and growing potatoes in their allotments, is now starting to benefit from tourism. No cars are allowed on the island, and in the sole village, the houses are huddled together for protection against the elements.

Two weeks in
Saint-Malo,
the city of privateers

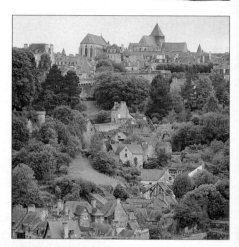

Saint-Malo (*above*), known in France as the 'Cité corsaire' (privateer's city) is the perfect point from which to explore Brittany. The old city, protected by its ramparts, is rich in seafaring tradition, as its nickname implies. There is the large beach at Sillon and the marina at Bas-Sablons, both delightful places to visit on foot (pp. 178–80). From Saint-Malo you can take short trips to explore the region, either in the vicinity of the town or along the Côte d'Émeraude. You can cruise to the islands or take a boat along the Ille-et-Rance canal, and from Saint-Malo there are regular sailings to the Channel Islands. If you are interested in technology you might want to visit the tidal power station on the Rance estuary (p. 171).

The Saint-Malo hinterland offers the possibility of delightful excursions to the *malouinières*, small 17th- and 18th-C. mansions built by wealthy merchants and ship-owners. Dinard in the west is a seaside resort that has something rather English about it and offers a variety of water-sports (pp. 176–67). Cancale (*below*), east of Saint Malo, is famous for its oysters (pp. 192–3). Between the two, on the Côte d'Émeraude, there is a succession of beaches and cliffs. Stop off at Cap Fréhel, which juts out 240 ft (72 m) into the sea and is topped by the fort of La Latte. There are many guided rambles, with explanations about the local fauna and flora (p. 173). Inland, you can take a trip down the river Rance, and if you do so, make a detour into the Dinan region (*top*) (p. 182–3). The feudal city of Dinan is the birthplace of Bertrand Du Guesclin (*c.*1320–80), a great military leader and the scourge of the English, whom he almost drove out of France. The town is one of the most beautiful in Brittany.

Two weeks in the
Land of legends

Brocéliande, Pontivy, Blavet valley

Exploring inland in Brittany is a very worthwhile pursuit. Your first stop should be the forest of Paimpont and mysterious Brocéliande, which is crisscrossed with bridle paths and footpaths. See if you can find the fountain of Barenton or the Val sans Retour (the valley of no return) and look for Vivian the fairy and Merlin the magician. If you visit the Château de Comper you will find the Arthurian Legend Centre (p. 275), which holds

exhibitions about the Arthurian legend, and will help you to understand the history of the region. The tourist office in the village of Tréhorenteuc organises guided tours of the area. Not far from the abbey and the lake, the Étang de Paimpont, where you can hire a pedalo, you may want to see the evil imp devil on the pulpit of the church at Campénéac. After a stop in

the Ploërmel forest (pp. 272–3), continue on to Josselin (pp. 268–9), where you can hire a boat and get to Pontivy and the Blavet valley on the canal that runs from Nantes to Brest. The river, whose flow varies in places from a slow-moving stream to a raging torrent, passes through superb landscapes, which can also be reached on foot. There are lots of ways to explore the valley. You can travel on horseback, in a landau, by bike, by canoe and even by microlight! This is also an ideal spot for angling, for the river Blavet is full of fish. If you travel a little further from the water, you will

find peace and solitude in Pont-en-Guern, a quiet resort, unspoilt by the pressures of modern life, which has an inn with bungalow accommodation, a swimming pool and recreational facilities for children. You might like to spend two or three days in the heart of one of the last surviving areas of the Breton *bocage* (wilderness). You can then travel on to Baud (pp. 242–3) and the beautiful and peaceful Camors forest.

Brittany à la carte

Megalithic sites 48

Religious heritage 54

Boating, sailing and yachting 18

Sporting holidays 24

Beaches and islands 30

Fishing and angling 36

Breton festivals 58

Boating, sailing and yachting

Where are the best places to berth in Brittany? Where can you watch regattas and yacht races? Where can you take a trip in a tall ship or a barge? Exactly what are the Stations Voile? Here are the answers.

① Brest

Moulin-Blanc marina (1325 berths). Sailing harbour
p. 122.

② Perros-Guirec

(600 berths on a pontoon). Stop-over point of the Tour de France à la Voile. Regattas.
p. 144.

③ Saint-Quay

New marina (1000 berths). Boat trips between Saint-Quay and Binic or in the estuary of the Trieux.
p. 159.

④ Pléneuf-Val-André

Dahouët harbour (313 berths).
p. 167.

⑤ Saint-Cast-le-Guildo

Fête de la Mer at Saint-Jacut (sea festival).
p. 175.

⑥ Saint-Malo

Sailing harbour of the Bas-Sablons (1200 places). Cruises on board *Le Renard*, replica of Surcouf's ship.
p. 180.

⑦ Morgat

Catamaran and surfboarding courses.
p. 205.

⑧ Douarnenez

Tréboul marina. Port museum (tall ships and old boats).
p. 215.

⑨ Bénodet

Sainte-Marine marina. Hiring reproductions of old barges to sail up the river Odet.
pp. 226-227.

⑩ Fouesnant

Port-la-Forêt marina (700 berths) and La Forêt-Fouesnant.
p. 231.

⑪ Pont-Aven

Marina.
p. 233.

⑫ Lorient

Water-sports in Larmor-Plage and Port-Louis.
p. 237.

⑬ Île de Groix

Port-Tudy marina.
p. 238.

⑭ Quiberon

Port-Haliguen marina. (900 berths). Regattas in summer. National sailing school of Saint-Pierre-Quiberon.
p. 247.

⑮ La Trinité-sur-Mer

Marina (1000 berths). Regattas, races.
p. 249.

⑦ *Towns that have Stations Voile status*

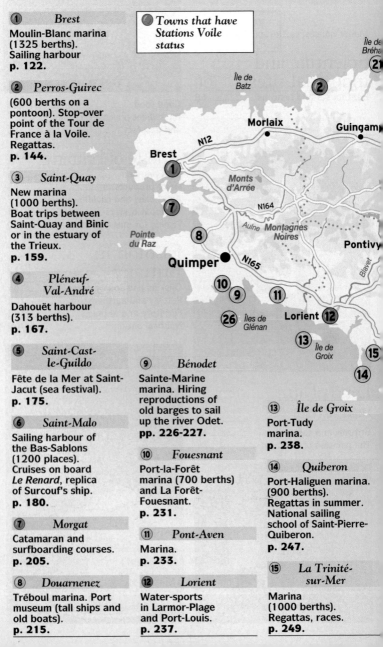

Île de Bréha

Île de Batz

Île de Groix

Morlaix

Guingam

Brest

N12

Monts d'Arrée

N164

Aulne Montagnes Noires

Pontivy

Pointe du Raz

Quimper

N165

Blavet

Lorient

Îles de Glénan

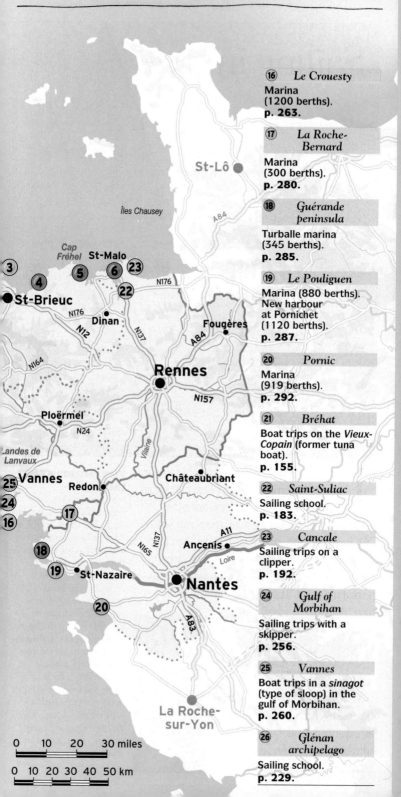

16 *Le Crouesty*

Marina
(1200 berths).
p. 263.

17 *La Roche-Bernard*

Marina
(300 berths).
p. 280.

18 *Guérande peninsula*

Turballe marina
(345 berths).
p. 285.

19 *Le Pouliguen*

Marina (880 berths).
New harbour
at Pornichet
(1120 berths).
p. 287.

20 *Pornic*

Marina
(919 berths).
p. 292.

21 *Bréhat*

Boat trips on the *Vieux-Copain* (former tuna boat).
p. 155.

22 *Saint-Suliac*

Sailing school.
p. 183.

23 *Cancale*

Sailing trips on a clipper.
p. 192.

24 *Gulf of Morbihan*

Sailing trips with a skipper.
p. 256.

25 *Vannes*

Boat trips in a *sinagot* (type of sloop) in the gulf of Morbihan.
p. 260.

26 *Glénan archipelago*

Sailing school.
p. 229.

Sailing in style

This special area, cut off from the Odet estuary, is a yachtsman's dream. The clear blue waters and the iridescent white sand make the Glénan islands a mecca for water-sports enthusiasts. The École des Glénans, founded in 1947 by Philippe Vianney, is not only a training school for yachtsmen but also a social centre for enthusiasts well-known around the world. The 10,000 or so trainees who have attended the school have entered a veritable temple dedicated to the sea. In its 50 years of existence, the school's training ships, the *Vaurien*, the *Caravelle*, the *Corsaire* and the *Mousquetaire*, have become legendary. Whether you are an experienced sailor or a novice, whether you sail a dinghy or a yacht, this is the place to learn.

Why Bretons are the best

From Marc and Yves Pajot from La Baule, Olympic sailing dinghy champions in 1972, to Anne and Maud Herbert, world windsurfing champions, Brittany keeps producing world-class water-sports athletes, in regattas as well as in off-shore racing. This is partly because of local tradition and the huge number of water-sports clubs all along the Brittany coastline. The main reason for this supremacy, however, lies in the fact that sailing and weather conditions in this part of the world are extraordinarily diverse. There are changing winds, strong currents, neap tides and an abundance of rocks. Nowhere else in the world will you be

able to find so many varied and often difficult conditions in which to learn how to handle a boat. 'If you can sail in Brittany, you can sail anywhere,' says the adage. And it is true!

50 years later

Nowadays, the École de Glénans has established branches in Corsica, on the French Riviera, in Baltimore and in Ireland. Every year, a thousand graduates volunteer to take beginners in hand and show them the ropes. The Glénans school has about 1,000 places on approximately 200 cruisers and 1,000 more on 300 sailing dinghies. There are also sailboards and coastal cruisers. The school publishes the *Glénans Navigation Course* of which 700,000 copies have been sold to date, and a teaching course is available on CD-ROM. These works are a sailor's bible, whether they are beginners or more experienced. You will have to book well in advance for a training course. (Centre Nautique des Glénans, Place Philippe-Vianney, 29900 Concarneau, ☎ 02 98 97 14 84.)

The Station Voile

Many towns in Brittany have been granted the title of *Station Voile* (sailing resort). They include Saint-Malo, Brest, Concarneau and Lorient, and the designation guarantees that the training and supervision are effective and that the trainees are well looked after. It also means that you can sail throughout the year. Wherever this title is granted, the town in question boasts several different water-

sports clubs and centres. They will all be listed at the local tourist office. Towns with *Station Voile* status are listed on pp. 18–19.

For beginners and for others

The 420 is a class of sailing dinghy that is easy to handle, fairly stable, lively but not oversensitive. Though it has rather fallen out of fashion, most yacht clubs still own some, and you could ask for a reduction if you choose to sail in one. Nowadays, many schools prefer small catamarans. These craft are practical, easy to handle, sensitive and respond to the slightest movement of the tiller.

They are also very forgiving and can therefore cope with beginners' errors. The size of the sail can vary, but you won't get up speed if there is little wind about. The vessels are excellent for teaching novices. Faster catamarans, with larger sails, are also available for more experienced sailors, and although they are much more difficult to handle they can produce a real thrill!

Yacht racing

Brittany is at the heart of yacht racing, whether as the point of departure, the point of arrival, or just as a stopover. The five major yacht races are the Spi *Ouest-France*, the most important French race, from La Trinité-sur-Mer; the Obélix Trophy in Bénodet; the Grand Prix du Crouesty; the Round the World in Eighty Days, or Jules-Verne Trophy race, which starts from Brest and finishes at Olivier de Kersauson (it can also start from the coast of England); and the Route du Rhum (rum road), held every four years, from Saint-Malo to Pointe-à-Pitre. The best place to see the tall ships set sail is at Cap Fréhel, but be advised that there will be a huge crowd! Two other important races are the Tour de France à la Voile, held in July, and the *Figaro*

Solitaire, an ultra-fast single-hull race, which usually sails round Brittany. Watching them is an unforgettable experience! (Information: UNCL, ☎ 01 46 04 17 80.)

Privateering and the privateers

P rivateering is not piracy, although the practices of piracy were its inspiration. The rules were laid down in the 17th C., when it was agreed that to provision a privateer the owner needed a 'war commission', a letter from the king, authorising him to 'hunt' enemy ships. Privateering (known in French as *la course*) is the continuation of trade in wartime. The privateer's goal was not to fight the enemy but to acquire spoils. This economic warfare enriched France and weakened the enemy.

The Intrépide, *boarding the brig* Maria-Stevens (1803)

The myth of Saint-Malo

Saint-Malo was the leading-privateering city in the 16th and 17th C. Its privateers pillaged the British, ransomed the Dutch and stole from the Spaniards, yet the booty they accumulated – a large part of which was delivered to the king of France – was a trifle compared with the wealth the town derived from cod-fishing off Newfoundland and the clandestine trade run from Saint-Malo, whose sailors rounded Cape Horn to deliver the basic necessities to the colonists of Peru. A bucket is worthless in itself, but it is worth its weight in gold if there are none to be had. In the 16th C. the Spaniards paid for such items in gold. The Falklands, known in Spanish as La Malvinas and in French as Les Malouines, are reminders of the trade with Saint-Malo.

René Duguay-Trouin

This famous sailor, whose dreams were realised, was a volunteer at 16, longing for fame and fortune, and a priva-

teering captain by the time he was 18! By the time he was 20, Duguay-Trouin's name inspired terror in the British. His greatest feat, an act of amazing audacity, took place in 1711. Leading a squadron of about 15 ships, he attacked Rio de Janeiro, a haven for the British and the Dutch. He destroyed the enemy ships, stole their cargoes and held the city to ransom. It was the greatest prize that had ever been collected by a privateer

The bastion of Hollande and the cathedral of St Vincent in Saint-Malo

and was never bettered. It was also the greatest loss ever suffered by the world's two largest merchant fleets.

The indispensable ship-owner

The privateer and his ship were largely dependent on the ship-owner, the key figure in ensuring the success of a mission. The owner financed the privateer's weaponry and was responsible for feeding the crew. In a way, the privateer was sailing on the owner's money. It was a risky business, because if the privateer were captured the ship would be sunk and all the money invested would be lost. But if the privateer took Rio or the *Kent*, the profits would be a hundredfold. René Duguay-Trouin would not have been as successful without his brother, Luc, who financed his expeditions. Two ship-owners from Saint-Malo, Nicolas Magon and Danycan de l'Épine, became so wealthy that they refloated 'at pressing

Robert Surcouf on board the Hasard, drawing by A. Paris

request' the king's own bankers and contributed generously to the nation's coffers.

Louis Garneray, privateer painter

Garneray is a unique figure in this strange history. He was a bold fighter who enlisted as a privateer at the age of 14, but was as adept with a paintbrush as he was with the

sword. He sailed the Indian Ocean with Surcouf and was taken prisoner by the British. Garneray then spent 8 years on the Portsmouth hulks, hideous floating prisons from which few men emerged alive. Garneray survived and told his story in *Voyages, Aventures et Combats* and *Mes Pontons* ('My Hulks'). He was also a talented artist who produced several paintings of ports and storms, some of which are exhibited in the Saint-Malo museum. The famous *Prise du Kent par la Confiance* ('Capture of the *Kent* by the *Confiance*'), is in La Rochelle musuem.

Robert Surcouf on the bridge of La Confiance, drawing by A. Paris

Surcouf's capture of the *Kent*

Surcouf first sailed as a cabin-boy on a privateer at the age of 13, and he continued his apprenticeship as a naval volunteer, taking command first of a slave-ship then of the privateer the *Émilie*, in the Indian Ocean. His courage and the deadly blows he dealt to British merchant shipping earned him the nickname 'The Ogre of Bengal'. His greatest feat was probably performed in

French privateers in the English Channel (1834)

1800 when his small brig, *La Confiance*, in which he sailed the seas from Madagascar to India, attacked the 1,200-ton, 40-gun British warship, the *Kent*. Through a series of rapid manoeuvres, Surcouf made it impossible for the British to use their artillery. The naval vessel was boarded and in the bloody battle that ensued, the privateer emerged the winner. At the age of 35, Robert Surcouf returned to Saint-Malo, where he became one of the wealthiest ship-owners in France.

Statue of R. Surcouf (1773–1827) on the ramparts of Saint-Malo

Sporting holidays

If you want a holiday with plenty of activity, here is a selection of the best places for water sports, horse-riding, climbing and aerial sports amongst others.
For sailing and sailboarding, refer to the Stations Voile on the map on pp. 18–19.

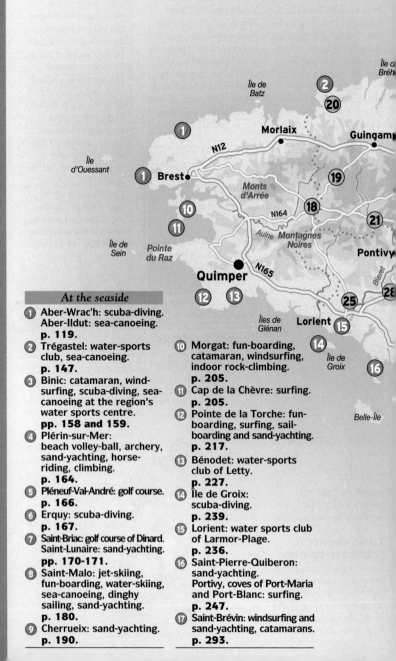

At the seaside

1. **Aber-Wrac'h: scuba-diving.
Aber-Ildut: sea-canoeing.
p. 119.**
2. **Trégastel: water-sports club, sea-canoeing.
p. 147.**
3. **Binic: catamaran, wind-surfing, scuba-diving, sea-canoeing at the region's water sports centre.
pp. 158 and 159.**
4. **Plérin-sur-Mer: beach volley-ball, archery, sand-yachting, horse-riding, climbing.
p. 164.**
5. **Pléneuf-Val-André: golf course.
p. 166.**
6. **Erquy: scuba-diving.
p. 167.**
7. **Saint-Briac: golf course of Dinard.
Saint-Lunaire: sand-yachting.
pp. 170-171.**
8. **Saint-Malo: jet-skiing, fun-boarding, water-skiing, sea-canoeing, dinghy sailing, sand-yachting.
p. 180.**
9. **Cherrueix: sand-yachting.
p. 190.**
10. **Morgat: fun-boarding, catamaran, windsurfing, indoor rock-climbing.
p. 205.**
11. **Cap de la Chèvre: surfing.
p. 205.**
12. **Pointe de la Torche: fun-boarding, surfing, sail-boarding and sand-yachting.
p. 217.**
13. **Bénodet: water-sports club of Letty.
p. 227.**
14. **Île de Groix: scuba-diving.
p. 239.**
15. **Lorient: water sports club of Larmor-Plage.
p. 236.**
16. **Saint-Pierre-Quiberon: sand-yachting.
Portivy, coves of Port-Maria and Port-Blanc: surfing.
p. 247.**
17. **Saint-Brévin: windsurfing and sand-yachting, catamarans.
p. 293.**

Îles Chausey

●St-Lô

Cap Fréhel   St-Malo

③ ⑤ ⑥
④
●St-Brieuc
⑦ ⑧
⑨
㉔   N176
㉓ Dinan   Fougères
㉒
N12
N164
Rennes
N137
N157
Ploërmel
㉖ N24
andes de
Lanvaux   **㉙**
㉗
Châteaubriant
●Vannes   Redon●
*Golfe du
Morbihan*

Ancenis
St-Nazaire   **㉖**
⑰
●Nantes
㉚   **㉛**
A83

La Roche-
sur-Yon

0   10   20   30 miles

0 10 20 30 40 50 km

Inland

⑱ Carhaix-Plouguer: canoeing and rafting. **p. 138.**

⑲ Callac: pedalos and swimming in the Verte Vallée; international cycling rally. **p. 141.**

⑳ Lannion: canoeing, rafting at the Stade d'Eau Vive. **p. 148.**

㉑ Guerlédan: dinghy sailing, pedalo, rowing, water-skiing, canoeing. **p. 160.**

㉒ Plœuc-sur-Lié: Avel-Dro paragliding club. **p. 163.**

㉓ Jugon-les-Lacs: swimming, dinghy sailing, pedalo. **p. 169.**

㉔ Dol-de-Bretagne: rock-climbing. **p. 194.**

㉕ Hennebont: canoeing and rowing. **p. 241.**

㉖ Ploërmel: water activities including canoeing, windsurfing, water-skiing. **p. 273.**

㉗ Rochefort-en-Terre: Île aux Pies, climbing, canoeing, mountain-biking. **p. 277.**

㉘ Baud: water-sports club Ével-Blavet: canoeing. **p. 243.**

㉙ La Gacilly: canoeing on the river Aff. **p. 279.**

㉚ Grand-Lieu lake and around Retz: microlight flights and canoeing on the rivers Tenu and Acheneau. **p. 295.**

㉛ Clisson: canoeing. **p. 301.**

Enjoy your favourite sport

N ot only will you be able to enjoy almost any water-based activity at any level in this region, but there are also many sports that do not depend on water, such as hiking, golf, horse-riding and cycling that you will be able to try during your stay. Contact the following addresses for more information.

sailing and windsurfing

For the best sailing conditions, try one of the *Stations Voile* (pp. 18–19), or any sailing school with the accreditation École Française de Voile, which guarantees the quality of the course.

Ligue de Bretagne de Voile
1 Rue Kerbriant
B.P. 39
29281 Brest
☎ 02 98 02 49 67

Nautisme en Finistère
11 Rue Théodore-Le-Hars, B.P. 1334
29103 Quimper Cedex
☎ 02 98 76 21 31
Information about any water sport in Finistère.

surfing

Surfing and surfboarding are taught and practised in clubs and surfing schools, which offer many training courses, so the bottom turn, roller and snap back will become a doddle!

Ligue de Bretagne de surf Croas an Dour
29120 Plomeur
☎ 02 98 58 70 69

Comité Départemental de Surf (Côtes d'Armor)
22 Rue de Nazareth
22100 Saint-Agathon
☎ 02 96 44 95 23

scuba-diving

Many clubs have activities for beginners, as well as guided explorations, visiting wrecks and even underwater photography courses.

Comité Interrégional Bretagne-Pays-de-Loire de PSM
39 Rue de la Villeneuve
56100 Lorient
☎ 02 97 37 51 51

Comité Départemental des Activités Subaquatiques (Côtes d'Armor)
B.P. 13
22560 Trébeurden
☎ 02 96 23 66 71

Comité Départemental d'Études et de Sports sous-marins (Ille-et-Vilaine)
Maison Départementale des Sports
13B Avenue de Cucillé
35065 Rennes Cedex
☎ 02 99 32 18 11

Comité Départemental de Plongée Sous-marine (Morbihan)
Rue du Lavoir,
56890 Saint-Avé
☎ 02 97 60 77 30

Sand-karting

It is no accident that Tadeg Normand, the sand-karting world champion, lives in Brittany. If you love speed, sand and wind, you will find them all in Brittany's 17 sand-karting clubs.

**Ligue de Bretagne de Char à Voile
12 Rue Frédéric-Mistral, 35200 Rennes
☎ 02 99 50 94 28**
(Same address as for the Comité Départemental de Char à Voile d'Ille-et-Vilaine (sand-karting committee).)

**Comité Départemental de Char à Voile
(Côtes d'Armor)**

**Centre Nautique Municipal, Saint-Efflam
22310 Plestin-les-Grèves
☎ 02 96 35 62 25**

Canoeing and kayaking

Whether you canoe at sea or on the river, a few beginner's classes will be enough to allow you to enjoy the world of water.

**Ligue de Bretagne de Canoë-kayak
8 Rue de Kermaria
22 300 Lannion
☎ 02 96 37 55 36**

**Comité Départemental de Canoë-kayak
(Côtes d'Armor)
6 Rue du 6-Août
22120 Plémet
☎ 02 96 25 77 02**

**Comité Départemental de Canoë-kayak
(Ille-et-Vilaine)
Maison Départementale des sports
13B Avenue de Cucillé
35065 Rennes Cedex
☎ 02 99 54 67 52**

**Comité Départemental de Canoë-kayak
(Morbihan) 8 Rue du Glévin 56150 Baud
☎ 02 97 51 02 70**

Hiking and rambling

The *sentier des douaniers* is a coastal footpath that passes through moorland and forest and is ideal for a ramble or hike in Brittany.

**Comité de Bretagne de Randonnée Pédestre
11 Rue de la Coudraie
– Brelivenez
22300 Lannion
☎ 02 96 48 94 71**

**Maison de la Randonnée
9 Rue des Portes Mordelaises
35000 Rennes
☎ 02 99 67 42 21**

Cycling and mountain-biking

Most tourist offices offer a variety of routes. Addresses are to be found throughout *Brittany* in the Close-up Section, pp. 110–307.

**Fédération Française de Cyclotourisme
Ligue de Bretagne
La Bouderie
35440 Dingé
☎ 02 99 45 00 86**

Horse-riding

Gallop along the beaches, canter through the forest or on the moor, or enjoy pony-trekking for a couple of days. All types of horseback riding are fun in Brittany!

**Association Régionale du Tourisme Équestre en Bretagne – ARTEB
38 Rue Laënnec
29710 Plonéïs
☎ 02 98 91 02 02**

**Ligue Équestre de
Bretagne
17 Rue du 62e-RI
56100 Lorient
☎ 02 97 21 28 58**

Parachuting

Several clubs offer this unique experience. Try seeing the region from another point of view!

**Ligue de Bretagne de
Parachutisme
Aérodrome de Vannes
56250 Moterblanc
☎ 02 97 60 78 69**

Microlighting

See p. 295.

Hang-gliding

See p. 163.

Climbing

Although Brittany's highest point, Tuchen Gador, is only 1260 ft (384 m), it has several rock faces that present quite a challenge.

**Club Alpin Français
13 Rue de Lorraine
35000 Rennes
☎ 02 99 59 28 76**

**Comité de Bretagne
de Montagne et
Escalade
32 Rue de la
Marbaudais
35700 Rennes
☎ 02 99 36 46 85**

Golf

If one of the great pleasures of golfing is to be in wonderful natural surroundings, you will enjoy the courses in Brittany, many of which are close to the sea.

**Ligue de Bretagne
de Golf
Parc de Lann Rohou
29800 Landerneau
☎ 02 98 85 20 30**

**Formule Golf
36–38 Rue de la
Princesse
78430 Louveciennes
☎ 01 30 78 47 75 and
☎ 08 00 26 07 91
(freephone number)**

Beaches and islands

This map will show you where the best beaches and the most picturesque islands are to be found and how to get to them.

① **Le Conquet**

Beaches of Trez-Hir and Blancs-Sablons.
pp. 116-117.

② **Saint-Pol-de-Léon**

Beaches of Sainte-Anne, Kersaliou and Pempoull.
pp. 130-131.

③ **Locquirec**

Ten sandy beaches.
p. 133.

④ **Perros-Guirec**

Beaches of Trestraou and Trestrignel.
p. 144.

⑤ **Pink Granite Coast**

Beaches of Ploumanac'h and Trégastel.
p. 147.

⑥ **Between Saint-Quay and Binic**

Beaches of Casino, Châtelet, Grève Noire, Comtesse and Port.
p. 158.

⑦ **Saint-Jacut**

Eleven beaches around the peninsula.
p. 175.

⑧ **Dinard**

Beaches of Écluse, Prieuré and Saint-Énogat.
pp. 176-177.

⑨ **Côte d'Émeraude**

Saint-Lunaire: beaches of Fosse-aux-Vaults, Longchamps, Grand-Plage, Port-Blanc. Saint-Briac: beaches of Salinette, Dame-Jouanne.
p. 170.

⑩ **Cancale**

Beaches of Port-Mer, Port-Pican, Port-Briac, Verger, La Touesse and the cove at Du-Guesclin.
pp. 192-193.

⑪ **Crozon peninsula**

Beaches of Morgat and Lanvéoc.
pp. 204-205.

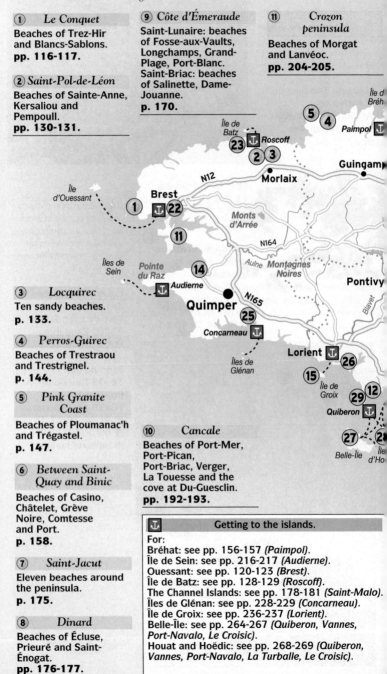

⚓ **Getting to the islands.**

For:
Bréhat: see pp. 156-157 *(Paimpol)*.
Île de Sein: see pp. 216-217 *(Audierne)*.
Ouessant: see pp. 120-123 *(Brest)*.
Île de Batz: see pp. 128-129 *(Roscoff)*.
The Channel Islands: see pp. 178-181 *(Saint-Malo)*.
Îles de Glénan: see pp. 228-229 *(Concarneau)*.
Île de Groix: see pp. 236-237 *(Lorient)*.
Belle-Île: see pp. 264-267 *(Quiberon, Vannes, Port-Navalo, Le Croisic)*.
Houat and Hoëdic: see pp. 268-269 *(Quiberon, Vannes, Port-Navalo, La Turballe, Le Croisic)*.

(14) **Tréboul**
Beach of Sables-Blancs.
p. 215.

(15) **Île de Groix**
Beaches of Grands-Sables and Sables-Rouges.
pp. 238-239.

(16) **The estuary of the Vilaine**
Pénestin: beaches of Mine-d'Or and of Damgan.
p. 280.

(19) **La Baule, Pornichet, Le Pouliguen**
10 m l (15 km) of beaches.
pp. 286-287.

(20) **Près de Saint-Nazaire**
Beaches of Sainte-Marguerite and Saint-Marc-sur-Mer.
p. 291.

(21) **Jade Coast**
Saint-Brévin, Saint-Michel-Chef-Chef, Préfailles: 5 m (7 km) of beaches.
pp. 292-293.

(22) **Brest**
Beach of Le Moulin-Blanc.
p. 122.

(23) **Roscoff**
Beaches of Traou-Erch, Saint-Luc, and cove of Perharidy.
p. 129.

(24) **Saint-Malo**
Beaches of Bon-Secours, Éventail, Môle, Sillon.
p. 180.

(25) **Concarneau**
Beaches of Cornouaille and Sables-Blancs.
p. 229.

(26) **Lorient**
Larmor-Plage.
p. 236.

(27) **Belle-Île**
Beaches of Port-Donnant, Herlin, Port-Maria, Grands-Sables.
pp. 266-267.

(28) **Houat**
Beaches of Treac'h-Er-Goured, Treac'h-Salus and Treac'h-Er-Venigued.
p. 268.

(29) **Quiberon**
Grande Plage and beach of Saint-Pierre-Quiberon.
p. 246.

(12) **Carnac**
Five beaches.
p. 249.

(13) **Rhuys peninsula**
Beaches of Kervert and Fogeo.
p. 263.

(17) **Le Croisic**
Beaches of Port-Lin, Saint-Valentin and Saint-Michel.
p. 282.

(18) **Guérande**
Beach of Grande-Falaise.
p. 285.

Tides and the sea

Brittany has a very large tidal range – that is to say, there is a significant difference between the level of the sea at high and low tide. At low tide the sea recedes for a long way and the exposed area of shore is called the *estran* in French. This area is used by fishermen looking for shellfish or by those who enjoy sand-yachting, speed-sailing and kite-flying.

What are tides?

The rise and fall of the water level in the oceans of the world are the result of the gravitational forces operating between the Earth, sun and moon.

Spring tide or neap tide

When the moon is new or full (syzygial), the sun is in line with the moon and the Earth and produces an additional attraction. The resulting tides, which are called 'spring tides', are then higher than usual. On the quadratures, that is when the line joining the moon to the Earth forms a right angle with the line joining the sun to the Earth – the attraction is reduced and the tides are lower. These are called the neap tides. During spring tides, the sea recedes a little further each day – and comes in a little further –

until the situation is reversed and the neap tide ensues. During this fortnight, the sea will recede a little less each day and will come in less far. This cycle is perpetual and affects every coast in the world.

Tide timetables

Confused by our explanation of spring and neap tides? Don't worry. If you want to take part in any form of water sport during your stay you will need to know when the tide is in, so all you need to do is buy a tide timetable. These are available in almost every shop, sometimes free, but otherwise costing just a few francs. Tidal ranges are counted from 0 to 120. The upper limit of 120 represents the high tide of the century, 0 is symbolic only, because it means that the tide never goes in or out, as is almost

the situation in the Mediterranean and other closed seas. The closer the tidal range is to 120, the further the sea will recede. The closer the tidal range is to 40 or 50, the smaller the differences between high and low tide will be.

Spring tides

There are several spring tides during the year. The best, as far as fishermen are concerned, occur during the equinox, when daytime and night-time are of equal lengths. There are two equinoxes a year, on 21 March and 23 September. Solstice tides (when the sun forms a wider angle with the earth) are also very strong and will often cause major storms. The winter solstice occurs on 21 December and the summer solstice on 21 June. At these times, an expanse of sea-bed is revealed that is rarely exposed to the sun. On the Breton coast, this is the signal for the start of the huge ormer hunt (pp. 40–41).

Marine currents

In Brittany the currents are strong, especially during spring tides, although their positions are well known. Every tourist office will have information on these. The most dangerous tides are in the bay of Mont-Saint-Michel at Cap Fréhel, in the area from Le Conquet to the Île-de-Sein and also in the gulf of Morbihan. On some west coast beaches near Brest, swimming is forbidden because of the existence of *baïnes*, fast-flowing currents, which propel swimmers into the open sea. Beaches with big rollers can also be danger-ous. When the tide goes out,

be careful: riding the breakers will not necessarily take you back to shore, and they have a very strong undertow. This is another good reason always to bathe where there is a coastguard. If you are

walking on the beach or taking a short cut at low tide, make sure you will not be cut off from the shore by incoming water. It is always better to be safe than sorry, especially with children.

YOUR HOLIDAY LOGBOOK

Each year an official logbook is published so that sailors can record every movement of their boats, every point they pass and each stopping-place. The log also contains a wealth of information about tides, currents and various ports as well as other problems you may encounter if you are sailing, all in French of course. You can use the book just as a holiday diary to record your personal notes, memories or sailing stories. The books are on sale at every ship's chandlers and in the ports, but you can also order one before you begin your trip from Interval Éditions, 3, Rue Fortia, 13001 Marseille (92 F + 30 F postage). If you are using it as a logbook on board a ship or boat, remember to chart the region to which you are sailing.

From island to island

islands that faces the mainland has a flatter landscape and fine, sandy beaches, whereas the northern-facing coasts, which look out to sea, are rocky and jagged. This rule is less applicable to the islands to the south of the Brittany peninsula, although they also have cliffs and rock formations, some of which are very striking, such as the steep rocks on Belle-Île.

T he islands off the coast of Brittany get many hours of sunshine and are the habitat of rare flora and fauna. The ecology of the islands is fragile, and weather conditions and the number of visitors vary widely, depending on the season. Breton islands are exposed to dangerous currents, violent storms and, often, to harsh living conditions. They sometimes look almost inaccessible, but all of them have a long heritage, and the inhabitants have an unparalleled spirit of hospitality and solidarity.

The Pointe de Poulains on Belle-Île

Obtaining water

Fresh water has always been a major problem for those islands that do not have a natural supply. The only way to get water to them is via underwater pipelines, for those that are close to the mainland, and desalination plants and rainwater collection tanks for those that are more remote. On Molène, for example, some very modern systems of water conservation have been introduced to ensure that every drop of water is collected. Three artesian wells have been bored to combat periods of drought by using underground water. Other islands do not have this option and are forced to ask for supplies in dry spells from water-tankers belonging to the French navy.

The reefs of Bréhat

Islands with a thousand faces

The Breton islands are scattered around a single massif, between the English Channel and the Atlantic Ocean. The islands are distinguished more by their differences than by their resemblances. In northern Brittany, the part of the

Alone on an island

Although the lack of entertainment and confined space have led to very active social groups and sporting associations, the isolation of

Île de Batz

Ouessant, Molène and Sein have lost more than the half their populations in less than 20 years. This situation is worsening with the proliferation of second homes for wealthy absentees, which have caused property prices to soar. In Bréhat land is more expensive per sq metre than it is in the fashionable 16th district of Paris! As a result, the population is ageing and is not being renewed.

The Treach-er-Goured beach on the Île d'Houat

the islands has some disadvantages. Staple goods, which have to be brought from the mainland, are generally as much as 30% more expensive on the island. Tourism means that boat crossings tend to favour the mainland to island direction rather than the other way round, consequently islanders sometimes have to spend a night on the mainland because there is no transport home in the evenings. Deep-sea fishermen leave their wives in very difficult living conditions and with extra work, although there is the compensation of a freedom that is experienced nowhere else.

Victims of depopulation

Faced with the decline of fishing and agriculture, and accompanied by mass emigration to the mainland, most of the islands have turned to tourism to survive.

Tourist invasion

Bréhat has 250 inhabitants in winter, but 6,000 visitors a day in summer. In season there are 10,000 a day on Belle-Île and 50,000 on the Ile-de-Sein, which has only 140 visitors out of season. These examples show the extent of the summer invasion. Although their ability to accommodate such numbers has improved over

the years, it is still a strain. The islanders have worked hard to preserve the islands, and cars cannot be taken to all of them. You are strongly advised, therefore, to leave your car on the mainland, and proceed by foot. Wear hiking boots because most islands have wonderful networks of footpaths, which allow you to explore them freely, on walks and rambles.

Ile de Batz

Fishing and angling

Brittany is, of course, famous for sea-fishing. It also has a number of rivers that are brimming with fish, creating a paradise for anglers, which the Maisons de la Pêche and the Maisons de l'Eau centres explain and promote.

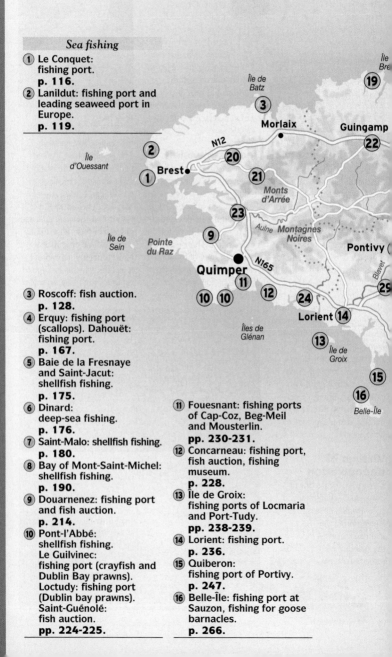

Sea fishing

① **Le Conquet:** fishing port. **p. 116.**

② **Lanildut:** fishing port and leading seaweed port in Europe. **p. 119.**

③ **Roscoff:** fish auction. **p. 128.**

④ **Erquy:** fishing port (scallops). Dahouët: fishing port. **p. 167.**

⑤ **Baie de la Fresnaye and Saint-Jacut:** shellfish fishing. **p. 175.**

⑥ **Dinard:** deep-sea fishing. **p. 176.**

⑦ **Saint-Malo:** shellfish fishing. **p. 180.**

⑧ **Bay of Mont-Saint-Michel:** shellfish fishing. **p. 190.**

⑨ **Douarnenez:** fishing port and fish auction. **p. 214.**

⑩ **Pont-l'Abbé:** shellfish fishing. **Le Guilvinec:** fishing port (crayfish and Dublin Bay prawns). **Loctudy:** fishing port (Dublin bay prawns). **Saint-Guénolé:** fish auction. **pp. 224-225.**

⑪ **Fouesnant:** fishing ports of Cap-Coz, Beg-Meil and Mousterlin. **pp. 230-231.**

⑫ **Concarneau:** fishing port, fish auction, fishing museum. **p. 228.**

⑬ **Île de Groix:** fishing ports of Locmaria and Port-Tudy. **pp. 238-239.**

⑭ **Lorient:** fishing port. **p. 236.**

⑮ **Quiberon:** fishing port of Portivy. **p. 247.**

⑯ **Belle-Île:** fishing port at Sauzon, fishing for goose barnacles. **p. 266.**

River fishing

20 Landerneau: salmon fishing in the river Élorn. **p. 124.**

21 Sizun: Maison de l'Eau, de la Rivière et de la Pêche, fly-fishing courses. **p. 135.**

22 Fishing for salmon and trout in the river Trieux. **p. 151.**

23 Châteaulin: salmon fishing in the river Aulne. **p. 209.**

24 Quimperlé: fishing for salmon and trout in the rivers Ellé and Laïta. **p. 235.**

25 Pontivy: fishing in the Blavet and in the Nantes to Brest canal, Maison de la Pêche. **p. 245.**

26 Ploërmel: fishing for perch, carp and pike in the duke's pond. **p. 273.**

27 Around Retz and Lac de Grand-Lieu, Passay: Observatory and fisherman's house. **p. 294.**

28 Ancenis: fishing for pike, pike-perch and sea eel in the Loire. **p. 306.**

29 Baud: fishing for pike, perch, salmon and trout in the Ével. **p. 242.**

17 La Turballe: fishing port (main port for sardine and anchovy), fish auction. Piriac-sur-Mer: fishing port. **p. 285.**

18 Pornic and the Jade Coast: fisheries. **p. 293.**

19 Tréguier: traditional fishing on the *Marie-Georgette*. **pp. 152-153.**

Sea- and fresh- water fishing

The diversity of marine life and the purity of river water in Brittany mean that fishing and angling are still fruitful occupations. The fishing industry was, with agriculture, the most important money-spinner in Brittany, employing about 10,000 men – more than half the fishermen of France. Freshwater fishing has many delights in store for the angler, who may be lucky enough to catch a salmon in the local rivers.

Sea-fishing techniques

Fishermen use different types of nets depending on the type of fish they intend to catch. The trawl is a sort of big purse or pocket that the boat drags in its wake. A distinction should be made between pelagic (surface) trawls and sea-bed trawls, which are the most destructive to the environment. The *fileyeurs* are boats that lay nets about 330 ft (100 m) long in the evening and pull them in the following morning or after a couple of days. The size of the mesh has been the subject of tough negotiations in Brussels. The *palangriers* reel out a long line to which a row of baited hooks is attached.

Above, top to bottom: mackerel, salmon and turbot

Right: unloading the catch at Saint-Guénolé

Sea fish

Sardines and, to a lesser extent, mackerel, have long been one of the main resources of the southern coasts of Brittany. Fishermen use a net called a *bolinche* or line-fish from ports such as Audierne, Douarnenez and La Turballe. Tuna, another staple fish, is nowadays trawled by factory fishing-boats sailing out of Concarneau or Lorient for the fishing grounds of the Azores or Ireland, or to the tropics for the fish that live in warmer seas. A few traditional boats continue to catch fish in the open sea during the summer, however. From July to September the unloading of the catch on the quays at Groix and Étel is always a big event, attracting tourists and locals alike, in search of really fresh fish.

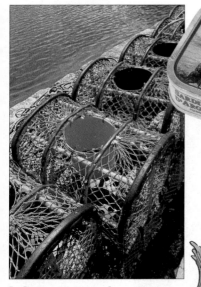

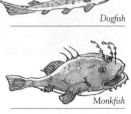
Pollack

Tuna

Dogfish

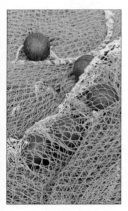

Monkfish

Lobster pots and crustaceans

A pot fisherman (*casayeur* in French) puts lobster-pots on the sea-bed in order to catch crustaceans. This type of fishing is essentially coastal. The boats are small – 26 to 40 ft (8 to 12 m) – and can be identified by their coloured buoys. Each boat may carry several dozen lobster-pots. Their catch consists of lobsters, which are now becoming rarer, edible crabs and spider-crabs. Dublin Bay prawns, the large shrimps that are the most popular shellfish in Cornouaille, are now exclusively caught with trawl nets.

Freshwater fishing

With 12,430 miles (20,000 km) of rivers, Brittany is not only a place for sea fishermen but it is also ideal for anglers. The *carte de pêche vacances* (holiday fishing registration card) is a permit that lets you fish on 15 consecutive days between 1 June and 30 September. Fees vary according to the *département* and the type of fishing. The easiest way to obtain a licence is to ask for it in angling shops or in the *relais* (cafés) sporting the *Saint-Pierre* sign, which lists the best fishing spots. There are about 15 such areas in Brittany. The list is also available from the **Comité de Tourisme Régional**, 1–3 Rue Raoul-Ponchon, Rennes, ☎ 02 99 28 44 30.

Trout and salmon

Although trout never left Breton rivers, the salmon is back after several lean years. Over the years the environment in which salmon thrive has been gradually restored to waters extending from the river Aulne to the Blavet in Morbihan, and the Élorn, the Éllé, the Ster, the Odet and the Trieux in the Côtes d'Armor. The biggest salmon are caught in March, and by June you may catch only a grilse, a young salmon that has spent only one year at sea. It is in the lower reaches of the river Aulne that salmon are at their most plentiful. As for trout, they bite from March to mid-September.

Shellfish fishing
'at the bottom of the water'

To go to the bottom of water' is the Breton expression used to describe fishing for shell-fish, one of the region's favourite activities. The coast abounds in shellfish, crustaceans and whitebait, which are all delicious. However, the would-be fisherman should be warned: everything is regulated. You must not use a rake to collect cockles; you are not allowed to collect very small shellfish; and fishing is only permitted in certain areas. Before you begin dipping into your chosen rock-pool, therefore, make sure it is not illegal (regulations are displayed in the tourist offices). The coasts are watched, and fines are always heavy.

Catching cockles

This type of fishing is as easy as it is pleasant! The cockles almost appear out of the sand when the tide goes out. If a cockle is buried a little deep-er, you can identify it by the little hole it digs and by the grey patch around it. Large sandbanks are their favourite

hiding places, and some of the best areas to find them are the bay of Mont-Saint-Michel in the north and the banks of the Étel in the south. The equipment you need could not be simpler – one bucket, a pair of eyes and your fingers!

Crabs and lobsters

Lobsters rule the rocky clefts in the sea-bed. Trawlers still bring back pots of them, but you will be very lucky if you manage to find one lurking between the rocks since they are now rare on the rocky seashore. Lobsters usually prefer to hide in rocky clefts with sandy bottoms, which is where they hide in order to moult. Velvet swimming crabs and edible crabs are far more numerous. The velvet swim-ming crab is a lively little crab found under stones. It pinches but does not hold on tight. The edible crab, on the other hand, holds on very tight. If one grabs your finger when you are hunting quickly break off the claw. Both the edible crab and the lobster would take off your fingers if they got half a chance.

The sand-eel, a slippery fish

One of the strangest of all the coastal fishing methods is one of the simplest, albeit some-what primitive. The sand-eel is a real will-o'-the-wisp, a shooting star. It jumps, rears up, twirls and finally buries

itself in wet sand under the astounded fisherman's nose. The Bretons catch it with a *cobêche*, a long shaft ending in a sort of hoe. As soon as the sand-eel jumps, flatten it with the *cobêche*. It will be slightly stunned and thus easier to catch. The beaches at Saint-Malo, Saint-Brieuc, south Finistère and the gulf of Morbihan are the best places to fish for sand-eels. Cook them by frying or baking them in batter.

Taking precautions

To be safe, only catch shell-fish or crustaceans that are still alive. If you are not sure how clean the water is where you are fishing (the Rance estuary, for instance), do not risk fishing there. If water is polluted to level 1, the shell-fish will be 20 times more polluted because they concentrate the toxic elements within them. Avoid catching crabs with soft-shells. Once collected, you will need to remove the sand. Wash the shell-fish thoroughly and leave them in salted water with added vinegar. This will make them eject their remaining sand.

King ormer

Ormer (abalone) fishing is forbidden in summer, and only ormer measuring more than 3 inches (8 cm) may be caught. It is forbidden to catch more than 20 ormers per person. Rules concerning the ormer are strict. For more than 20 years ormers were few and far between, and it was only at the beginning of the 1990s that stocks began to be replenished. They can be found during spring tides in deep cracks. Their colour merges with that of the rock, and you will be lucky if you do manage to find 20 of them. They should be sliced, beaten, then sautéed in oil, with garlic and parsley. Ormers are often considered the best seafood.

Excursions and walks

Quite apart from the well-known GR 34 footpath (*le Sentier des Douaniers*), whic runs along much of the coast, Brittany has numerous trails and bridle paths. The rivers also provide a way to explore the region. If you want to try something a bit different, hire a horse-drawn caravan as a novel way to see the countryside.

On the water

1. Brest: trips in the harbour with the Vedettes Armoricanes.
   p. 121.
2. Paimpol: mini-cruises on the Trieux estuary.
   p. 157.
3. Dinard: boat trips on the river Rance.
   p. 176.
4. Dinan: boat trips on the Ille-et-Rance canal, the river Rance or Nantes canal in Brest.
   p. 183.
5. Châteaulin: cruise on the Aulne on board the former sand-carrying barge, the *Notre-Dame-Rumengol*.
   p. 208.
6. Bénodet: cruise on a launch or on a barge on the river Odet.
   p. 226.
7. Auray: mini-cruises on a pleasure boat to visit the estuary of the Loch, the Etel or the Gulf of Morbihan.
   pp. 252-253.
8. Gulf of Morbihan: boat trips around the gulf on a pleasure boat or motorboat.
   p. 256.
9. Josselin: cruises on the Nantes canal in Brest.
   p. 270.
10. Redon: cruises on the Vilaine, the Oust and the Aff.
    pp. 278-279.
11. Brière National Park: barge trip on the canals.
    p. 289.
12. Nantes: boat trips on the river Erdre.
    p. 299.

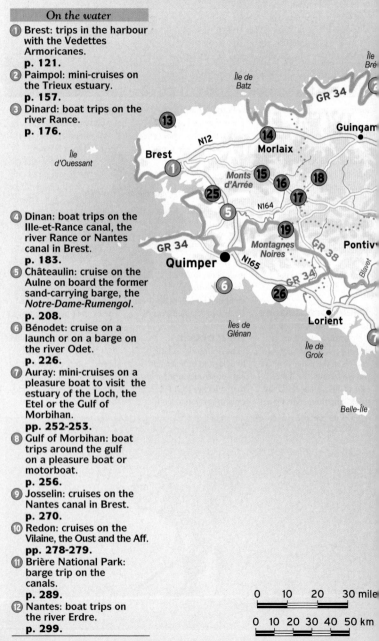

Île de Batz

Île d'Ouessant

Île Bré

GR 34

N12

Brest

Morlaix

Guingam

Monts d'Arrée

N164

Quimper

Montagnes Noires

GR 34

N165

GR 34

GR 38

Pontiv

Lorient

Îles de Glénan

Île de Groix

Belle-Île

13 14 15 16 18 25 17 5 19 26 6

| 0 | 10 | 20 | 30 mile |

| 0 | 10 | 20 | 30 | 40 | 50 km |

On dry land

13 Côte des Abers: hiking trails.
p. 118.

14 Morlaix: marked walks around the bay (GR 34).
p. 132.

15 Monts d'Arrée: walks with a donkey and along footpaths
p. 134.

16 Huelgoat: pony trekking and walking. Locmaria-Berrien: caravan hire.
p. 137.

17 Carhaix-Plouguer: hiking tours.
p. 138.

18 Callac: mountain-biking in the Verte Vallée and marked trail leading to the Gorges du Corong.
pp. 140-141.

19 Montagnes Noires: trails and marked, narrow paths.
p. 142.

20 Forest Plédran: marked trails for pony trekking, hiking and mountain-biking.
p. 165.

21 Lamballe: horse-riding, pony-trekking, biking and hiking tours.
p. 168.

22 Bay Mont-Saint-Michel: pony-trekking in the bay or hiking, following the course of the river Couesnon.
p. 190.

23 Rennes: marked hiking tours.
p. 199.

24 Fougères: hiking, pony-trekking and mountain-biking in the forest.
p. 201.

25 Landévennec: hiking to Ménez-Hom.
p. 207.

26 Quimperlé: walks on the banks of the river Ellé.
p. 235.

27 Rhuys peninsula: 50 m (80 km) of marked trails.
p. 262.

28 Paimpont forest: marked trails leaving from the Tréhorenteuc.
p. 275.

29 Grand-Lieu Lake and around Retz: footpaths and long walks.
pp. 294-295.

30 Blain: Gâvre forest, rambling, pony-trekking or biking.
p. 303.

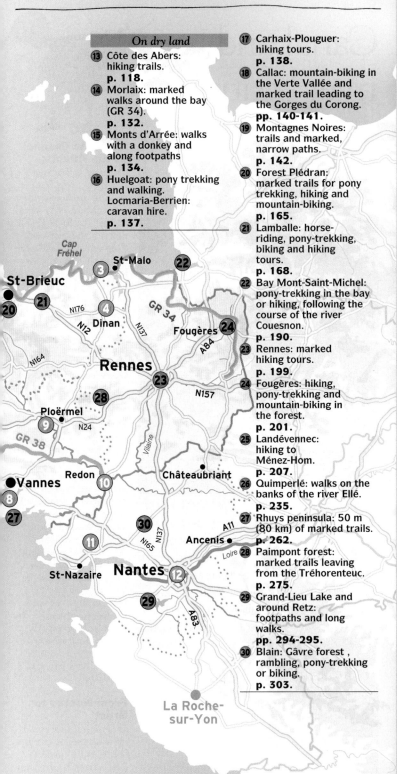

Canal and river boating

Brittany has more than 370 miles (600 km) of navigable canals and rivers, an exceptionally extensive network. From east to west and from north to south, there are landscapes which can be seen only from the water – granite and red shale peaks, deep forests and small valleys. River and canal trips take you far from the noise and bustle of the cities. You can travel at a leisurely pace, stopping at locks garlanded with flowers and mooring along the way to explore the mysterious castles and standing stones that you glimpse as you pass.

From the Channel to the Atlantic

Cruises set off from Saint-Malo for La Roche-Bernard, via Dinan and Redon – the main crossroads of the waterways and popular centres for river and canal craft – and go along the Ille-et-Rance canal following the course of the river Vilaine. From Rennes to Redon, the Vilaine is lined with half-timbered farmhouses, windmills, châteaux and manor houses buried in deep valleys overlooked by wooded hilltops and steep ridges. Le Corbinière, near the port of Guipry-Messac, is considered one of the great beauty spots of inland Brittany.

Boat hire

A wide range of boats can be hired. They are all easy to steer and do not require a licence to operate. The river launches and the small barges can hold between four and 12 people. Small barges, with a wide top deck, lend themselves better to slow trips than the launches, which are rather like floating caravans. You can moor wherever you fancy, go off on a jaunt to a village or take an excursion into the countryside. The cost of hire for a weekend or a week varies according to the type of boat and the period, but it will range from 2,000 F to 19,000 F.

From Nantes to Brest

The Nantes to Brest canal is not fully navigable, since it is bisected by the Guerlédan dam, but it offers exceptional opportunities for a cruise. After Nantes you sail through the beautiful Erdre valley before crossing the Gâvre forest and the marshes, which are rich in wildlife. Beyond Redon there is the Oust valley, with the delightful tranquillity of the Île aux Pies (p. 277, Rochefort-en-Terre). You can watch the rock-climbers as they scale the granite cliffs or hire a horse and ride along the bridle paths on the island. Next is Malestroit, with its many bridges spanning the river and its Gothic and Renaissance houses. Josselin is next, with its magnificent château, and it is followed by the lush green-ery of the Blavet valley. Between the harbour at Brest and Carhaix, the river Aulne, well known for its excellent fishing, is also navigable.

to the same level as the river upstream. The process usual-ly takes about 20 minutes. When the water reaches the required level in the lock, the upstream gates will open and you can carry on sailing.

Where and how to set off

Several routes are suggested by the river tourism com-panies. There are departures points from Sucé-sur-Erdre, near Nantes, from Redon and Messac in Ille-et-Vilaine, as well as from Josselin and Rohan, in Morbihan and from Dinan.

You can also hire a genuine river barge, the *Neptune*, piloted by its captain. He will take you from Chapelle-aux-Filtzméens in Ille-et-Vilaine. The waterways are generally closed to shipping from 15 October to 15 March. For more informa-tion, contact the tourist office in Redon at the Place de la République, 35600 Redon ☎ 02 99 71 06 04.

Going through the locks

If you are sailing upriver, the lock gates usually remain open to allow ships to enter the lock. Once in the lock, the lock-keeper will crank the lock-gate shut allowing water to enter and to raise the boat

Walking and hiking

With almost 3,100 miles (5,000 km) of bridle paths and footpaths, Brittany is a paradise for hikers, ramblers or the casual walker. The famous *Sentier des Douaniers* (customs officers' path) offers an unbeatable view of the sea, but there are many other routes that lead inland to such places as the mysterious Monts d'Arrée, where fog rolls around the fantastical rocks which cover the moor. Coastal paths, tow paths, footpaths, bridal paths – there are many different routes to explore for healthy and scenic days out.

Lighthouse (above) and Belle-Île beach (top)

Sentier des douaniers

Created in 1791 to combat smuggling, the *Sentier des Douaniers* (customs officers' path) was gradually abandoned over the years, and it was only restored in the early 1980s. You can now walk along the entire Breton coast from Cancale in the north to Brière in the south. In fact, the shore is part of the public coastal area, which means that those owning land beside the path must leave a 10 feet (3 m) strip between the end of their land and the limit of the highest tides. This is good news for hikers! The coastal path is, in addition, under the special protection of the Conservatoire du Littoral

(coastline conservation) in some areas, such as the bird sanctuary at Cap Sizun. Some parts of the path are unforgettable: between the Fort La Latte and Cap Fréhel the path is more than 160 feet (50 m) above sea level.

Long hikes

The longest trails for hikers are marked with white and red beacons. The GR 34, one of the longest, often merges with the coastal path, but does diverge from it at some points. The path passes between heathland and moorland through areas of remote countryside that are almost unexplored. The GR 380 path leaves the Armorican Regional Nature Park in the

Finistère region and ends in the Monts d'Arrée – definitely a trip worth making. Finally, the GR 37 path follows the canal from Nantes to Brest. Following the route from start to finish would involve several full days' walking, but the route can easily be followed in stages. There are plenty of places to stay along the way (for

information, contact: ABRI-Maison de la Randonnée, 9 Rue des Portes Mordelaises, 35000 Rennes, ☎ 02 99 67 42 20).

Paths for ramblers

Paths suitable for ramblers are marked in yellow. These routes can take from 1–2 hours or up to a whole day. The suggested routes often have a tourist attraction or a *gîte* as their starting point. They are not particularly arduous and are perfectly suitable for short walks or for families with young children. The islands, where vehicular traffic is often restricted, or even prohibited altogether, are among the most delightful places to discover on foot.

Specific routes, local paths

The most famous route is probably the Tro-Breiz, the pilgrimage any Breton wanting to reach heaven had to perform. It involved visiting the graves of the seven saints who founded the bishoprics

of Brittany. Brought up to modern standards in 1994, the path in May offers the opportunity of a beautiful tour of Brittany, taking in Quimper, Saint-Pol-de-Léon, Tréguier, Saint-Brieuc, Saint-Malo, Dol-de-Bretagne and Rennes. In the same way, several specific routes link various elements of Brittany's architectural

heritage (lighthouses and beacons around Brest, p. 69), culinary heritage (the Route du Cidre in Cornouaille, information at the Quimper tourist office, ☎ 02 98 53 04 05), or the cultural heritage (Cornouaille Artists' Route, information at the Groupement Touristique de Cornouaille, 145 Avenue de Kéradennec, BP 410, 29330 Quimper Cedex, ☎ 02 98 90 75 05). The local footpaths are identified by red and yellow beacons and consist of one-week walks, which will allow you to acquire a deeper knowledge of the cultural heritage of the region. This way, you can explore the Brocéliande forest or the Montagnes Noires around Gourin.

Megalithic sites

Brittany is full of megaliths, or standing stones. Follow the map and you will be able to tell the difference between menhirs, henges, dolmens and cairns.

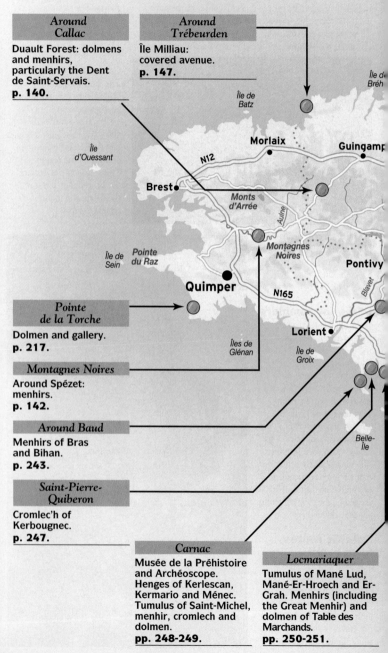

Around Callac

Duault Forest: dolmens and menhirs, particularly the Dent de Saint-Servais.
p. 140.

Around Trébeurden

Île Milliau: covered avenue.
p. 147.

Pointe de la Torche

Dolmen and gallery.
p. 217.

Montagnes Noires

Around Spézet: menhirs.
p. 142.

Around Baud

Menhirs of Bras and Bihan.
p. 243.

Saint-Pierre-Quiberon

Cromlec'h of Kerbougnec.
p. 247.

Carnac

Musée de la Préhistoire and Archéoscope. Henges of Kerlescan, Kermario and Ménec. Tumulus of Saint-Michel, menhir, cromlech and dolmen.
pp. 248-249.

Locmariaquer

Tumulus of Mané Lud, Mané-Er-Hroech and Er-Grah. Menhirs (including the Great Menhir) and dolmen of Table des Marchands.
pp. 250-251.

Île de Bréh
Île de Batz
Île d'Ouessant

Morlaix
Guingamp
N12
Brest
Monts d'Arrée
Aulne
Montagnes Noires
Pontivy
Blavet
Île de Sein
Pointe du Raz
Quimper
N165
Lorient
Îles de Glénan
Île de Groix
Belle-Île

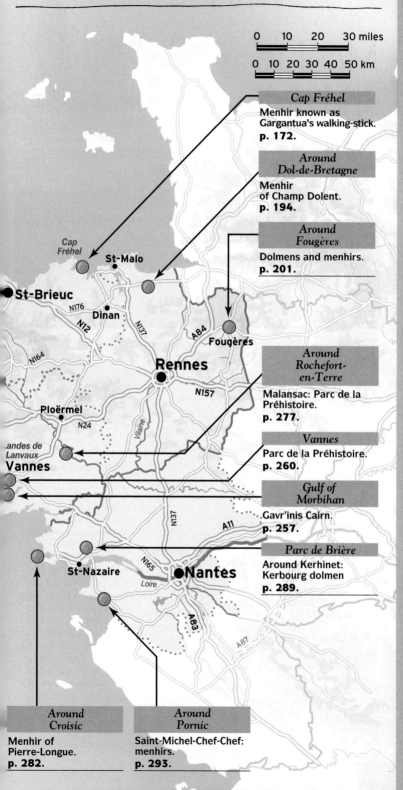

Cap Fréhel

Menhir known as Gargantua's walking-stick. **p. 172.**

Around Dol-de-Bretagne

Menhir of Champ Dolent. **p. 194.**

Around Fougères

Dolmens and menhirs. **p. 201.**

Around Rochefort-en-Terre

Malansac: Parc de la Préhistoire. **p. 277.**

Vannes

Parc de la Préhistoire. **p. 260.**

Gulf of Morbihan

Gavr'inis Cairn. **p. 257.**

Parc de Brière

Around Kerhinet: Kerbourg dolmen **p. 289.**

Around Croisic

Menhir of Pierre-Longue. **p. 282.**

Around Pornic

Saint-Michel-Chef-Chef: menhirs. **p. 293.**

Menhirs and dolmens

A menhir

The Kerlescan alignments

A dolmen

Brittany is a favourite place for archaeologists and historians because of the large number of megaliths – which means literally 'big rocks' – some of which date from more than 5000 years BC. For long a source of great fascination, it is now known that menhirs – the standing stones made popular by Obélix, a character in the Asterix cartoons – and dolmens – stone tables that often belonged to a larger grouping – were used as burial sites or places of worship.

Dolmens

A dolmen is a term used for either a simple stone table or a more complex arrangement, marking a collective burial place and consisting of several megaliths. These funerary monuments, some of which are incredibly large, were partially buried in the ground or erected on the surface and later covered with soil, creating a tumulus. Many dolmens consist of a long corridor leading to either one or several rooms formed from large stone slabs. They may also be surrounded by dry stones, when they are called cairns.

Cairns

Cairns are the most impressive of the megalithic monuments in the sense that they may consist of several dolmens, which are arranged in a very specific order. The Barnenez cairn, in the bay of Morlaix, dates from 5000 BC and is one of the most beautiful examples. The equally impressive Gavrinis cairn in the gulf of Morbihan used about 10,000 tonnes of stone and would have taken up to three years to build.

5000 years BC

Most of these monuments date from a period between 5000 and 2000 years BC. The way in which these stone monuments were built indicates that burial rites were very well developed at this time. The people who built them lived under the protection of a fortified camp and had given up hunting and gathering for agriculture and animal husbandry.
Their method of construction remains a mystery when one considers the dimensions of some dolmens and menhirs which weigh up to 350 tonnes, as well as cairns 230 feet (70 m) long.

A cairn

A cromlech

Alignments

Landing strips for extraterrestrials, petrified armies or a hail of asteroids? These are just some of the interpretations of these mysterious alignments. In addition to the funerary nature of numerous megalithic monuments, some menhirs, which may be as

much as 23 feet (7 m) tall, may well have served as landmarks. Moreover, very precise astronomical data seems to have been used in the alignment of the Carnac menhirs. They are oriented according to the summer and winter solstices and have cromlechs, or stone circles, at each end, the purpose of which is unknown.

Ornamentation

It has been possible to date megalithic monuments thanks to the engravings in the stone. In the 4th millennium BC these consisted of snakes, axes and other carvings, but 1,000 years later, these themes were replaced by those of daggers and relief carvings of female breasts decorated with necklaces.

Fashionable jewellery

Digs conducted at tumuli have revealed not only many objects and jewellery of remarkable beauty but also polished jade and fibrolite axes as well as precious stones. Some of these finds can be seen in the museums at Vannes and Carnac. There are beautiful necklaces made of callais, a sort of turquoise, as well as pearl pendants and other jewels that will amaze you by their sophistication and 'modernity'. These objects serve only to deepen the mystery surrounding this civilisation, about which so little is known.

The Kermario alignments

Celts versus Romans

The Celts arrived in Armorica (the Celtic name for Brittany) around 600 BC. Later, at the peak of their civilisation, they overcame the Romans. It was at the time of this important victory that their chieftain Brennus uttered the famous words 'Woe betide the defeated!' to the terrified enemy. The integration of the Celts into the existing population of Armorica split the area into different tribes: the Coriosolites, the Osimes and the Veneti. Armorican resistance to the Roman invasion was very strong, which explains how Celtic culture survived so well in the region. The best example of the Celtic cultural heritage is the Breton language, which is closely related to both Welsh and Cornish.

Incredible wealth

The golden masks, splendid weapons and abundance of jewellery found in Celtic tombs indicate the wealth and magnificence of their civilisation. There are also indications of the sophistication of Celtic daily life, and they were probably among the first peoples in Europe to use the chariot in war. In his *Gallic Wars* Julius Caesar records his surprise at the effectiveness of the war chariots. In the same way, while the Romans used the amphora as a large container, the Celts had already invented the barrel.

Necklace dating from the 5th C. BC, in the museum of Quimper

This was a such a revolution that it is comparable to the discovery of the wheel. The barrel remained the most convenient container for transporting large volumes until the mid-20th C.

17th C. engraving of Julius Caesar

The druids

The druids were the link between the Celts and the Gauls. They were a combination of warrior-priest and witch-doctor, and the Celts never took important decisions without consulting them. Druids believed in the immortality of the soul. The religious tradition was transmitted orally from one druid to another in a 20,000-line poem that was never written down. The great annual convocation of the druids took place in the Forest of Carnutes near Chartres. Certain plants, such as mistletoe, which they cut with a golden sickle, were invested with divine powers. In the same way the oak tree represented the deity. In Celtic hierarchy, the bards ranked just below the druids.

The heritage of the Celts

Armorica became more or less subject to the Roman Empire, until the disintegration of the latter in the 4th C. It then became a place of refuge for the inhabitants of the island of Britain, who were fleeing from the invasions of the Angles and the Saxons. The name 'Breton' dates from this period. The Celts and Bretons intermarried, and this union left lasting traces, particularly on the language. For instance, *lann*, in Celtic, means monastery or religious community, and *plou* designates a group of warriors. When you travel through Brittany you will notice many Breton place-names with these prefixes. These will seem unusual at first, but as you travel through the region you will soon get used to them. For example, Landivisiau or Landerneau were created by monks whereas Plougastel or Plouguerneau were founded by warriors. In both cases, the name of the monk or of the clan's chief often follows the prefix. Lannion was founded by the monk Ion, Ploudaniel, by the chieftain Daniel.

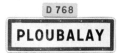

Breton family names

Breton surnames are very often Celtic in origin. You will notice how like Welsh they are. *Gwen* (or Guen) means 'white'. Le Guen, a very common Breton surname, is the equivalent of the French name Leblanc or the English name White. *Du* means 'black', *coz* means 'old' and *penn* means 'end', which will enable you to translate more

Vercingetorix addressing the Gauls

Breton family names. There are also some quaint Breton place-names, such as Aber-Wrac'h, which means literally 'estuary of witches'. As you can see, the similarity to Welsh is striking.

Religious heritage

Like other regions of France, Brittany contains many places of worship – Romanesque or Gothic chapels, churches, cathedrals, priories and abbeys. It also has its own special religious architecture, in the form of parish closes (see p. 57) and calvaries (see p. 56).

Churches, chapels, abbeys, calvaries

(1) Daoulas: abbey.
p. 127.

(2) Parish closes of Trémaouézan, Pencran, Dirinon and La Roche-Maurice.
p. 125.

(10) Pointe du Raz: Pont-Croix, Notre-Dame-de-Roscudon church. Pointe du Van: Saint-They chapel.
pp. 212-213.

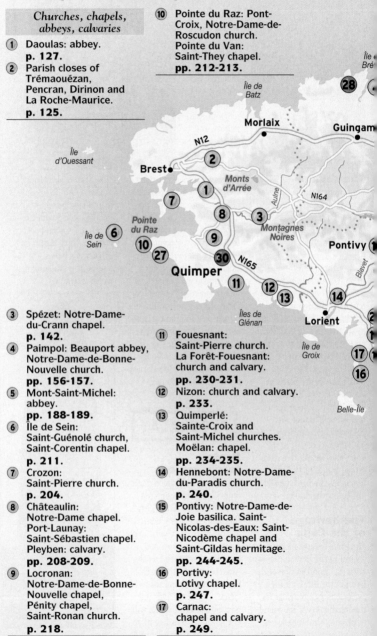

(3) Spézet: Notre-Dame-du-Crann chapel.
p. 142.

(4) Paimpol: Beauport abbey, Notre-Dame-de-Bonne-Nouvelle church.
pp. 156-157.

(5) Mont-Saint-Michel: abbey.
pp. 188-189.

(6) Île de Sein: Saint-Guénolé church, Saint-Corentin chapel.
p. 211.

(7) Crozon: Saint-Pierre church.
p. 204.

(8) Châteaulin: Notre-Dame chapel. Port-Launay: Saint-Sébastien chapel. Pleyben: calvary.
pp. 208-209.

(9) Locronan: Notre-Dame-de-Bonne-Nouvelle chapel, Pénity chapel, Saint-Ronan church.
p. 218.

(11) Fouesnant: Saint-Pierre church. La Forêt-Fouesnant: church and calvary.
pp. 230-231.

(12) Nizon: church and calvary.
p. 233.

(13) Quimperlé: Sainte-Croix and Saint-Michel churches. Moëlan: chapel.
pp. 234-235.

(14) Hennebont: Notre-Dame-du-Paradis church.
p. 240.

(15) Pontivy: Notre-Dame-de-Joie basilica. Saint-Nicolas-des-Eaux: Saint-Nicodème chapel and Saint-Gildas hermitage.
pp. 244-245.

(16) Portivy: Lotivy chapel.
p. 247.

(17) Carnac: chapel and calvary.
p. 249.

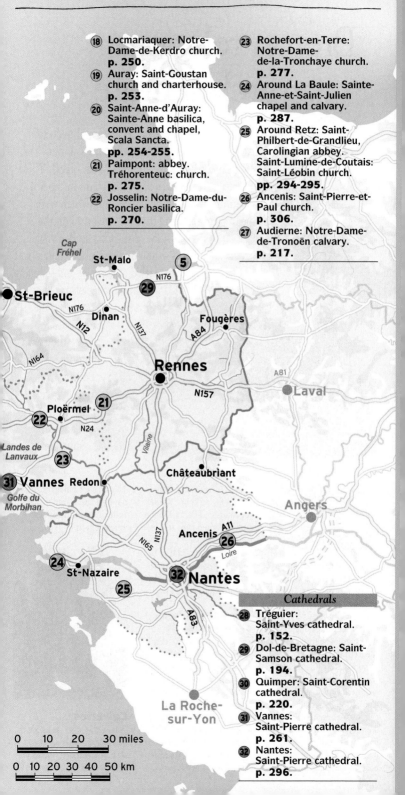

Cathedrals

0   10   20   30 miles

0 10 20 30 40 50 km

Breton religious architecture

The first period of Breton religious architecture dates from the time of the megaliths, and engraved pagan steles (upright stone slabs). These monuments were 'recovered' by Christians in the 4th C. The menhirs of Brignogan or Trégunc (which were topped by crosses), and the cross engraved on the stone of the Coq de Pont-Aven, show how successive religions tried to conquer and supplant their predecessors. The Romans also used the standing stones to celebrate their own divinities, as can be seen in the stele to five gods in the Quimper museum.

The Lanmeur crypt
The Perguet de Bénodet, the collegiate church of Loctudy and the Locmaria church in Quimper are considered the most beautiful examples of Romanesque architecture of the 11th and 12th C. Unfortunately, the rebuilding to which they were subjected on the pretext of restoration, especially after the wars, often conceals the architecture of the period in which the church was built. This does not apply, however, to Lanmeur, where the 10th-C. crypt was restored in keeping with its original appearance. This vast colonnade, adorned with snakes, is Brittany's oldest Christian sanctuary. The portal of the church of Saint-Sauveur at Dinan is a classic example of Romanesque architecture.

The golden age of Gothic style
The jewels of Breton's religious architecture date mostly from the 15th C. They include the basilica of Folgoët (1423), Notre-Dame-des-Carmes at Pont-Labbé, which dates from the early 15th C., and Saint-Nonna de Penmarc'h (1489), a Flamboyant Gothic masterpiece with glorious stained-glass windows of the period. The delicacy and lightness of the style lasted until the late 16th C., when the parishes were enclosed.

Calvaries
Although parish closes are to be found in other regions, such as Aquitaine, the calvary itself is typically Breton and

originates from Lower Brittany. A calvary is a sculpture of a group of figures representing a scene from the gospels. Calvaries flourished in Brittany from 1450 (Troënen de Saint-Jean-Trolimon) to 1610 (the date of the last great calvary in Saint-Thégonnec). The calvary of Plougonven in the Finistère region (1554) consists of 100 figures, representing scenes from the life of Christ and the Passion. Try to identify the Three Wise Men and the horned Devil. Plougonven is also the only large calvary to be signed by the sculptors, Henry and Bastien Prigent, who called themselves *ymageurs*.

NOTRE DAME DE PITIÉ

Sacred fountains

Traditionally symbols of purification, fountains were reputed to have medicinal properties. They are so numerous in Brittany that they ought to be able to cure almost every illness on earth! Often the fountains are intricately carved, such as the ones at Le Folgoët in Saint-Nicodème-en-Pluméliau and Logonna-Daoulas. They usually matched the prevailing architectural style, but sometimes they are merely outlets for springs, as at the Rocher-des-Trois-Évêques (three bishops' rock) in the Monts d'Arrée. The illnesses treated always have some connection with the life of the saint commemorated by the fountain, and as many Breton saints are reputed to be able to cure back pain, blindness and gastric problems, there is a wide choice for sufferers who seek a cure.

THE PARISH CLOSES

From the late 16th C. some villages in northern Finistère became wealthy by growing flax and making linen, which they then exported to England, Portugal and even South America. In addition, the sea route between Flanders and Italy passed through the region. Ships would stop in the area so that passengers could buy the linen, which was famous for its quality. The trade considerably increased the wealth of these villages, which was piously invested in building a close (or enclosure) around the church with a triumphal arch or portal, a calvary and an ossuary. Such parish closes can be seen throughout Brittany, especially in the Trégor, but most are to be found around the river Élorn, which separates Léon from Cornouaille. La Martyre, Sizun, Landivisiau and Lampaul-Guimiliau are all on the same route and are well worth a visit. ☎ 02 98 68 48 84.

The church

The cemetery

The ossuary

The calvary

The portal

Breton festivals

The sea, the *crêpes* and even the patron saints of the many little villages all offer opportunities for celebrations in Brittany. There are also several internationally famous events which are held here.

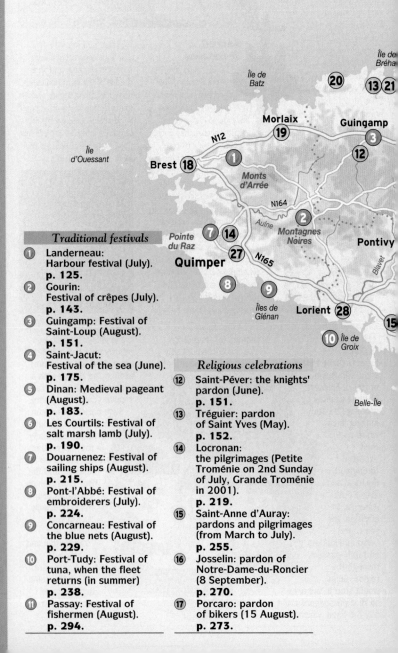

Traditional festivals

1. **Landerneau:** Harbour festival (July). p. 125.
2. **Gourin:** Festival of crêpes (July). p. 143.
3. **Guingamp:** Festival of Saint-Loup (August). p. 151.
4. **Saint-Jacut:** Festival of the sea (June). p. 175.
5. **Dinan:** Medieval pageant (August). p. 183.
6. **Les Courtils:** Festival of salt marsh lamb (July). p. 190.
7. **Douarnenez:** Festival of sailing ships (August). p. 215.
8. **Pont-l'Abbé:** Festival of embroiderers (July). p. 224.
9. **Concarneau:** Festival of the blue nets (August). p. 229.
10. **Port-Tudy:** Festival of tuna, when the fleet returns (in summer) p. 238.
11. **Passay:** Festival of fishermen (August). p. 294.

Religious celebrations

12. **Saint-Péver:** the knights' pardon (June). p. 151.
13. **Tréguier:** pardon of Saint Yves (May). p. 152.
14. **Locronan:** the pilgrimages (Petite Troménie on 2nd Sunday of July, Grande Troménie in 2001). p. 219.
15. **Saint-Anne d'Auray:** pardons and pilgrimages (from March to July). p. 255.
16. **Josselin:** pardon of Notre-Dame-du-Roncier (8 September). p. 270.
17. **Porcaro:** pardon of bikers (15 August). p. 273.

St-Lô

Îles Chausey

Cap Fréhel

St-Malo

St-Brieuc

Dinan

Fougères

Rennes

Ploërmel

andes de Lanvaux

Vannes

Redon

Châteaubriant

Golfe du Morbihan

Ancenis

St-Nazaire

Nantes

La Roche-sur-Yon

N176 N12 N164 N137 N157 N165 N83 N84 A84 A83

Vilaine

0   10   20   30 miles

0 10 20 30 40 50 km

Festivals and festivities

⑱ **Brest**: Festival of short films (November). **p. 122.**

⑲ **Morlaix**: Wednesday festival in the streets (July–August). **p. 132.**

⑳ **Perros-Guirec**: Festival of comic strips (July), Festival of the city of hydrangeas (August). **p. 145.**

㉑ **Tréguier**: Festival of kites (July–August). **p. 153.**

㉒ **Loudéac**: Race meeting (August). **p. 162.**

㉓ **Dinard**: British film festival (October). **p. 177.**

㉔ **Saint-Malo**: Festival of comic strips (end of October), travel show (May). **p. 179.**

㉕ **Hédé**: Festival of theatre and music (August). **p. 187.**

㉖ **Rennes**: Festival of travelogues (1st week in January or February), Festival of Breton art (July), The Transmusicales (early December). **pp. 198-199.**

㉗ **Quimper**: Cornouaille Festival (July). **p. 222.**

㉘ **Lorient**: Festival of Celtic art and music (August). **p. 237.**

㉙ **Nantes**: International Summer Festival (early July), Three Continents festival (November), Rendezvous on the Erdre (September). **p. 299.**

Feast-days, pardons, and other festivals

There are few parts of France in which the feast-days that enrich village life are so deeply entrenched in religious roots. The first feast-day is in May, when Bretons march behind a cross in a procession that always begins with a mass. In the evening the feast becomes more pagan. Prayers give way to toasts to the traditional gods Chouchen and Hydromel, and the festivities often continue until daybreak, with dancing to the traditional *biniou* and the not-so-traditional electric guitar.

Pardons: a living tradition

From May and throughout the summer, the Bretons run from pardon to pardon. The feast-day, called the pardon, starts with a solemn mass in the name of the patron saint of the local church or chapel. The worshippers form a procession behind the banners or the vessels containing the saint's relics which are paraded for the occasion. The route and ceremonials vary in length, and the folklore behind the tradition now attracts a great number of tourists. The pardons range from traditional to ultra-modern, from the pardon of the horsemen of Saint-Péver (p. 151), to the pardon of the bikers in Porcaro (p. 273) and the Pardon of Notre-Dame-la-Garde in Pléneuf-Val-André, when the mass is always celebrated on a trawler.

La Grande Troménie

The **Petite Troménie** of Locronan (tourist office, ☎ 02 98 91 70 14) takes place every year, but the **Grande Troménie**, the only Breton pardon to last a whole week, only takes place every six years. The *troménie* is based on an ancient Celtic rite, the *Nemeton*, meaning 'a temple under the holy vault of the sky'. The procession passes round the Nemeton, which has been renamed Minihy by the Bretons, and means 'space in which the right of sanctuary is perpetuated'. On the way to the *Grand Troménie*, it is not unusual to see women lying on a huge granite stone, the famous *jument de pierre*, which is reputed to make women fertile and provide them with a husband! The evening celebrations are not religious. The next *Grande Troménie* will take place in 2001.

The Spézet sculpture

This sculpture in honour of the Virgin is made of butter, and is displayed each Trinity Sunday at Spézet (Town Hall, ☎ 02 98 93 80 03). Until recently, women used to go from farm to farm collecting slabs of butter large enough to be carved. Today they ask for money and buy a huge slab which the women work on for hours. The sculpture depicts animals, landscapes and patterns.

Dancing and festou-noz

Religious fervour often gives way to popular celebrations, the *festou-noz*. Breton dances originally combined business with pleasure because the dancers' clogs stamped down the earthen floors of the houses! Breton culture was extremely popular in the 1970s but has since fallen out of favour. Now these popular festivals are being revived and are beginning to attract young people again, who are ready to hold each other by the little finger and dance the gavotte and the *en dro* in a chain, or

dance a *plinn* in couples to frantic rhythms. A few bands, like Ar Re Yaouank, have brought the old melodies up to date in a dynamic way.

Breton music and musicians

Having nearly disappeared from the musical stage, players of traditional Breton music have made a comeback, and their melodies are now played in the region and throughout France. The performances of Alan Stivell, who plays and promotes the Celtic harp, of Tri Yann or of Dan Ar Braz, the initiator of the *Héritage des Celtes*, are all part of this grow-ing trend. At the same time, the *bagadous*, traditional ensembles of players, including drummers, bagpipe players, and bombard (bassoon-like instrument) players, have expanded their musical reper-toire. There is a newer and larger public for Celtic music, especially at such events as the Interceltic Festival at Lorient (p. 237), the largest festival of its kind not only in France, but in any country with a Celtic tradition.

Manor houses and castles

The castles, châteaux, fortresses and manor houses of Brittany are one of its best-kept secrets, as are its military fortifications. Many of these buildings can be visited, and some contain museums or are used for temporary exhibitions.

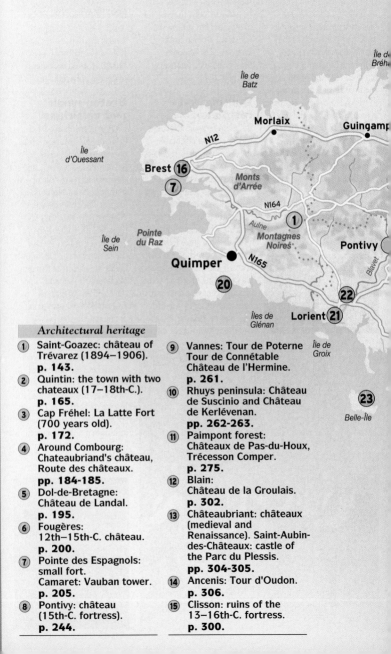

Architectural heritage

1. **Saint-Goazec: château of Trévarez (1894–1906).** p. 143.
2. **Quintin: the town with two chateaux (17–18th-C.).** p. 165.
3. **Cap Fréhel: La Latte Fort (700 years old).** p. 172.
4. **Around Combourg: Chateaubriand's château, Route des châteaux.** pp. 184-185.
5. **Dol-de-Bretagne: Château de Landal.** p. 195.
6. **Fougères: 12th–15th-C. château.** p. 200.
7. **Pointe des Espagnols: small fort. Camaret: Vauban tower.** p. 205.
8. **Pontivy: château (15th-C. fortress).** p. 244.
9. **Vannes: Tour de Poterne Tour de Connétable Château de l'Hermine.** p. 261.
10. **Rhuys peninsula: Château de Suscinio and Château de Kerlévenan.** pp. 262-263.
11. **Paimpont forest: Châteaux de Pas-du-Houx, Trécesson Comper.** p. 275.
12. **Blain: Château de la Groulais.** p. 302.
13. **Châteaubriant: châteaux (medieval and Renaissance). Saint-Aubin-des-Châteaux: castle of the Parc du Plessis.** pp. 304-305.
14. **Ancenis: Tour d'Oudon.** p. 306.
15. **Clisson: ruins of the 13–16th-C. fortress.** p. 300.

Manor houses, castles and farms

Almost every path in Brittany leads to a farmyard. At the same time, there is hardly a hamlet or village that does not have a traditional manor house. Whether in the north or west, on the coast or inland, the rural architecture is astonishingly diverse. Keep an eye out for these signs of a thriving farming community. Sadly, though, many *longères* (long, narrow stables and cowsheds), which blend into the landscape, have been replaced by the ugly sheds of modern agriculture.

Penty and Ty Braz

Typical Breton hamlets often consist of buildings grouped together rather haphazardly – homes, stables, cowsheds, barns and stores for farm tools – but there is a reason for it. The buildings surround a square courtyard either in a semi-circle or at right angles to it, to give protection against the wind. These one-storey farmhouse buildings are the most typical kind of Breton dwellings. When they are joined in a long row and covered by a single roof, they are called *longères* in French, or *Ty Braz* in Breton. Single houses are *penty*.

Slate and thatch

The grey-blue slate roof remains the typical image of Brittany. But once again, regional diversity has to be taken into account. In the south Finistère region, for better wind-resistance, the slates are embedded in mortar. If the slates are thick, they are laid in tiles of decreasing size from top to bottom. On the coast of the Côtes-d'Armor region, the roofs are covered with tiles, which were imported from Britain during the 19th C. The Morbihan region, on the other hand, boasts many thatched roofs. The thatch is made of wheat, rye or *hèdre*, a kind of native wild gladiolus from the Redon marshes.

A festival of colour

If ochre is typical of the earthhouses around Rennes, the purple shale colours the farmhouse walls around Brocéliande in a wine-red hue. In the Morlaix region you can also find shale houses which are almost black. By contrast, smooth, pink sandstone with white speckles is typical of the country houses around Erquy. Grey granite is also a very common building material. It is found on beaches in the form of pebbles or in the small, irregular stones used to build the walls of the small houses on the Quiberon peninsula.

Above: Nicolazic house in Sainte-Anne-d'Auray
Below: Brière cottage in Kerhinet

The story of the manor houses

The architecture of the manor houses, which are so numerous in the north of Brittany, dates back to the 14th and 15th C., before the influence of the Renaissance in the 16th C. These stately homes of the landed gentry and wealthy middle classes usually have a large room on the ground floor, a staircase in a tower built onto the side of the house, a few apertures with granite surrounds (sometimes carved) and an imposing main entrance. Bull's-eye windows and family emblems also adorn these buildings, which have all the outward trappings of the wealth of an aristocracy that not only looked after the tenants but also kept a close eye on them.

Castles and enclosures

From the 14th C. onwards changing alliances and feuds between leading members of the aristocracy led to the building of fortresses, castles and enclosures throughout Brittany. From Saint-Malo to Clisson, and from Vitré to Brest, different architectural styles were used in succession or concurrently. There are watchtowers (Solidor Tower in Saint-Malo), medieval fortresses (La-Latte Fort) and hunting lodges (Suscinio), as well as mansions in the Renaissance and Classical styles. Sadly, the rich heritage represented by these dwellings is rarely appreciated, and they greatly deserve to be rediscovered and renovated.

Scientific and industrial sites

From tide-mills to the tidal power station on the Rance, from ancient forges to the ultra-modern processing of seaweed, Brittany offers the opportunity to learn about the techniques of yesterday and today.

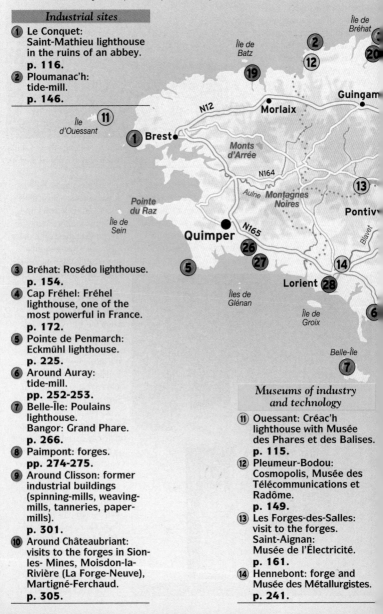

Industrial sites

1. Le Conquet: Saint-Mathieu lighthouse in the ruins of an abbey. p. 116.
2. Ploumanac'h: tide-mill. p. 146.
3. Bréhat: Rosédo lighthouse. p. 154.
4. Cap Fréhel: Fréhel lighthouse, one of the most powerful in France. p. 172.
5. Pointe de Penmarch: Eckmühl lighthouse. p. 225.
6. Around Auray: tide-mill. pp. 252-253.
7. Belle-Île: Poulains lighthouse. Bangor: Grand Phare. p. 266.
8. Paimpont: forges. pp. 274-275.
9. Around Clisson: former industrial buildings (spinning-mills, weaving-mills, tanneries, paper-mills). p. 301.
10. Around Châteaubriant: visits to the forges in Sion-les- Mines, Moisdon-la-Rivière (La Forge-Neuve), Martigné-Ferchaud. p. 305.

Museums of industry and technology

11. Ouessant: Créac'h lighthouse with Musée des Phares et des Balises. p. 115.
12. Pleumeur-Bodou: Cosmopolis, Musée des Télécommunications et Radôme. p. 149.
13. Les Forges-des-Salles: visit to the forges. Saint-Aignan: Musée de l'Électricité. p. 161.
14. Hennebont: forge and Musée des Métallurgistes. p. 241.

Îles Chausey

Cap Fréhel

St-Malo

●St-Brieuc

Dinan

N176
N12
N137

N164

Rennes

Ploërmel
N24

N157

andes de Lanvaux

●Vannes

Golfe du Morbihan

Redon

Châteaubriant

Ancenis ●

St-Nazaire

Nantes

La Roche-sur-Yon

Factories and workshops

19 Saint-Pol-de-Léon: Algoplus (seaweed cultivation and processing), Blzien coachworks. **p. 131.**

20 Pleubian: Centre d'Études et de Valorisation des Algues. **p. 153.**

21 Saint-Malo: Naval dockyard. **p. 181.**

22 Côte d'Émeraude: dam and tidal power station on the river Rance, Josse company (old materials). **p. 171.**

23 Saint-Léger-des-Prés: cabinet-maker's workshop, restorer of historic houses. **p. 185.**

24 Fougères: Minelli and J.-B. Martin shoe factories. **p. 201.**

25 Rennes: Ricard factory, Citroën factory, Ouest-France newspaper. **pp. 198-199.**

26 Port-la-Forêt: CDK Technologie (construction of racing boats). **p. 231.**

27 Concarneau: trawler and home-made preserves. Rosporden: Globes-Exports (seaweed cultivation and processing). **p. 229.**

28 Lorient: Kerguilet dairy factory. **p. 236.**

29 La Gacilly: Yves Rocher factory. **p. 279.**

30 Muzillac: Domaine de Pen-Mur, paper mill. **p. 281.**

15 Ploërmel: Musée des Sciences Naturelles and horloge astronomique. **p. 272.**

16 Redon: Musée de la Batellerie. **p. 278.**

17 Saint-Nazaire: Ecomusée, Chantiers de l'Atlantique. **p. 290.**

18 Nantes: Planetarium. **p. 298.**

Lighthouses and beacons

The code of the sea

Ar-Men, the Vieille, the Kéréon, and Jument are names that have fascinated and terrified Breton seafarers. These are the names of lighthouses that were originally built far out to sea but which are now automated and their lights computer-controlled from land. They are symbols of an heroic past, when a variety of systems were used to protect sailors. The Lighthouses and Beacons Service in Brest has been responsible for them since Napoleon's time.

North   South   East   West

The cardinal beacons

The Saint-Mathieu headland

Lights and lighthouses

Now that the oil lamp is obsolete, halogen lamps light the way for seamen at night. Each light has its own properties by which it can be distinguished from its neighbour. Both the colour – white, green, red or purple – and the rate at which it flashes make each light different from another. The beam may be fixed or flashing, there may be longer alternate light and dark phases, whose intervals vary or isophase (equal phase), or there may be sparkling lights.

Beacons and marker buoys

Whether they are floating or fixed, beacons and marker buoys allow mariners to determine their position and avoid any risks that could be encountered near the coasts, such as wrecks, submerged rocks or sandbanks. Every fixed and visible object, such as a church steeple, a water-tower or a lighthouse, can be used as a landmark. Taken as a compass reading and located according to pre-determined alignments, landmarks, seamarks and beacons enable navigators to follow a carefully charted route and avoid hidden dangers.

'Bacyrouge' and 'tricovert'

At the entrance to a harbour or channel, the rule is to pass the cylindrical red markers to port (left) and the conical green markers to starboard (right). French sailors use a mnemonic to remember the procedure: *bacyrouge* for the red beacons and *tricovert* for the green ones. This rule is the most widespread and is part of the A system. But there is also a B system, which is exactly

the reverse – just to complicate matters! So, if the green light is to starboard in Brest, it will be to port in New York!

Who sees Ar Men

About 7 miles (12 km) off Sein there is a famous lighthouse that was feared by every lighthouse-keeper in the region. There was an adage: 'He who sees Ar Men, is in trouble again.' Construction began in 1867 and took 14 years due to the ferocity of the storms and waves striking the rock. The lighthouse used to be occupied by the keepers, who sometimes remained trapped there for weeks at a time. Since 10 April 1990

Ar Men has been entirely automated, like every lighthouse along the Breton coast, and it is now not visited for anything but brief repairs or routine maintenance.

The SNSM, St Bernard of the sea

Along the 1,120 miles (1,800 km) of coastline, from the mouth of the Couesnon near Mont-Saint-Michel to the Loire estuary, the Société Nationale de Sauvetage en Mer (SNSM) has 250 stations. It is run by 4,000 volunteers, most of whom are retired merchant seamen or fishermen, who man the lifeboats. They are helped by the French navy, the customs service and the coastguard. The SNSM rescues about 10,000 people and about 2,000 ships annually.

The lighthouses and beacons tour

This fascinating tour, created by the Brest tourist office, involves visiting a dozen lighthouses in the Nord-Finistère

region. It can be done in two ways: either sailing from Brest to Ouessant, or taking the road and coastal paths from Brest to Brignogan. The towers of the lighthouses dominate the glorious landscapes. Some lighthouses can be visited, including the Saint-Mathieu and Trézien lighthouses, as well as the one on the Île Vièrge and the Île de Stiff. For further information contact the tourist office in Brest, 8 Avenue Georges-Clemenceau, ☎ 02 98 44 24 96.

Beacons indicating a hazard

The lighthouse at Poulains headland on Belle-Île

Land of art and artists

Many artists have come from Brittany, and its landscapes have inspired a great number of painters, writers and film directors. The map indicates the places on which they have left their mark and the museums dedicated to them.

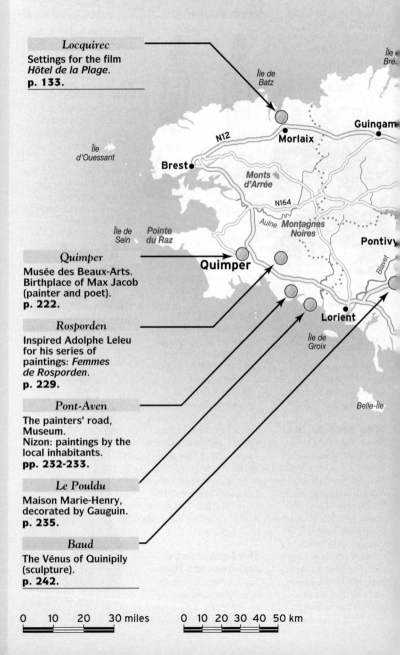

Locquirec

Settings for the film *Hôtel de la Plage*.
p. 133.

Quimper

Musée des Beaux-Arts. Birthplace of Max Jacob (painter and poet).
p. 222.

Rosporden

Inspired Adolphe Leleu for his series of paintings: *Femmes de Rosporden*.
p. 229.

Pont-Aven

The painters' road, Museum.
Nizon: paintings by the local inhabitants.
pp. 232-233.

Le Pouldu

Maison Marie-Henry, decorated by Gauguin.
p. 235.

Baud

The Vénus of Quinipily (sculpture).
p. 242.

Île Bré.

Île de Batz

Guingam

N12

Morlaix

Île d'Ouessant

Brest

Monts d'Arrée

N164

Île de Sein

Pointe du Raz

Aulne Montagnes Noires

Pontivy

Blavet

Quimper

Lorient

Île de Groix

Belle-Île

0   10   20   30 miles

0   10 20 30 40 50 km

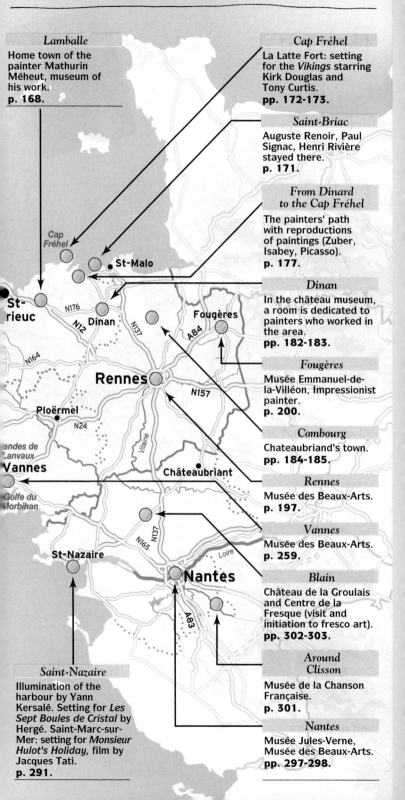

Lamballe

Home town of the painter Mathurin Méheut, museum of his work.
p. 168.

Cap Fréhel

La Latte Fort: setting for the *Vikings* starring Kirk Douglas and Tony Curtis.
pp. 172-173.

Saint-Briac

Auguste Renoir, Paul Signac, Henri Rivière stayed there.
p. 171.

From Dinard to the Cap Fréhel

The painters' path with reproductions of paintings (Zuber, Isabey, Picasso).
p. 177.

Dinan

In the château museum, a room is dedicated to painters who worked in the area.
pp. 182-183.

Fougères

Musée Emmanuel-de-la-Villéon, Impressionist painter.
p. 200.

Combourg

Chateaubriand's town.
pp. 184-185.

Rennes

Musée des Beaux-Arts.
p. 197.

Vannes

Musée des Beaux-Arts.
p. 259.

Blain

Château de la Groulais and Centre de la Fresque (visit and initiation to fresco art).
pp. 302-303.

Around Clisson

Musée de la Chanson Française.
p. 301.

Nantes

Musée Jules-Verne, Musée des Beaux-Arts.
pp. 297-298.

Saint-Nazaire

Illumination of the harbour by Yann Kersalé. Setting for *Les Sept Boules de Cristal* by Hergé. Saint-Marc-sur-Mer: setting for *Monsieur Hulot's Holiday*, film by Jacques Tati.
p. 291.

Brittany in a sentence

In addition to the beauty of its scenery and the adventurous nature of its people, Brittany has also supplied French literature with some of its greatest writers. Chateaubriand, Lamennais, Queffelec and Pierre-Jakez Hélias are just some of those who have upheld the black-and-white Breton flag. Writing in French or in Breton, their native countryside has inspired them, as it now inspires the poets and novelists who follow in their footsteps. Further afield, Jack Kerouac (real name Jacques Lebris de Kerouac), the author of *On The Road*, was born to an immigrant Breton family in Canada.

Land of memoirs and adventure

From François-René, Viscount of Chateaubriand, who spent most of his youth in Saint-Malo and Combourg, to Jules Verne, who came from Nantes, Brittany has celebrated the success of famous writers. More recently, Pierre-Jakez Hélias has made Brittany live through his stories, and is the most famous contemporary author to write in the Breton language. His *Horse of Pride* has been translated into 20 languages. He also set his stories further afield in the Antarctic, Peru and Mauritius, as well as on the moors of Lanvaux, the Fréhel cliff and the Saint-Malo ramparts. Roger Vercel (*Faces of the Privateers*), André Le Gall (*King of the Dogs*) and Bernard Simiot (*These Gentlemen of Saint-Malo, The Carbec Trilogy*) reveal the

faces of Brittany in their historical novels. Their captivating stories of adventure on the high seas bring to life the intriguing tales of the privateers. This tradition of writers of adventure stories continues with authors such as Yann Queffelec.

Land of comic strips

Comic strips are another Breton speciality. Bécassine, the Breton peasant woman with plenty of common sense, was created in 1905 by the writer Caumery and the artist Pinchon and continues to be successful. Two writers manage to laugh at Brittany while understanding it so well. The first is Cr'haen; his *Bout d'homme* (runt) is sensitively written in a language full of images taken from Brittany's culture and legends. You can delight in the adventures of this little boy who will never grow up. The storyline is original and the drawings attractive, and *Bout d'homme* has established the author as one of the greatest French creators of a comic strip. In *Mulot* De Forest and Bignon describe with mischief rather than malice the adventures of a Parisian writer who has decided to live in the depths of Brittany in order to solve a magic puzzle which his brother, a priest, has given him. In this book, Brittany is caricatured with good nature. You can find these books all

over France, of course, but if you happen to be in Saint-Brieuc, don't miss the Dédicaces bookshop (12 Rue Saint-Goueno, ☎ 02 96 33 92 93) where an admirer of the genre will explain to you why, thanks to Loisel, Cr'haen and Lidwine amongst others, Breton comic strips are at least as good as Belgian ones.

Breton and Gallo

Thanks to the creation of the *Diwan* schools for teaching Breton, and the bilingual

PUBLISHING AND THE PRESS

Ouest-France is the leading daily newspaper. It is a traditional, Christian-Democrat publication with a daily circulation of one million, and it has become a pillar of regional culture that cannot be ignored. The *Télégramme de Brest*, based in Morlaix, is also a defender of regional interests. Several new publications have recently emerged, such as *Armen* and *Le Chasse-Marée*, which are based in Douarnenez and are outstanding journals specialising in ethnology. Publishing in general is well-developed in Brittany and more than 1,000 books are published annually in French and Breton.

classes founded by the Ministry of National Education, the Breton language is increasing in popularity again. Today 300,000 Bretons, most of them from the Finistère region, still speak this ancient Celtic tongue, which has regional variations. The other local language, Gallo, which is of Roman origin, was once commonly spoken in eastern Brittany but has survived only in the patois used in a few places in the Ille-et-Vilaine and Morbihan *départements*.

The Chasse-Marée bookshop in Douarnenez

The painters of Brittany

Claude Monet, 'The Reefs of Belle-Île'

With its constantly changing skies and wonderful light, Brittany provides artists with an endlessly fascinating source of inspiration. It is also a land of legend and tradition, and for all these reasons has long been a favourite with painters from all over the world. The Pont-Aven school, which was founded by Paul Gauguin and Émile Bernard in 1888, has had a major influence on local art, but Brittany has also produced and adopted artists whose styles are very diverse.

P. Gauguin, La Belle Angèle, *1889*

Mathurin Méheut (1882–1958)

Mathurin Méheut is probably the best-known native Breton painter. The author Henri Polles said of him that he was 'the most Breton artist of all time'. Méheut was an illustrator and ethnologist, as can be seen in the collection of his work portraying everyday life in Brittany at the beginning of the century. In order to capture the sailor, the peasant and the craftsman as they were engaged in their everyday occupations, the artist travelled throughout the region. He left a valuable record, of which fine examples can be seen in the museum at Lamballe, his birthplace.

The Pont-Aven school

In his desire to escape from Paris and the bustle of the city, Paul Gauguin (1848–1903) visited Pont-Aven in 1886, in search of authenticity and a fresh approach. The next 10 years were productive for the painter who, surrounded by about 20 artists, including Émile Bernard, Paul Sérusier and Maurice Denis as well as Dutch and Irish painters, broke with Impressionism and laid the foundations for a new style, Symbolism, which would lead later painters into Abstractionism.

THE FAVOURITE HAUNTS OF PAINTERS

While the region has attracted artists as famous as Monet, Corot, Renoir and Matisse, they tended to favour certain areas. In 1863 a small colony of artists established itself in Douarnenez. Eugène Boudin (1824–98) preferred Faou and Camaret. Belle-Île and the Guérande peninsula were the favourite haunts of numerous artists, and Picasso's holidays in Dinard proved to be particularly productive. However, in the ranking of favourite places for artists, Cornouaille, from Quimper to Pont-Aven, is the most popular.

A great forerunner

As early as 1826 the famous English landscape painter William Turner (1775–1851), the great forerunner of Impressionism, loved to paint in Brittany. Turner set out on a long sea voyage that took him right round the coast of the Armorican peninsula, before sailing up the river Loire. Throughout the trip, Turner kept busy painting, producing watercolours of Nantes that are among the most important artistic records of the so-called city of dukes.

Y. Tanguy, Infinite Divisibility

Symbolism according to Gauguin

Vision after the Sermon and *The Yellow Christ* are just two of the masterpieces that Paul Gauguin painted in Brittany. The vivid colours are laid on in a flat tint with a black outline, which is reminiscent of enamel-work or a stained-glass window. The Symbolist poet Édouard Dujardin used the term 'cloisonism' for this type of work. 'Can you see this blue shadow?' Gauguin asked his followers, continuing 'then use the most beautiful blue tint on your palette'. In a more subtle way, these paintings, with their simplified designs, inspired by religion or scenes from everyday life, were influenced by Japanese prints.

Some well-known Breton painters

In addition to Mathurin Méheut, leading Breton painters include Jean-Julien Lemordant, whose panel *Contre le Vent* is exhibited in the Quimper museum, and Pierre Jacob, known as Tal Coat (1905–85), who came from Pouldu. The Surrealist artist Yves Tanguy (1900–1955), who was born in Locronan, also deserves mention. The young artist Jean-Charles Blais, who is from Rennes, started to draw on torn posters; today his work is highly sought after in the contemporary art market.

P. Gauguin, A Mill in Brittany

P. Bernard, Breton women in a Meadow

Nature in Brittany

Fauna and flora are as diverse in Brittany as their habitats are. There are coasts, marshland, moorland and forests, which can be either wild and untouched or carefully tended. Brittany always has something wonderful to offer.

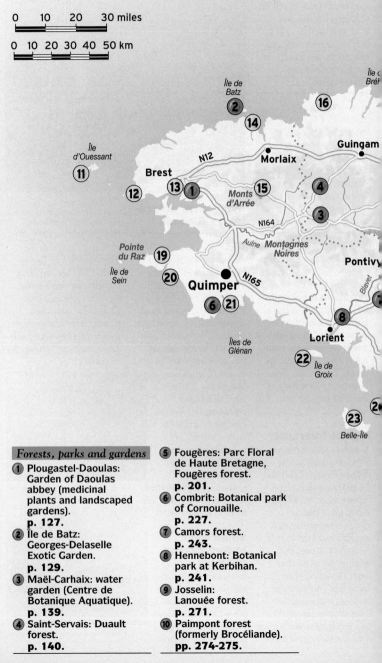

Forests, parks and gardens

① Plougastel-Daoulas: Garden of Daoulas abbey (medicinal plants and landscaped gardens). **p. 127.**

② Île de Batz: Georges-Delaselle Exotic Garden. **p. 129.**

③ Maël-Carhaix: water garden (Centre de Botanique Aquatique). **p. 139.**

④ Saint-Servais: Duault forest. **p. 140.**

⑤ Fougères: Parc Floral de Haute Bretagne, Fougères forest. **p. 201.**

⑥ Combrit: Botanical park of Cornouaille. **p. 227.**

⑦ Camors forest. **p. 243.**

⑧ Hennebont: Botanical park at Kerbihan. **p. 241.**

⑨ Josselin: Lanouée forest. **p. 271.**

⑩ Paimpont forest (formerly Brocéliande). **pp. 274–275.**

Discovering the natural environment

⑪ **Ouessant:** Centre d'Étude du Milieu (ornithology, botany and entomology course). **p. 115.**

⑫ **Le Conquet:** departure port for the glass-bottomed launch to see the sea-bed and the Molène archipelago. **p. 116.**

⑬ **Brest:** Océanopolis, every aspect of the sea. **p. 123.**

⑭ **Roscoff:** oceanological observatory. **p. 129.**

⑮ **Monts d'Arrée:** Beaver sanctuary in the Monts d'Arrée. **p. 134.**

⑯ **Perros-Guirec:** The Sept-Îles bird sanctuary. **p. 144.**

⑰ **Cap Fréhel:** La Fauconnière bird sanctuary. **p. 173.**

⑱ **Saint-Malo:** Grand Aquarium (visits, conferences, shop). **p. 181.**

⑲ **Cap Sizun:** nature reserve (migratory and nesting birds). **p. 213.**

⑳ **Audierne:** Maison de la Baie (ornithological discoveries and guided tours). **p. 216.**

㉑ **Penfoulic:** Maison du Marais (explanation of the fauna and the flora), nature walks. **p. 231.**

㉒ **Île de Groix:** Ecomusée de Port-Tudy and Pen-Men nature reserve. **p. 239.**

㉓ **Belle-Île:** Koh-Kastell bird sanctuary. **p. 266.**

㉔ **Vannes:** aquarium and butterfly farm. **pp. 259-260.**

㉕ **Golfe du Morbihan:** Falguérec nature reserve (former salt marshes of Séné). **p. 257.**

㉖ **Houat:** Ecomusée (growing of plankton and underwater ecosystem). **p. 269.**

㉗ **Le Croisic:** Océarium. **p. 282.**

㉘ **Parc de Brière:** wildlife park, Maison de l'Éclusier (history and tradition of the marshes). **pp. 288-289.**

㉙ **Saint-Philbert-de-Grandlieu:** Maison du Lac (lakeside wildlife). **p. 295.**

㉚ **Île de Versailles:** Maison de l'Erdre (explanation of the river ecosystem). **p. 299.**

㉛ **Gâvre forest:** Maison Benoist (flora, fauna, woodland occupations). **pp. 302-303.**

Seabirds

You can often hear them calling, even though you can't see them. In the ploughing season, they form huge white streaks that float above the furrows which are made behind the tractors. When the wind is too strong for them, they seek refuge in towns. From Cap Fréhel to Cap Sizun, from the gulf of Morbihan to the mouth of the river Loire, seabirds, such as common gulls, tern and black-headed gulls, can be spotted throughout Brittany. You only have to look up to see their incessant ballet as they wheel and turn in the sky, so don't forget to pack your binoculars!

Seagull

Common gull or black-headed gull?

This question is constantly asked by inexperienced observers. In fact, it is not important because the Latin word *larus* (gull), which indicates the species, does not differentiate between them. Moreover in France, the word *mouette* refers mainly to the small species of gull, whose wingspan rarely attains 3 feet (1 m), whereas the true common gull's wingspan can reach 6 feet (2 m). The kittiwake is a species that breeds in Brittany but spends most of its time out at sea, but large colonies of black-headed gulls are more commonly seen.

Following the seasons

Spring is the mating season for most seabirds, when gulls, kittiwakes, cormorants and shags settle for many weeks in enormous colonies on the sheerest cliffs. In summer the adults forage for food for their young in fishing ports, on beaches and on rubbish tips, where food is abundant and the pickings are easy. When the young are old enough, they will accompany their parents on these forays. In the autumn, the season of migration, almost all the species gather at the mouth of the estuaries before they fly to Africa for the winter, returning the next year.

Gannet

Breeding and migratory birds

The herring gull, which is the commonest gull and probably the first white bird that you will see in Brittany, reproduces in colonies which can number up to several thousand pairs. This breeding bird is different from its cousin, the lesser black-backed gull, which is also a migratory bird, which spends the winter in Africa. Gannets, the largest seabird, and cormorants, the crows of the sea, about which Breton sailors weave stories, remain attached to their customary breeding grounds. The common terns – sometimes called the swallows of the sea – are the greatest migratory birds in the world, as they fly from one hemisphere to another twice a year!

From clifftop to sea level

While the seagull chooses the tops of rocky islands as a resting-place between catches, the waters of the gulfs and other bays are frequented by numerous species of duck, such as the red-breasted merganser, half of whose entire population winters in France, especially in the gulf of Morbihan. The Brent goose and shelduck are also well represented in this area. Other species, such as the ringed plover and the oyster-catcher, patrol the shores in

Ringed plover

search of small prey, whereas the gull-like fulmar lives mainly on the high seas.

Puffins

The puffin is very photogenic, and its beak makes it resemble a clown. This bird has become a symbol of wildlife in Brittany and has given its name to many bistros. Arriving in March from the open sea, it reproduces mainly on the Sept-Îles archipela-

Puffin

go, in the bay of Morlaix, and on the Ouessant rocks. It suffered from the increased levels of pollution in the sea and from an increase in the gannet population, and has almost disappeared. Only a few hundreds pairs still fly to Brittany in order to perpetuate the species.

Wigeon

Red-breasted merganser

Seaweed from the Côte des Abers

There is no other French coastal area where sea and land interact in quite the same way. Around the islands and in the bays and coves, sea- and freshwater intermingle, and the effects of the tide can often be noticed far inland. These conditions promote the growth of seaweed and, for this reason, Brittany has one of the largest deposits of seaweed in the world, producing 90% of the 80,000 tonnes of seaweed harvested each year in France. More and more uses are being found for seaweed, and in recent years many companies have been formed to develop new foodstuffs and therapeutic and cosmetic products that are based on seaweed.

The Sainte-Marguerite peninsula

Rias and abers

The *ria* is a geographical feature of the Iberian peninsula, and the word itself is Spanish. By extension and association, the word has become a synonym in French for an *aber*. However, the meaning of *ria* is much more precise. It refers to an ancient valley overrun by the sea, either after a landslide or due to a rise in the sea level. Étel in the Morbihan region and Tréguier in the Côtes d'Armor are both examples of *rias*. *Aber*, on the other hand, is a Breton word, which simply means 'mouth', as it does in Welsh. It has been applied to this part of the coast of Brittany, leading to such names as Aber-Wrac'h, Aber-Benoît and Aber-Ildut. These inlets are sometimes several miles long. There are other types of estuary in Brittany, but what makes the *aber* different is that it is more of a sea inlet than a river. The sea prevails, and the freshwater is reduced to a trickle at low tide.

Bladderwrack

This type of coast, like that of Haut Léon, is the best place in

Europe for gathering bladderwrack, and this area actually accounts for 80% of French production. Seaweed seems to have always been gathered and used in Brittany. Nowadays, specially equipped tractors and boats have replaced pitchforks and horse-drawn carts. Bladderwrack (*Fucus vesiculosus*), which is easily distinguished by the

The small port and seaside resort of Aber-Wrac'h

bladders containing air that allow it to float on the surface, is still used as fertiliser.

The scoubidou

In the past special boats used to be equipped with a kind of long scythe, which would sever the seaweed from the rocks or sea-bed to which it was attached. Since the 1970s such boats have been fitted with a *scoubidou*, a rotating hook attached to hydraulic lifting gear that grips the seaweed and wraps it around itself, much like wrapping spaghetti around a fork. The seaweed, mostly horsetail kelp, is then stowed in a tangled mass in the hold and unloaded mechanically in the harbour to be transported to the processing industries. In Brittany about 3,000 acres (1,200 ha) of under-water seaweed fields are harvested in this way.

Drink it or eat it

Seaweed is very rich in trace elements, mineral salts and vitamins, and it can be eaten as a vegetable, in salads or as a flavouring, as well as being

dehydrated or pickled. Nowadays, gourmet food shops and health food stores stock bread and noodles to which seaweed has been added, and you can even purchase seaweed snacks. Some isotonic beverages for sportsmen and women contain seaweed as an ingredient. However, the market for edible seaweed remains marginal in France, where it represents only 4–5% of total production. In Japan the proportion is 95%!

Seaweed: tastes and colours

There are up to 700 species of red, blue or brown seaweed, growing along the Breton coast, but only a dozen are permitted for human consumption. The

Lanildut fishermen in the North Finistère region mainly collect carrageen (*Laminaria digita*), which is used as a gelling agent and thickener in a wide range of applications, from pharmaceuticals to the food industry. This is the seaweed that, with a few others, is represented by the letters E401, E402 or E404 in the ingredients list of numerous processed foods produced in the European Union. Wakame, the seaweed that is eaten mainly in Japanese dishes such as sushi, is cultivated in the open sea on ropes, rather like mussels are, and is gathered at low tide.

The Ar Goat,
forest and moorland

A few thousand years ago Brittany was covered by a huge forest, the *Ar Goat*, which means 'the world of the interior' as opposed to the *Ar Mor*, which refers to the world of the sea. The Romans began a process of deforestation, which has never stopped. Some woodland was cleared by Breton landowners and divided into farmland, and some was left fallow. As the humus was deprived of air by new scrub and undergrowth, the cleared land became the famous Breton moor (*lande*). Moorland predominates in the rural areas of Ille-et-Vilaine and Morbihan, and has become a beautiful feature of the landscape.

September each year to make delicious blackberry jam. Daffodils grow wild in Brittany and are picked in early spring. The great forests consist mainly of oaks and beeches. Beech is a favourite wood of carpenters and craftsmen because of its strength and tight grain. Around Redon, in particular, there are also many sweet chestnut trees, which come into their own at the Fête des Marrons (chestnut festival; p. 278). On the coast, pine and yew trees are abundant. In the days when shipbuilding required huge amounts of wood, the trees chosen were lashed together with stays, so that the trunks to be used for the hulls grew in a natural curve.

On Breton hills

Most of the moorland is in drier hill country, where the soil is poor and only a few types of vegetation will grow. This includes a variety of moor grass, which sometimes makes the moor appear yellow. The wildflowers native to the

Woods and forests

The scrubland or undergrowth is a good place to find wild food – wild mushrooms, of course, as well as wild berries, such as blackcurrants, blackberries and bilberries. Bramble bushes are a favourite with the Bretons who brave their prickles in late

covers the moor with a purple carpet on slightly damp slopes. The common heather (*Calluna vulgaris*) is also a species that grows in highland and lowland moors, but the wettest parts are covered with ling and bog-myrtle. White heather is quite a find because it is reputed, especially by gypsies, to bring good luck.

moorland of Brittany include gentians and spotted orchids, which are protected species and must not be picked. Many of the protected cliffs, such as Cap Fréhel, the Pointe de Grouin Headland and Cap Sizun, are covered in heather and gorse, which are frequently replanted.

A yellow and purple flora

Gorse is a shrub that has thorns instead of leaves, thus distinguishing it from broom, and it is one of the most common plants of the Breton moor. The European gorse bush (*Ulex europaeus*) can grow to more than 6 feet (2 m) in height and flowers in the spring, giving the moor the appearance of a huge yellow carpet. It also has a sweet and delicate scent. Western or dwarf gorse (*Ulex galii*) starts to grow in August or September and has no particular smell. In the past gorse bushes were ground up and used as fodder for cattle. Heather is another typical plant of the moor. Bell heather grows in the driest parts, whereas Scotch heather

Moorland birds

The greenfinch, a small songbird with yellow feathers, builds its nest in the highest bushes of the moorland, but the linnet remains the most typical moorland bird, although it is migratory. It returns to the moors of Brittany in early April after a long flight from southern Spain or Morocco. Two other songbirds which nest in grassland and in moorland where the vegetation has been cut back are the meadow pipit and the stonechat. The Dartford warbler likes living in the *garrigues*, the scrubland of southern France, as much as it enjoys the Breton moors.

The curlew, a long-beaked bird related to the pheasant and with a distinctive call, had become a rarity on the bare moorland that it favours, but by the end of the 20th C. it had begun to return. Moorlands are the favourite haunts of many raptors, including the hen harrier, the kestrel and Montagu's harrier, which nests in France almost exclusively in the Monts d'Arrée. Their numbers will increase if they are able to find suitable prey.

Food and drink

Brittany is celebrated for its fresh seafood, but it also has a lot of other special dishes. Here are the locations of a few of the best places in which to sample the cuisine of Brittany. Details and addresses are on the following pages.

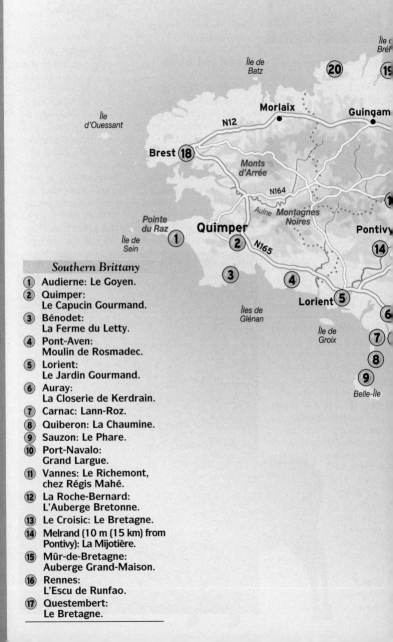

Southern Brittany

1. Audierne: Le Goyen.
2. Quimper:
   Le Capucin Gourmand.
3. Bénodet:
   La Ferme du Letty.
4. Pont-Aven:
   Moulin de Rosmadec.
5. Lorient:
   Le Jardin Gourmand.
6. Auray:
   La Closerie de Kerdrain.
7. Carnac: Lann-Roz.
8. Quiberon: La Chaumine.
9. Sauzon: Le Phare.
10. Port-Navalo:
    Grand Largue.
11. Vannes: Le Richemont,
    chez Régis Mahé.
12. La Roche-Bernard:
    L'Auberge Bretonne.
13. Le Croisic: Le Bretagne.
14. Melrand (10 m (15 km) from
    Pontivy): La Mijotière.
15. Mûr-de-Bretagne:
    Auberge Grand-Maison.
16. Rennes:
    L'Escu de Runfao.
17. Questembert:
    Le Bretagne.

Northern Brittany

⑱ Brest: Ma Petite Folie.
⑲ Paimpol:
Le Domaine de Kerroc'h.
⑳ Perros-Guirec:
Les Feux des îles.
㉑ Saint-Brieuc:
Aux Pesked.
㉒ Erquy: L'Escurial.
㉓ Dinan:
Les Grands Fossés.
㉔ Cancale:
Maison de Bricourt.
㉕ Plancoët:
Chez Jean-Pierre Crouzil.

Îles Chausey

Cap
Fréhel

㉔

㉒

St-Malo

N176

㉕

St-Brieuc

N176

㉓

Dinan

N12

N137

A84

Fougères

N164

Rennes
⑯

N157

Laval

A81

Ploërmel

N24

Vilaine

Vannes

⑪

⑰

Redon

Châteaubriant

Golfe du
Morbihan

⑫

Angers

N137

N165

A11

Ancenis

Loire

⑬

St-Nazaire

Nantes

A83

A87

La Roche-
sur-Yon

A83

0   10   20   30 miles

0 10 20 30 40 50 km

Good food

Brittany is a real paradise for lovers of fish and seafood. However, local specialities are not restricted to these particular foods – there are many others to delight visitors to the region, including the famous *andouille de Guémené* (chitterling pork sausage).

The top four

Cancale

Maison de Bricourt
1 Rue Duguesclin
☎ 02 99 89 64 76
Closed on Tue. and Wed. lunchtime and from mid-Dec. to Mar.
This is quite simply one of the best restaurants in the whole of France. Olivier Roellinger's cooking, which combines fresh local produce with exotic spices, is world-famous. But the incredible thing is that his prices are not prohibitive. So go on, treat yourself! Menus from 280F.

Plancoët

Chez Jean-Pierre Crouzil
20 Rue Quais
☎ 02 96 84 10 24
Closed on Sun. evening and Mon. out of season and from 1 to 8 Oct.
Visit this great chef to enjoy hot and iced oysters in a Vouvray savoury custard and carrots, or the Breton lobster flamed with lambic (a strong Belgian beer)… all in a setting to match. Menus from 290F.

La Roche-Bernard

L'Auberge Bretonne
2 Place Duguesclin
☎ 02 99 90 60 28
Closed Thu. and Fri. lunchtime, first fortnight in Jan. and from 22 Nov. to 9 Dec.
This temple of the culinary arts serves such unique creations as truffled scallops *en surprise* and spider-crab charlotte in a vinaigrette sauce with cockles and broad beans. It also serves traditional dishes such as *kouign aman* (Breton butter cake) topped with vanilla ice cream. Menus from 150 F (weekdays).

Questembert

Le Bretagne
13 Rue Saint-Michel
☎ 02 97 26 11 12
Closed Mon. and Tue. lunchtimes except in July, Aug. and Jan.
The decor is delightful because Georges Paineau is also a painter in his spare time. While he waits for success as an artist, his culinary talent attracts the attention of gourmets from near and far. How could anyone resist steamed oysters with tarragon, baked red tuna with stewed rhubarb served with a clam juice vinaigrette, or cabbage stuffed with lobster with tomato coulis? Menus from 210 F.

Other recommendations

Brest
Ma Petite Folie
Port de Plaisance
☎ 02 98 42 44 42
Closed from 11 to
25 Aug. and from 22
Dec. to 6 Jan.
Dine on this former lobster
boat and savour the crab
rillettes (potted minced crab),
navarin de lotte (braised monkfish), or the Breton lobster
grilled *à ma façon* (in my
own way). Menus from 110 F.

Paimpol
Le Domaine de Kerroc'h
29 Quai Morand
☎ 02 96 20 50 13
Closed Tue. and Wed.
lunchtime out of season
and from 1 Jan. to 15 Feb.
Louis Le Roy is a fisherman's
son, so you are sure to be
eating the best and the
freshest catch that Brittany
has to offer. Inventive cookery in an 18th-C. mansion.
Menus from 125 F.

Perros-Guirec
Les Feux des îles
53 Boulevard Clémenceau
☎ 02 96 23 22 94
Closed Sun. evening and
Mon. at lunchtime out of
season from 1 to 8 Feb.
and from 1 to 6 Oct.
Line-caught sea bass
flavoured with cider and
cooking apples, *blanquette de
lotte* (monkfish in white

The chef of Ferme du Letty (see p. 88)

sauce) with vegetables,
fillet of beef braised with
marrow and Chinon red
wine are on the menu.
Antoine Le Roux celebrates
the delicious combination
of foods from land and sea.
Menus from 128 F.

Saint-Brieuc
Aux Pesked
59 Rue du Légué
☎ 02 96 33 34 65
Closed Sat. lunchtime, Sun.
evening and Mon., and
from 25 Dec. to 15 Jan.
The dishes are typically
Breton, from Cancale
oysters and orange-flavoured
crêpes (pancakes) with *lait
ribot* (buttermilk), *cocos de
Paimpol* sorbet and *andouille*

de Guémené (chitterling
sausages). Menus from 108 F.

Erquy
L'Escurial
29 Boulevard de la Mer
☎ 02 96 72 31 56
Closed Sun. evening and
Mon. out of season and
from 25 Nov. to 7 Dec.,
as well as the first week
of school holidays in Feb.
Here, the art of cookery has
been handed down from
mother to daughter for three
generations. Turbot, john
dory and monkfish are all
delicious. Menus from 98 F.

Dinan
Les Grands Fossés
2 Place du Général-Leclerc
☎ 02 96 39 21 50
Closed Thu.
Try Alain Colas' buckwheat
profiteroles stuffed with crab
and calf sweetbreads fried
with *andouille de Guémené*
(chitterling sausages). Menus
from 90 F.

The lobster stew by Alain Colas at the Grands Fossés in Dinan

Audierne

Le Goyen
Place Jean-Simon
☎ 02 98 70 08 88
Closed Mon. out of season, from mid-Nov to the end of Dec. and from mid-Jan. to early Feb.
Straight from farmer to table. The owner farms the oysters and lobsters so freshness is guaranteed! Menus from 120 F.

Quimper

Le Capucin Gourmand
29 Rue des Reguaires
☎ 02 98 95 43 12
Closed Sun. evening and Mon.
You can trust this Capuchin monk because Jacques Pichon's restaurant is said to be one of the best in town. You are sure to agree after sampling his warm *far* (pudding), typical of the Pont-l'Abbé region, served with a *pommeau* (applejack) sauce. Menus from 115 F, lunch from 95 F.

Bénodet

La Ferme du Letty
Le Letty Izella
☎ 02 98 57 01 27
Open from 15 Feb. to 15 Nov.
The *Fest Aw Hoc'h*, a selection of cold pork or ham, the black pudding salad *à la fouesnantaise*, the bread from the Pont l'Abbé region and the poached pears are among the specialities of this farm,

where simple fare has been revived by a great chef. Menus from 98 F.

Pont-Aven

Moulin de Rosmadec
Centre-ville
☎ 02 98 06 00 22
Closed Wed. and Sun. evening out of season and from the last two weeks in Nov. to Feb.

Harmony between first course and main dish is the order of the day here. The langoustine bisque cannot be separated from the goat's cheese and morel ravioli, and delicious potato pancakes are accompanied by roast loin of lamb with herbs. There is always a warm welcome, so you are sure to want to return! Menus from 162 F.

Lorient

Le Jardin Gourmand
46 Rue Jules-Simon
☎ 02 97 64 17 24
Closed Sun. and Mon., the first fortnight of Aug. and during the school holidays in Feb.
Arnaud Beauvais-Pelletier is your host in this pastel-coloured setting. His wife, Nathalie, who is from Lorient, is in charge of the kitchen. She always finds the freshest produce, and the

dishes she prepares combine innovation and tradition in the most delicious way. Her *gigot de lotte braisé au cidre de Guidel* (monkfish braised in cider) is an absolute must! Menus from 98 F.

Auray

La Closerie de Kerdrain
20 Rue Louis-Billet
☎ 02 97 56 61 27
Closed Sun. evening and Mon. out of season and the second fortnight of Nov.
Everything here is a delight, whether it is the pale green decor or the seafood dishes. The scallops gratin will confirm this. Menus from 105 F.

Carnac

Lann-Roz
36 Avenue de la Poste
☎ 02 97 52 10 48
Closed Sun. out of season and from 5 Jan. to 5 Feb.
To remind you of exactly where you are, the decor consists of Quimper earthenware, antique Breton furniture and watercolour seascapes. The cuisine is just as typical – for instance, the *ragoût aux petits légumes* (spring vegetable stew) is served with lobster. Menus from 95 F.

Quiberon

La Chaumine
Quartier le Manémeure
☎ 02 97 50 17 67
Closed Sun. at lunch time and Mon. out of season, and from 15 Nov. to 15 Dec.
This restaurant is in the heart of the fishermen's district. The traditional home cooking is greatly appreciated by the locals. Menus from 80 F.

Sauzon (Belle-île)
Le Phare
Quai Guerveur
☎ 02 97 31 60 36
Closed from 12 Nov. to
25 Dec. and from 3 Jan.
to 27 Mar.
Mussels, crabs, langoustines,
and other shellfish are picked
straight out of the sea. It is
well worth stopping here!
Menus from 85 F.

Port-Navalo
Grand Largue
Embarcadère
☎ 02 97 53 71 58
Closed Mon. at lunchtime
in season, Tue. out of
season and from mid-Nov.
to Christmas and in Jan.
From the jetty you have a
marvellous view over the
open sea. As for the food, the
chef knows how to liven up
seafood dishes with a subtle
and original mixture of spices.
His recipes are a great secret.
Menus from 95 F.

Vannes
**Le Richemont,
chez Régis Mahé**
Place de la Gare
☎ 02 97 42 61 41
Closed Sun. evening,
Mon, second fortnight of
Nov. and during school
holidays in Feb.
One of the best places to eat
in Brittany. Régis Mahé has a
fertile imagination. Try his
sole meunière with roast potatoes and mozzarella. Menus
from 165 F.

Le Croisic
Le Bretagne
11 Quai de la Petite-
Chambre
☎ 02 40 23 00 51
Closed Sun. evening and
Mon. out of season and
from 15 Nov. to 15 Dec.
Here you can enjoy fresh fish
caught in the morning,
accompanied by fresh local
produce. The sea-bass in a salt
crust will remind you that the
salt pans are not far away.
Menus from 99 F.

a brochette of scallops
cooked on a wood fire.
Bon appétit! Menus from
80 F.

Nathalie Pelletier in Lorient

Ancenis
**La Toile
à Beurre**
82 Rue Saint-Pierre
☎ 02 40 98 89 64
Closed Sun. evening
and Mon.
Trained by Maximin,
Rostang, Chibois and Passard,
Jean-Charles Baron is one
of the rising stars of the
culinary world. In his bistro-
like restaurant, he cooks
smoked eel turnovers with
Gamay-flavoured butter, roast
tuna with fresh tomato sauce
and, to finish, fried apples
with Layon wine. Menus
from 98 F.

Melrand
La Mijotière
15 km from Pontivy
Quenetevec
☎ 02 97 27 72 82
Closed Sun. evening,
Mon. and in Feb.
Welcome to the manor
house! The spit-roasted leg
of lamb is already waiting for
you, turning slowly in the
hearth. Or you might prefer

Mûr-de-Bretagne
**Auberge
Grand-Maison**
☎ 02 96 28 51 10
Closed Sun. evening,
Mon, and from 15 Feb.
to 1 Mar.
Traditional recipes and local
dishes are transformed by
Jacques Guillo's inventive-
ness. His *galette* (buckwheat
pancake) filled with smoked
mackerel, his *crème océane*
and the delectable potato
dishes flavoured with caviar
sauce and sea-urchin purée
are all delicious, as is his
baked Coulommiers cheese
with honey. Menus from
140 F.

Rennes
l'Escu de Runfao
11 Rue du Chapitre
☎ 02 99 79 13 10
Closed Sun. evening.
One of the very best
restaurants in Rennes. Try
the turbot with chanterelle
mushrooms and the sweet-
breads and lobster with
Sauternes. Menus from 125 F.

Buckwheat pancakes,
crêpes and desserts

From a tiny stall in a marketplace selling crêpes and buckwheat *galettes* (pancakes) to the most sophisticated restaurant, it is impossible to avoid the hundreds of places that serve pancakes in Brittany. Although this food is relatively simple, it is sufficient to form the basis of a good and balanced meal when served with a crunchy salad. Your meal could, for instance, consist of a *traditionnelle complète* (buckwheat *galette* with egg, ham and cheese) followed by the classic *beurre-sucre* (butter and sugar) *crêpe*. The Bretons know how to combine these two types of pancake in one meal, and they can make them into a variety of delicious dishes. Enjoy a large glass of the local cider with your meal to help wash it down.

Crêpes or galettes ?

Which do you prefer, *crêpes* or *galettes*? These Breton specialities are so similar that people sometimes get confused between them and simply call both of them *crêpes*. The main difference is the flour used to make them and whether they are sweet or savoury. Wheat flour is used for the sweet *crêpes*, which are usually eaten as a dessert, and buckwheat is used to make a genuine *galette*, which can be enjoyed at any time of the day, with a sausage, some *lait ribot* (buttermilk) or simply while it is still warm with a nut of slightly salted butter.

The Buckwheat Road

Buckwheat is much older than white wheat flour, which became widely available only in the 20th C. It was first introduced by the Crusaders and soon became a popular crop in Brittany, thanks to its high yield on poor soil. It fell into disfavour for a while, but growth has revived significantly, with some 250 growers harvesting 5,000 acres (2,000 ha) of buckwheat a year in the five Breton *départements*. The Buckwheat Road is a tour of about 65 miles (100 km), organised by the Armorican Regional Natural Park, which covers several ecological museums, including the Kerouat windmills in Commana (☎ 02 98 68 87 76), and the Champs à Saint-Ségal museum (☎ 02 98 73 01 07), which holds various events every summer. For information ☎ 02 98 73 17 03.

Lacy pancakes – Crêpes dentelles

Invented in 1888 in Quimper, the *crêpe dentelle* is a subtle combination of granulated sugar and fine wheat flour, producing a light, paper-thin, lacy pancake. The cooking process is an art in itself. The pancakes are then cut into strips and rolled up around a knife blade to give the finished product. The Gavottes factory in Dinan produces some of the best *crêpes dentelles* in Brittany. The shop is at 9 Rue du Château and is open from Tuesday to Saturday and on Sundays in July and August (☎ 02 96 87 06 48).

Kouign aman – Brittany buttercake

This rich mixture of the finest wheat flour, butter and sugar will tempt even the most dedicated weight-watcher. This delicious sweet cake had its origins in Douarnenez in 1865, when the recipe was invented by a baker called Scordia. All the best Breton bakers offer the *kouign aman*. It is the traditional cake for celebrations, for Sundays and for communion, but the Bretons are so fond of it, they will eat it on any occasion.

The far breton

You might come across this pudding filled with raisins or apricots, but remember that the true *far breton* is made with prunes. A creamy *crêpe* batter, delicately flavoured with apple brandy and cinnamon, is poured over stoned prunes before being baked in the oven. In the Finistère region, 3½ oz (100 g) of butter is generally added as well as some slices of apple. The origin of the *far* goes back to the Romans except that they used to salt the batter.

Cider, chouchen and cervoise

Cider is an important element in Breton cuisine, and it is a good accompaniment to any dish. However, the only cider to benefit from an *appellation d'origine contrôlée* (AOC) is cider that comes from the Fouesnant region of Cornouaille and from the Bigouden area. Numerous cider makers are to be found in Brittany, some of whom still work in the traditional way (p. 230). *Chouchen* is a type of mead of Celtic origins, a fermented honey drink, but be careful – it has quite a kick! Honey is also an ingredient in *cervoise* (barley beer), which is made from hops. But you have to be really clever to guess the six other plants that give it its powerful taste and and its amber colour. Of course, all these alcoholic beverages should be consumed in moderation!

A taste of Brittany

Where can you buy all the delicious foods that Brittany produces?
Growers, breeders, cooks and producers will be happy to open
their doors for you. Just follow the guide.

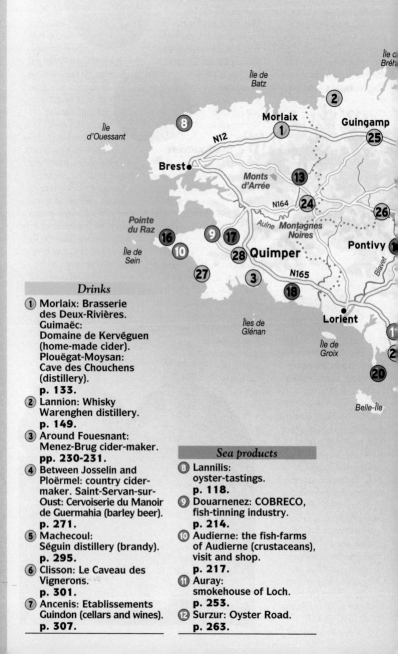

Drinks

1. Morlaix: Brasserie des Deux-Rivières. Guimaëc: Domaine de Kervéguen (home-made cider). Plouëgat-Moysan: Cave des Chouchens (distillery). **p. 133.**
2. Lannion: Whisky Warenghen distillery. **p. 149.**
3. Around Fouesnant: Menez-Brug cider-maker. **pp. 230-231.**
4. Between Josselin and Ploërmel: country cider-maker. Saint-Servan-sur-Oust: Cervoiserie du Manoir de Guermahia (barley beer). **p. 271.**
5. Machecoul: Séguin distillery (brandy). **p. 295.**
6. Clisson: Le Caveau des Vignerons. **p. 301.**
7. Ancenis: Etablissements Guindon (cellars and wines). **p. 307.**

Sea products

8. Lannilis: oyster-tastings. **p. 118.**
9. Douarnenez: COBRECO, fish-tinning industry. **p. 214.**
10. Audierne: the fish-farms of Audierne (crustaceans), visit and shop. **p. 217.**
11. Auray: smokehouse of Loch. **p. 253.**
12. Surzur: Oyster Road. **p. 263.**

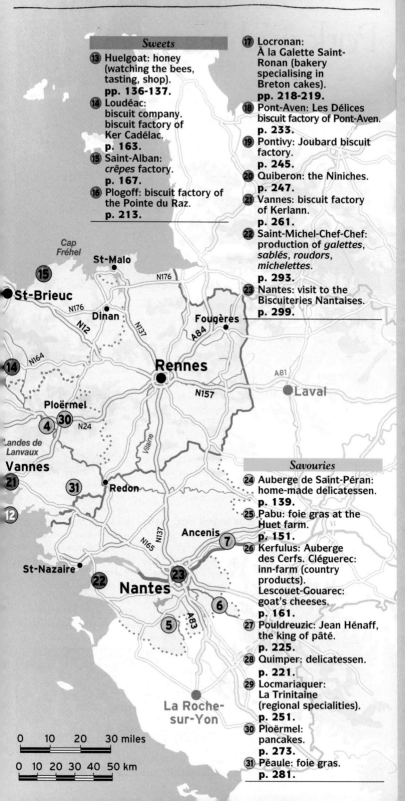

Sweets

13 Huelgoat: honey (watching the bees, tasting, shop).
pp. 136-137.

14 Loudéac: biscuit company. biscuit factory of Ker Cadélac.
p. 163.

15 Saint-Alban: *crêpes* factory.
p. 167.

16 Plogoff: biscuit factory of the Pointe du Raz.
p. 213.

17 Locronan: À la Galette Saint-Ronan (bakery specialising in Breton cakes).
pp. 218-219.

18 Pont-Aven: Les Délices biscuit factory of Pont-Aven.
p. 233.

19 Pontivy: Joubard biscuit factory.
p. 245.

20 Quiberon: the Niniches.
p. 247.

21 Vannes: biscuit factory of Kerlann.
p. 261.

22 Saint-Michel-Chef-Chef: production of *galettes*, *sablés*, *roudors*, *michelettes*.
p. 293.

23 Nantes: visit to the Biscuiteries Nantaises.
p. 299.

Savouries

24 Auberge de Saint-Péran: home-made delicatessen.
p. 139.

25 Pabu: foie gras at the Huet farm.
p. 151.

26 Kerfulus: Auberge des Cerfs. Cléguerec: inn-farm (country products). Lescouet-Gouarec: goat's cheeses.
p. 161.

27 Pouldreuzic: Jean Hénaff, the king of pâté.
p. 225.

28 Quimper: delicatessen.
p. 221.

29 Locmariaquer: La Trinitaine (regional specialities).
p. 251.

30 Ploërmel: pancakes.
p. 273.

31 Péaule: foie gras.
p. 281.

Cap Fréhel
St-Malo
N176
St-Brieuc
N176
N12
Dinan
N137
Fougères
A84
N164
Rennes
A81
Laval
Ploërmel
N24
N157
Landes de Lanvaux
Vannes
Redon
Vilaine
Ancenis
N137
N165
St-Nazaire
Nantes
A83
La Roche-sur-Yon

0 10 20 30 miles
0 10 20 30 40 50 km

Pork and ham

Brittany produces 240,000 tonnes of specialist pork and ham products annually, more than a quarter of France's total production. The region has long known how to make good food from virtually every part of the pig, and the various pork products are still among the best specialities of the region making it a feast for meat-eaters.

The red label and free-range pork
The *label rouge* (red label of quality for meat) criteria are extremely strict. Piglets must be free-range, and three-quarters of their food must consist of cereals. Antibiotics are strictly forbidden. This label produces two more appellations, *porc fermier de Bretagne* (free-range Breton pork) and *porc fermier de l'Ar Goat* (free-range pork from the Ar Goat, inland Brittany).

The andouille
There can be no doubt that the tastiest *andouille* (chitterling sausage) comes from Guémené-sur-Scorff in Morbihan. It can be easily recognised by the concentric circles of the cooked, salted chitterlings. Once cooked, the *andouille* is dried and smoked, which gives it a dark skin. This sausage is usually eaten cold on a slice of buttered bread, but can also be grilled or fried and eaten in a buckwheat *galette*.

Sausages and ham
The 100% pork sausage occupies a special place in the pork produce of Brittany. It is grilled, then rolled inside a buckwheat *galette*, a real institution in the region. In addition to sausages, pork products include cooked, smoked or raw ham, with or without the rind, salamis and garlic sausages, black puddings and tripe with prunes.

The pig in disgrace
Brittany's freshwater sources

have become tainted due to the pig. Once a real economic life-saver for the region, pigs are now in disgrace. Almost 80 towns have been classified as 'areas of natural excess' because of the surplus slurry and farmyard manure they are producing, which is threatening to harm the water supply. The whole region has mobilised to find a solution to the problem.

Dairy products
la crème de la crème

In spite of the quotas imposed by Brussels, dairy production continues, especially in the Léon region, which still produces excellent quality dairy cows. Most of the livestock currently farmed (mainly Charolais and Charentais cows) will, however, eventually be sold for beef.

Slightly salted butter

Brittany is about the only place where you will taste it, but the Bretons can hardly bring themselves to eat anything else! Salt used to be added to preserve the butter, but now the salt content varies between 0.5 and 3%. Bridel and Besnier are large industrial producers, which continue to concentrate most of their production on unsalted butter for 'export' – that is, to be sold throughout France, where the preference is for the unsalted variety.

Full-cream milk

The colour of this milk, known in French as *gros lait*, is slightly yellower than that of ordinary milk as well as being thicker and creamier. 200 tonnes are produced each year. Consumption is still mainly local, and is a part of the Breton rural tradition. This milk once came only from the famous Breton pied cows, but for some years the producers have managed to obtain the milk from other breeds.

Buttermilk

Buttermilk is slightly fermented and should be drunk ice-cold. It has a slightly sour taste, which makes it particularly thirst-quenching. It is called *lait ribot* locally, *ribot* meaning a churn. Be careful, however, because the word *ribot* on the bottle does not necessarily mean that the contents are buttermilk. Ribot is the name of a dairy and it is the brand-name for other products, including ordinary milk. Only bottles labelled *fermenté* contain real buttermilk.

The pedigree pied cow

There is a saying that this cow is 'useful for the rich man, providence for the poor'. The Breton pied cow is a champion dairy cow. You will come across a few herds on your walks in the area around Cap Sizun as some breeders refuse to give them up, despite the quotas for dairy products that have made this pedigree breed almost extinct. Sturdy and small, with hindquarters higher than the forequarters, the distinctive black-and-white colouring makes this cow easily recognisable. Be careful if you are crossing fields in which these cows are grazing, for like most dairy cattle, the pied cow is bad tempered, and beware especially of the pied bull.

Artichokes and cauliflowers Breton specialities

Pictures of local government offices being bombarded with potatoes or cartloads of cauliflowers being thrown into the streets of Quimper or Morlaix by angry growers are regular sights on the front pages of French newspapers. Indeed, Brittany, as the premier vegetable-growing region of Europe, producing one million tonnes annually on 173,000 acres (70,000 ha) of cultivated land between Brest and Saint-Malo, is greatly affected by fluctuations in world prices.

The 'golden belt'

For three centuries the Léon hills have been devoted to the cultivation of globe artichokes and cauliflowers. The hills are bathed in the warm air rising from the Gulf Stream and are therefore protected from the worst of the winter cold as well as from excessive summer heat. The famous Breton artichoke, which is produced from October to May, is quite fleshy and must be cooked. A new variety, the purple artichoke, has been introduced recently, and this is eaten raw with a sprinkling of salt. Artichokes and cauliflowers can be stored for several days in the vegetable rack of the refrigerator. When cooked, artichokes are suitable for home freezing.

Potato varieties

Potatoes were introduced to Belle-Île by the Irish in the 18th C. They were despised at first but soon became a staple dish and one that has lasted for generations. Many varieties of potatoes are produced. The coastal growing regions specialise in early potatoes, which have a delicate hazelnut flavour and are served simply browned in butter.

The Sirtema, Ostara and Starlet varieties are fairly soft and arrive in the markets in May, whereas the Nicolas and Charlotte varieties are firmer and can be purchased only in June. Potatoes grown inland are lifted in the autumn for longer storage.

The empire of the farmer-turned-manager

Alexis Gourvennec, one of Brittany's recent success stories, was labelled a 'farmer-turned-manager' before he became managing director of Brittany Ferries. In 1961 he had the idea of bringing all the vegetable growers into a single federation so that they would have more clout in the marketplace. Sica, as it is known, is now the main group of producers, with 3,500 members marketing 400,000 tonnes of vegetables a year. This organisation also manages the *marché au cadran de Kerivel* in Saint-Pol-de-Léon, which fixes the price of vegetables daily for the growing region.

Traditional vegetables and edible flowers

The Léon producers, always at the forefront of innovation, have brought several traditional vegetables up to date in order to diversify their

production. For instance, the round cauliflower has been in competition for five years with its pointed counterpart, which originates from an old Roman variety, the romanesco. Some vegetable growers are also growing edible flowers to add to salads, including begonias, marigolds, pansies and nasturtiums. Millions of flowers are now packaged in punnets and exported all over the world. They can be bought in the wholesale market at Rungis, in Paris for 10 F a punnet of 15 flowers, or try some at a top restaurant.

Seeing the vegetables grow

Throughout the year the Haut Léon district arranges guided tours for groups that wish to visit some of the major growers, including the Compagnie Bretonne de l'Artichaut (the Breton artichoke company), which produces canned and deep-frozen foods. Here, you will learn that 5 lb (2 kg) of fresh cauliflower are needed to give 2¼ lb (1 kg) of deep-frozen florets, and that the artichoke heart represents only

10% of the vegetable. Information and booking: Pays du Haut Léon, Place de l'Évêché, 29250 Saint-Pol-de-Léon (☎ 02 98 29 09 09).

Breton tomatoes

After a difficult start, Breton tomatoes have now achieved a high status in the regional horticulture stakes. The best known are those from Nantes or Rennes. Try serving them *à la bretonne*. For this, you need to choose some small, quite round, firm tomatoes. Finely chop some onions (the ones from Roscoff are highly recommended) and cook them in butter until they are transparent, then add the peeled and seeded tomatoes. This makes a good side-dish to serve with meat, fish or buckwheat *galettes* (Breton pancakes). Bon appétit!

All about oysters

Each year Brittany provides 30% of the 140,000 tonnes of oysters produced by France. Production is split between two major areas: northern Brittany, including the bays of Cancale, St Brieuc and Morlaix, and southern Brittany and the Morbihan estuaries. The Bretons enjoy eating oysters throughout the year, but they are particularly associated with Christmas and New Year, and oyster-farmers make about half their turnover during the festive season.

How to recognise types of oyster

The European or 'flat' oyster, *huître plat* (*Ostrea edulis*), and the giant or 'convex' oyster, *huître creuse* (*Crassostrea gigas*), are two distinct species. The European oyster is native to Brittany, whilst the giant oyster arrived accidentally when a Portuguese ship carrying oyster spats to Britain was shipwrecked off the coast in 1868. The baby oysters found a favourable site and began to breed. Unfortunately, this species of oyster was decimated by a

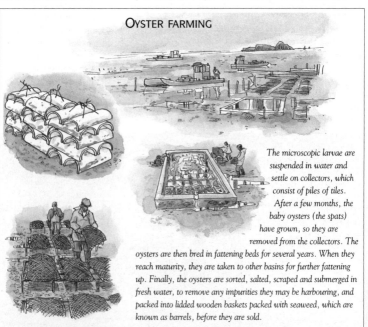

OYSTER FARMING

The microscopic larvae are suspended in water and settle on collectors, which consist of piles of tiles. After a few months, the baby oysters (the spats) have grown, so they are removed from the collectors. The oysters are then bred in fattening beds for several years. When they reach maturity, they are taken to other basins for further fattening up. Finally, the oysters are sorted, salted, scraped and submerged in fresh water, to remove any impurities they may be harbouring, and packed into lidded wooden baskets packed with seaweed, which are known as barrels, before they are sold.

virus in 1973 and has since been replaced by spats imported from Japan. This larger, Pacific oyster is not as well liked in France as the

smaller European type, as its flesh is not considered to be as flavoursome.

Oysters from Paimpol, Morlaix or Cancale

In Brittany oysters, like great wines, are classified by their origin. The fleshy Paimpol oyster contains a high level of iodine; the Morlaix oyster has delicate flesh; and the Cancale convex oyster is fleshy and very salty. The *fine de claire* and the flat Belon oyster, which have excellent reputations, are produced in southern Brittany; they have a faintly nutty aftertaste. Marennes oysters, which have a green tinge, are farmed in the Vendée region. In France oysters are usually eaten raw with a vinegar dressing containing shallots and a dash of lemon juice. They can also be stuffed and cooked.

How to buy oysters

Most supermarkets concentrate on selling oysters in the Christmas season, but fishmongers sell them throughout the year. More oysters are sold in markets than in any other type of outlet. European oysters are classified into nine categories, depending on their size, and convex oysters into eight. In France oysters are bought by the dozen and mussels by the litre (1¼ imperial pints, about 2 US pints). It is also possible to buy oysters and mussels by weight.

When to eat oysters

Despite superstitions to the contrary, oysters and mussels can be eaten at any time of the year. Oysters are fleshiest during the fattening period – from May to August – and are a good source of vitamins. The ban on eating oysters at certain times of the year is based on an edict issued by Louis XV. This did not actually ban the consumption but rather the transport of oysters in months not containing the letter 'r', because these are the hottest months of the year. The labels on the oyster barrels at the fishmonger indicate the origin, size and date of catch. For mussels, you can ask for the public health label showing the date on which the mussels were shipped and confirming that they are fit for consumption.

Storing oysters

To keep oysters fresh, you need to keep them from opening their shells. The best way to do this is simply to pile them up and put a weight on the top. The bottom shelf of the refrigerator or the window sill in winter are both adequate for storage. The shellfish will keep in this way for about 10 days after they are taken from the water. Always throw away oysters that do not contain water and any whose mantle (the darker, outer part) does not react when pricked with the tip of a knife. Do not open oyster barrels if you are not going to eat the oysters immediately.

Oyster farms

Les Viviers de la Forêt, La Cale La Forêt-Fouesnant
☎ **02 98 56 96 68**
Ring for information on opening hours.
Les Huîtrières du Château de Belon, Port de Belon, Riec-sur-Belon
☎ **02 96 06 90 58**
Open all year.
(*See also the Oyster Road p. 263.*)

Fishing for mussels

Mussels, like oysters, are bivalve molluscs, and they have been the delight of gourmets since the dawn of history. Mussels can be divided into two species, the small mussel (*Mytilus edulis*) and the larger mussel (*Mytilus galloprovincialis*), which lives in the Mediterranean Sea. Mussels are either male or female, but some oysters can change their sex. Both mussels and oysters are said to have aphrodisiac properties ...

Gourmet France

The French desire for mussels is so great that the annual production of 70,000 tonnes is not enough to satisfy demand, and so nearly 40,000 tonnes of mussels are imported annually, mainly from the Netherlands, Spain and Ireland. French mussels are mostly farmed, and they are much tastier than the imported fished mussels. Always check the origin of the shellfish you intend to buy at the fish-monger or in a restaurant.

Collecting mussels

It is still possible to collect mussels in Brittany, but ask first at the tourist office because collecting is strictly controlled. Above all, do not pick the clusters of shellfish that you see stuck to the rocks on the seashore in easily accessible and heavily populated areas as they are often unfit for human consumption. It is dangerous to eat shellfish of uncertain origin as they tend to collect and concentrate any impurities from the water in which they live.

starfish and winkle. The stakes are inspected and replaced on a regular basis, and collecting may be done by hand or by machine.

barges, which can carry five or six tonnes of oysters, or curved rowing-boats, known as *yoles* (gigs), which are smaller and easier to handle.

Moules marinières

Pour some white wine (*gros-plant* from the Nantes region is ideal) into a deep pot over thinly sliced shallots or onions. Add a bouquet garni, chopped parsley and butter. Sprinkle with freshly ground black pepper. Bring to the boil and cook at a rolling boil for about five minutes, then add the mussels, which should have been carefully washed and scraped. Cover the pot. The mussels are ready when they have opened by themselves and are best served piping hot. Discard any whose shells have not opened. Mussels can also be eaten plain, cooked without water, and served simply with some chopped parsley, onions, a sprig of thyme, a bay leaf and butter. For a main course allow about 1 lb (500g) per person. You can eat as many as you like – the energy content is barely nine calories and they full of minerals and trace elements.

Mussel beds

In the Mediterranean mussels are usually bred on flat beds. In Brittany the most frequent farming method is called *bouchot*. This consists of planting lines of oak stakes, 165–330 feet (50–100 m) long and about 13–20 feet (4–6 m) high, firmly into the sand at the limit of low tide. The mussel spat is bred on ropes, which are rolled around the stakes when the larvae have turned into young mussels. It takes two years for mussels to reach the minimum size of 1¼ in (4 cm). The spat requires continuous care in order to protect it from predators such as gulls, green crabs,

Shellfish farming craft

Most mussel or oyster breeding activities are carried out using strange-looking craft, the oddest being the wheeled-boat, mostly used for mussel picking in the bay of Mont-Saint-Michel. These curious vessels are amphibious floating workshops, enabling fishermen to work on the mussel beds, whatever the level of the tide. Oyster collection from the beds is performed using either flat-bottomed

Arts and crafts

There is a huge choice of local and traditional clothing, sailing gear and accessories, so there are plenty of holiday souvenirs for you to purchase. If you want to find out more about their origins, visit the local arts and folklore museums.

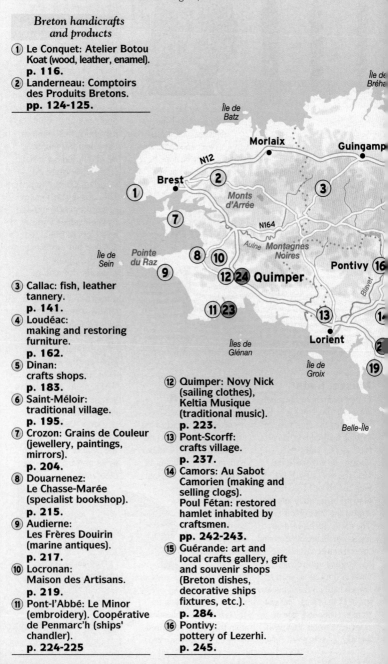

Breton handicrafts and products

1. Le Conquet: Atelier Botou Koat (wood, leather, enamel). **p. 116.**
2. Landerneau: Comptoirs des Produits Bretons. **pp. 124-125.**
3. Callac: fish, leather tannery. **p. 141.**
4. Loudéac: making and restoring furniture. **p. 162.**
5. Dinan: crafts shops. **p. 183.**
6. Saint-Méloir: traditional village. **p. 195.**
7. Crozon: Grains de Couleur (jewellery, paintings, mirrors). **p. 204.**
8. Douarnenez: Le Chasse-Marée (specialist bookshop). **p. 215.**
9. Audierne: Les Frères Douirin (marine antiques). **p. 217.**
10. Locronan: Maison des Artisans. **p. 219.**
11. Pont-l'Abbé: Le Minor (embroidery). Coopérative de Penmarc'h (ships' chandler). **p. 224-225**
12. Quimper: Novy Nick (sailing clothes), Keltia Musique (traditional music). **p. 223.**
13. Pont-Scorff: crafts village. **p. 237.**
14. Camors: Au Sabot Camorien (making and selling clogs). Poul Fétan: restored hamlet inhabited by craftsmen. **pp. 242-243.**
15. Guérande: art and local crafts gallery, gift and souvenir shops (Breton dishes, decorative ships fixtures, etc.). **p. 284.**
16. Pontivy: pottery of Lezerhi. **p. 245.**

Antiques

⑰ Saint-Malo:
marine flea-market.
p. 180.
⑱ Combourg:
antique shops.
p. 184.
⑲ La Trinité-sur-Mer:
marine items.
p. 249.
⑳ Rochefort-en-Terre:
Au Bon Vieux Temps
(antiques and traditional
items).
p. 276.
㉑ Soudan: L'Occasion
Soudanaise (antiques).
p. 305.

Local arts, crafts and traditions

㉒ Rennes: Musée Breton.
p. 197.
㉓ Pont-L'Abbé:
Maison du Pays Bigouden.
p. 224.
㉔ Quimper: pottery works,
Musée Départemental
Breton.
p. 222.
㉕ Sainte-Anne d'Auray:
Musée du Costume
Breton.
p. 255.
㉖ Lizio:
Écomusée de la Ferme
et des Vieux Métiers.
pp. 270-271.
㉗ Batz-sur-Mer: Maison du
Sabot and Musée des
Marais Salants.
p. 283.
㉘ Guérande:
Maison des Paludiers
and Maison du Sel.
p. 285.
㉙ Kerhinet: open-air
museum (costumes
and old tools),
Maison des Artisans.
Île de Fédrun:
Maison de la Mariée.
p. 289.
㉚ Bourgneuf-en-Retz:
Musée du Pays de Retz.
p. 295.
㉛ Blain: Musée des Arts
et Traditions Populaires.
p. 303.

Oilskins and sou'westers
Breton clothes

Rain, wind and sea spray are not unknown in Brittany, and traditional Breton clothing takes account of the roughest weather conditions. Strength, warmth and comfort are the essential features of the clothing, and several manufacturers have designed ranges of weatherproof clothes that are suited to the rough living conditions endured by fishermen. Practical and easy to wear, these garments have become popular with recreational sailors and tourists.

and Poupon. Today, the clothing factory at Trégunc (Pont-Minaouët, 29910 Trégunc, ☎ 02 98 97 66 79) is an expanding industry with over 150 employees. The factory does not admit visitors. However, from 30 June onwards, you can buy the previous year's collections at bargain prices.

The Cottens' saga

This success story started in the early 1960s, when Guy Cotten decided to manufacture clothes for fishermen. His friends, most of whom were fishermen themselves, described the kind of clothes they would like to be able to buy – strong, as waterproof as an oilskin, but as comfortable as a suit. Guy and Françoise Cotten started to design and manufacture garments which the trainees at the Rosbraz watersports centre were the first to try out. They were an immediate success, and the famous Rosbraz jacket was born. Since then it has sailed the seven seas and has been worn by famous yachtsmen such as Colas, Tabarly

Oilskins and sou'westers

The standard light and strong yellow oilskin now always has a hood attached to it, but the traditional sou'wester is still worn too. This is an oilskin hat with a very wide brim, turned down flat at the back in order to cover the collar of the jacket and stop rain from running down the back of the neck. It has a certain outdated charm and is still worn by fishermen, mainly in southern Finistère. It is comfortable to wear, since it is lined with corduroy or a smooth fabric. And costing less than 100 F it makes a good souvenir from Brittany too. You can find them in such places as Moussaillon in Concarneau (Avenue Biele, Seld-Zenne, ☎ 02 98 97 09 22).

The reefer and sailor's pullover

The French sailor's pullover was all the rage in the 1960s. It has changed somewhat but is just as comfortable. This warm, woollen sweater is buttoned on the left shoulder; it is long and fairly tight fitting, but you can move freely in it. A 'genuine' French sailor's pullover will cost about 400 F. The reefer or pea jacket is more popular with fishermen than with tourists because the cloth is thick and strong enough to withstand bad weather. The collar is wide enough to be turned up and buttoned to the neck.

The sea jacket

You can wear one of these jackets (*vestes de quart*) anywhere: at sea off Iroise or on the Champs-Élysées. They really started to become fashionable in France in the early 1990s. Waterproof, strong and easy to wear, they are made in bright colours so that the sailor is clearly seen from afar. It is much more than a mere jacket: it is almost part of the survival kit. The price is rather steep (you will hardly find one for less than 700 F), but the comfort and style suit any

kind of weather conditions and they are now popular worldwide. Beware of imitations. All the ship's chandlers sell the *veste de quart*, but if you are looking for the genuine article, a real investment that will last a lifetime, you should look out for the Helly Hansen, Aigle, Botalo or Guy Cotten brands.

Pottery and earthenware

Earthenware and china seem to have always been part of Brittany's heritage. One of the best-known makers is H.B. Henriot, and the pottery made by the factory is as closely associated with Quimper as porcelain is with Limoges. It dates back to 1690, when an earthenware maker from Provence, Jean-Baptiste Bousquet, set up the first pottery factory in the area of Locmaria. Others emulated him, and Quimper pottery has now become famous all over the world, and is especially popular in the United States.

Designs

As early as 1850 the traditional earthenware of Quimper featured floral designs as well as the 'little Breton' with his *bragou braz* (wide breeches), hat and long hair. These primitive figurines, painted in bright colours, are entirely handmade. They are created by applying small brushstrokes and lines with a paintbrush in the shape of a raindrop to draw flowers and leaves. In the late 19th C., under the influence of Alfred Beau, who was an outstanding artist, these designs were enriched with numerous scenes from country life, such as weddings, dances, markets and pardons.

Manufacturing

First a special mix is prepared, using a combination of clay, dolomite, talc, glass dust and silica. This is made into a thick liquid, the consistency of porridge, and then kneaded into a thick, round block, which will lose 75% of its water content. The paste must now be kneaded again until it becomes firm and can then be cut into several pieces by the mould-makers and put into moulds. The pieces are hand-dried, smoothed and fired before being dipped into vats of enamel. They are then fired again to fix the colours.

are manufactured using industrial pastes, which are white and more friable.

A word of warning

Plates, bowls, lamp bases, statuettes, vases – all kinds of objects in daily use and tableware may be made of Quimper earthenware.

Although most are not marked that they are not dishwasher safe, it is unwise to put cake-servers or butter knives in the dishwasher. A special range of dishes has been created that is heat resistant and can be used in convection ovens or microwave ovens. Do not use any other Quimper earthenware dishes in an oven, because they are unlikely to be heat-resistant and may crack.

VISITING THE FACTORIES

The most famous factory of all is H.B. Henriot, situated in Ruc Haute, in the Locmaria district. This is where the Quimper industry was born. The factory runs guided tours (admission charge), which will take you to the workshops (Mon. to Fri. from 9.15am to 11.15am and from 1.15pm to 4.15pm, reservations required, group reservations: ☎ 02 98 90 09 36). The Faïencerie d'Art Breton, which is managed by Pierre Henriot, is at 50 Route de Locronan (Free guided tours; Tues. to Fri. from 9am to 11.30am; Groups only with reservations, ☎ 02 98 53 72 72).

Antique earthenware

Before the end of the 19th C. dishes were rarely signed. Later they were stamped with the most prestigious marks – H.R., H.B., Henriot or Éloury-Porquier. Less expensive items, which are much more attractive than the modern products, date from the 1950s or 1960s, when natural clay was still in use. To determine when the pottery was made check the underneath of the item. If you are lucky, you will find genuine bowls, ashtrays and small pots that are made of earthenware dating from this period for no more than 100 F or 150 F. Today, the items, though still hand-painted,

Furniture and antiques

A traditional wardrobe or a Breton chest made of carved, dark wood is a beautiful piece of furniture to take back with you. But for anyone who feels that this is too much of an encumbrance, there is a wide range of small, typical, though original, items available, which will remind you of your holidays once you are back home.

Furniture

Even though such traditional furniture as box-beds or sideboards are becoming quite difficult to find, and therefore more expensive, a number of Louis XV or Louis Philippe wardrobes and chests of drawers can still be found. This furniture has been adapted to Breton style and is of modest proportions. In the Côtes d'Armor there are wardrobes with typical cornices called 'pigs ears'. Prices vary between 3000 and 7000 F for a simple piece that has not been restored, but remember to take into account what it will cost to get it home.

Platters, spoons and bowls

Butter moulds, butter pats and various types of cake moulds can still be found in second-hand shops and stalls. The same applies to the series of little wooden spoons of beech or boxwood, from the plainest design to those inlaid with pewter or brass. Some can even be folded so that they could be taken along to a wedding. Locally made simple but decorative earthenware platters and bowls, can also be found quite easily for only a few hundred francs. You might also find sets of Breton bowling balls, known locally as *boulou-pok*, which are made entirely of wood, and could be used as an original pair of bookends, for example.

Biscuit tins

These are sought-after collector's items and this has caused the prices to rise. A biscuit tin from the LU factory featuring the famous schoolboy (*petit écolier*) is one of the most sought-after, as are biscuit tins in the shape of the Eiffel tower or a train. Given the numerous biscuit factories in the region, many biscuit tins, dating from various periods, are likely to be found in the area, which will suit every taste and price range.

Nautical antiques

Cruising in a sailing ship was once an elegant way of life. Comfort and luxury used to be the standard onboard large cruisers and liners. The exotic woods and copper fittings associated with cruise liners can, of course, be found on dry land now.

computer that is less decorative but can precisely calculate the position of the ship. It is, therefore, possible that you will find a sextant, the symbol of sailing on the high seas, in an antique shop or at auction.

The sextant

This is the handsomest sailing accessory. For this reason prices are very high (around 3,000 F for a sextant made of stainless steel in a wooden case). Nevertheless, the price is justified by the intricate mechanism. For a long time, the sextant was indispensable for measuring the sun's angle to the Earth. Pointing it at the skyline would give the longitudinal position of the ship. The sextant is gradually being replaced now by GPS, a pocket-sized

Treasure ships

There is treasure to be found on every ship. Copper barometers, varnished tillers, finely carved sea-chests and trunks ... you will find all of this on dry land. Try to avoid the souvenir shops if you want to purchase the genuine item. Skippers and ship-owners get their supplies from the elegant boutiques in the ports, too. It is a guarantee of quality.

Knot pictures

Everybody is keen on knot pictures, so prices have rocketed. An attractive example may cost almost 3000 F, and even the least expensive will cost about 500 F. For a

cheaper alternative buy 10 sq feet (1 m²) of blue velvet, a small piece of plywood, a sheet of plexiglass of the same size, 6 ft (2 m) of thin rope and, for less than 30 F, a booklet explaining how to make your own knots. Then get to work!

Brittany in detail

Northern Brittany

Southern Brittany

Brittany in detail

On the following pages you will find details of the most interesting places to visit in Brittany. For your convenience, the region has been divided into zones. The colour code will enable you to easily find the area you are looking for.

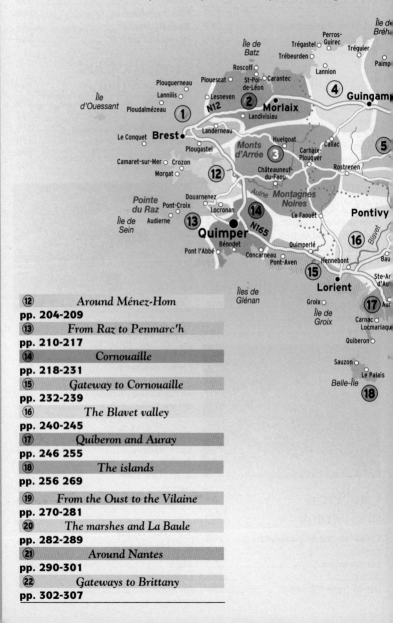

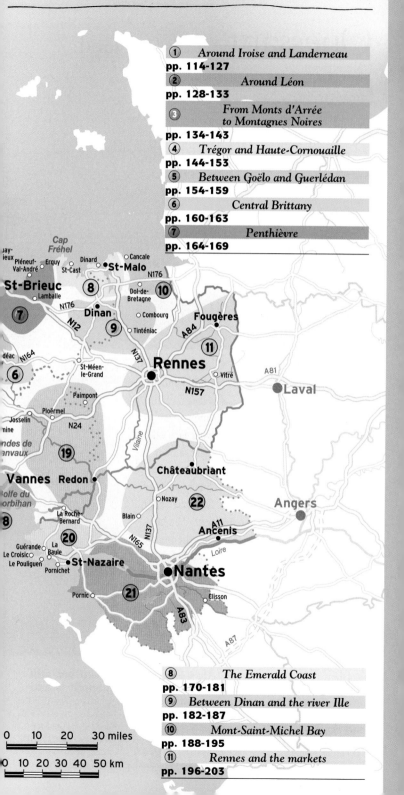

Cap Fréhel

uay-ieux · Pléneuf-Val-André · Erquy · St-Cast · Dinard · Cancale · St-Malo

N176

St-Brieuc · Lamballe

⑧

N176 · Dol-de-Bretagne · ⑩

⑦

N12

Dinan · Combourg · Fougères

déac · N164

⑨ · Tinténiac · A84

⑥

St-Méen-le-Grand · N137 · Rennes · ⑪ · Vitré · A81

Laval

Paimpont · N157

Josselin mine

Ploërmel · N24

Vilaine

ndes de anvaux · ⑲

Châteaubriant

Vannes · Redon

olfe du orbihan

Nozay · ㉒

Angers

⑧

La Roche-Bernard · Blain

Guérande · Le Croisic · La Baule · ⑳ · N165 · N137 · Ancenis · A11

Le Pouliguen · Pornichet · St-Nazaire

Loire

Pornic · ㉑ · Nantes · Clisson

A83

A87

0   10   20   30 miles

0 10 20 30 40 50 km

Ouessant, a distant land…

Ouessant is at the world's end, a magical place, where sea, land and wind commune with each other under the gaze of man, who has adapted to the extra-ordinary power of the elements. The people of Ouessant have always been almost completely self-sufficient. The men spent most of their lives at sea, while the women farmed the barren land. Ouessant society has therefore always been dominated by women because of the long and repeated absences of the men. Until the beginning of the 20th C., for example, women used to ask for the men's hand in marriage! Nobody would have dared to do otherwise.

right by the sea. As the aircraft makes its final approach, you feel certain that it will miss the airfield altogether and you will end up in the sea. It's quite a hair-raising experience, but don't worry, the pilot is used to it.

Getting there

From the coast (departures are from Brest), two ferry companies (**Penn Ar Bed** ☎ 02 98 80 24 68 and **Finist'Mer** ☎ 02 98 89 16 61) operate to the island. The only air service is **Finist'air** (from Brest-

Guipavas airport ☎ 02 98 84 64 87). The flight to Ouessant takes only 20 minutes, but it is an unforgettable trip. You get the impression that the plane is going to land on a gigantic mass of foam, then, as you approach, you are able to make out the tiny airfield

A wild but still unspoilt island

No cars are allowed on the island. You can either walk or ride a bicycle (hire one from the tourist office, Place de l'Église, ☎ 02 98 48 85 83). The island is listed as a 'reserve of the Iroise biosphere', and no pollutants are permitted. A tour of about 7 miles (12 km) departs from the church of Lampaul, in the

direction of Grand'Roche, an enormous natural sea barrier situated right in the middle of a small bay, then visits the little harbour of **Bougezenn**, where cranes winch boats out of the water so they can be repaired. You will then see the magnificent **Pointe du Pern** and the famous **Créac'h lighthouse**. You return to Lampaul through the little village of Niou Uhella.

Créac'h lighthouse

☎ 02 98 48 80 70 or
☎ 02 98 48 85 83
Open daily May to Sept.
10.30am–6.30pm.
Out of season 2–4pm, except Mon.
Admission charge.
Créac'h also features the **Musée des Phares et des Balises** (museum of lighthouses and beacons), which traces the history of a variety of markers and warning lights since ancient times. This is the most appropriate place for such a museum since so many ships have been wrecked on the rocks of Ouessant.

Ouessant Ecological Museum

Maison du Niou Uhella
☎ 02 98 48 86 37 or
☎ 02 98 48 85 83
Open daily May to Sept.
from 10.30am–6pm.
Out of season 2–4pm, except Mon.
Admission charge.
The museum consists of a traditional mid-19th-C. Ouessant house, where the daily life and the island traditions will be explained to you in detail. You will also find out why the domesticated animals on Ouessant – horses, cows and sheep – were so small. Sadly, apart from the black sheep, these dwarf animals have all become extinct.

The sheep fair

The weather is bitterly cold, the wind is blowing a gale, it is raining heavily and the sea is raging. In other words, it is a typical February day on the island. On the first Wednesday of the month, the sheep that were set free to roam on Michaelmas (29 September) are gathered in again. Each farmer recognises his own sheep thanks to the branding on their ears. Sheep that have not been recognised are sold at auction, and in the true spirit of the island, the proceeds go to islanders who have suffered from damage caused by winter weather. There are few tourists at this time of year, but it is the best time to experience the spirit of solidarity of the Ouessant islanders.

ORNITHOLOGICAL CENTRE

Centre d'Étude du Milieu
☎ 02 98 48 82 65
Ouessant is an exceptionally favourable site for the study of birds, especially in autumn, when flocks of migratory birds arrive at the island. The Centre for the Study of the Environment offers several residential courses to improve your knowledge of ornithology, entomology and botany. Some of the courses are booked up in advance, but you can also make individual bookings, and the centre will organise accommodation for you.

Le Conquet and Saint-Mathieu headland,

the tip of France

The restaurant here is quite popular, so you will probably have to book in advance, but you absolutely must taste the seafood platter at dusk at the Saint-Mathieu headland (☎ 02 98 89 00 19; menus between 150 F and 320 F). When night falls you will be able to see all 15 of the nearby lighthouses lighting up, one after the other. At the end of your meal, walk along the promenade at the foot of the lighthouse or around the ruins of the abbey, and experience the glow of the lighthouses, the wind and the noise of the sea 100 feet (30 m) below.

Le Conquet, a small fishing port

This is an extraordinarily busy port, or perhaps it only seems so because it is so small. One reason is that fishing has always been practically the only source of livelihood here, and thus village life is centred on the port. Just sit for a few minutes on a terrace in front of the port and let your eyes wander from one boat to the next, from a bird to a lobster-pot. The time will fly past. The little town of Le Conquet and its steep lanes are also interesting to wander around. Visit the **Atelier Botou Koat** (☎ 02 98 89 12 08), in front of the church, in which you will probably find some tiny Breton souvenirs made of leather or earthenware, or traditional clogs?

Kermorvan and the Corsen headland

Leave the town of Le Conquet by crossing over the suspension footbridge that links it to the peninsula and the longest beach of the region, les **Blancs-Sablons**. Not only does it have 1¼ miles (2 km) of sand, but it is protected by steep cliffs from the wind and has the most magnificent views. **Corsen headland**, in the north, can be reached via a footpath. Once there, you can say that you have reached the tip of France. To symbolise its isolated position, two signposts indicate that Moscow is 1,900 miles (3,010 km) away to the east, and New York 3,200 miles (5,080 km) to the west. A great photo opportunity!

The Aquafaune motorboat

☎ 02 98 89 17 66
Daily cruises Apr. to Oct. Reservation required. Why not take a trip to the **Molène archipelago**? You just have to board the *Aquafaune* motorboat, which has underwater viewing facilities that enable you to look at the seabed around the islands of Béniguet, Quéménès, Trielen, Molène and Balanec. You will also be able to watch seals and dolphins in their natural environment. There are three tours, one of which includes a stop at the island of Molène.

Boarding is from the Sainte-Barbe pier in the port of Le Conquet.

The cove of Bertheaume

Daily trips in season. The cove is sheltered and has several attractive beaches, overlooked by an impressive fortress. Fort de Bertheaume is known as the 'fort at the world's end'. Its isolated position and the violence of the elements that continuously rage around it will help you understand why.

Le Trez-Hir

Saint-Tropez in Brittany

About 4½ miles (7 km) E of Le Conquet

Trez-Hir is where the people of Brest go for their holidays, and some of them even have second homes here, for it is close to the town. The longest beach, overlooked by Fort de Bertheaume, is called Saint-Trop'-sur-Rade, and the tiny

Spotcheck

A2

Finistère

Things to do

Hiking on the coast
The *Aquafaune* motorboat

For the children

Keringar's farm

Tourist office

Le Conquet:
☎ 02 98 99 11 31

KERINGAR'S FARM

On your way back to Le Conquet, why not stop off at Keringar's farm (Lochrist, Le Conquet; ☎ 02 98 89 09 59). It is both a playground and a place where children, aged from 4 to 12, can learn all about life in the country. Several endangered species are bred at the farm, and children can have a go at the various tasks that need to be done for the animals, as well as weaving and basket-making. Mini-camps featuring tepees are also set up and supervised by trained instructors. As for the parents, delicious farmhouse produce is available for purchase.

seaside resort is an entertaining place. It could claim to be Brittany's answer to fashionable Saint-Tropez on the Côte d'Azur, although the weather does not always live up to it.

The Côte des Abers
The Armorican coast

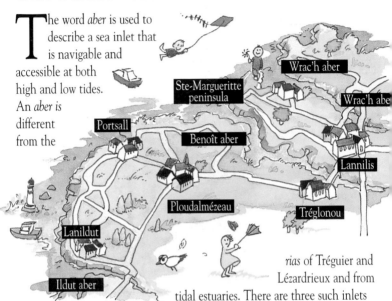

The word *aber* is used to describe a sea inlet that is navigable and accessible at both high and low tides. An *aber* is different from the *rias* of Tréguier and Lézardrieux and from tidal estuaries. There are three such inlets in Brittany, all of them close to each other – Wrac'h, Benoît and Ildut. They are important natural shelters, protecting small, inland ports, whose glorious trading days may be over but are still charming and interesting places to visit.

Tréglonou

Getting about on foot

From Tréglonou, near the head of the Benoît *aber*, a footpath runs to the sea and offers a succession of superb views, which are of particular interest to birdwatchers. If you walk along the path at low tide you should be able to see

grey herons, egrets and sandpipers on the mudflats. There are many other routes for walkers (brochure available from the Lannilis tourist office, 1 Place de l'Église, ☎ 02 98 04 05 43).

Lannilis

Above the abers

Lannilis is a pretty little town, which is situated between the *abers* of Wrac'h and Benoît. Its speciality is oysters, which you can taste straight from **Bescond**'s oyster farm (Beg ar Vill, Le Passage, Landéda, ☎ 02 98 04 93 31). The Krach bridge, which begins in Lannilis, was paved as long ago as the Iron Age and is said to be the result of the pact a miller signed with the devil, so that he no longer had to skirt right around the *aber* to

deliver his flour. From here, a small, winding path brings you to the banks of the *aber*.

Benoît aber

Windmill country

Towards the end of the 19th C. there were more than 100 windmills operating here, and they provided the whole region with flour. Because they stood beside rivers, these windmills have now become second homes and some are restaurants. Nevertheless, they remain outwardly unchanged. There is a signposted walk from the **Mesnaod mill**.

Wrac'h aber
By boat

The Wrac'h is the most famous *aber* of all, as well as being the largest. When the Wrac'h fairy gave it its name, she could not have known that it would become one of the most popular tourist spots in northern Brittany. As the tides rise and fall, the landscape and the colours of the Wrac'h *aber* change.

into the waters of one of these inlets, which are protected from the wind and the swell by the sheltering banks that enclose them.

A **boat trip** is the perfect way to discover the beauty of the area (Lannilis tourist office, 1 Place de l'Église, ☎ 02 98 04 05 43). If you are not a good sailor you could spend time on the superb beach of the Sainte-Marguerite peninsula and ramble through the sand dunes or visit the small port of **L'Aber-Wrac'h** and the Baie des Anges (angel's bay), both of which are very busy during the peak summer season.

Diving into the abers
Port de L'Aber-Wrac'h
☎ 02 98 04 81 22

The sea-beds of the *abers* are among the most diverse in the whole of Brittany, and you will find muddy, rocky or sandy conditions. This may be a good time to take a dip

Portsall
A bitter memory

The rocks of Portsall are the symbol of the largest oil-slick ever experienced by Brittany. On 16 March 1978 the *Amoco-Cadiz* sank with all her cargo, and 220,000 tonnes of crude oil escaped from her hull. Of course, all surface traces of the oil have completely

disappeared, but some of the microscopic species that lived deep in the sea have been lost forever. Even though the Bretons have received compensation for the disaster, the law-suits to find out who was responsible have lasted for years. The gigantic anchor of the tanker can still be seen at the end of the pier in Portsall as a reminder of the disaster.

BY KAYAK

As you enter the Ildut *aber*, you are welcomed by the charming little town of Lanildut, which has the distinction of being Europe's premier seaweed port. It is fascinating to see the heavily laden rowing-boats on their way back to port in the early afternoon bearing their strange harvest. Some go as far as the island of Ouessant to prospect for fields of seaweed. A pleasant way to experience the delights of the *aber* is to explore it by sea-kayak. The Lanildut watersports centre offers guided trips (☎ 02 98 04 40 56).

Brest, last stop before America!

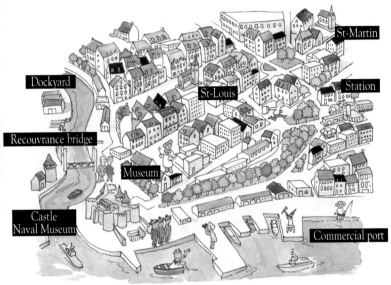

This is the French port closest to the American continent and a strategic site of prime importance. Brest is not a well-known tourist destination, but it is rich in folklore that bears witness to the spirit of its inhabitants, whose reputation for hospitality remains unsullied. Brest is also the starting point for several tours, including one of the lighthouses.

The dockyard and harbour

Porte de la Grande-Rivière
☎ 02 98 22 23 68
Open daily 15 June to 15 Sep. and school holidays 9–11am and 2–4pm.
Free admission (identity card or passport required).

The dockyard is the symbol of the town. Brest is the head-quarters of the maritime

préfecture of France's longest coast, extending from Granville to Biarritz. The others are at Cherbourg, for northern France, and Toulon,

for the Mediterranean area. Naval launches, frigates, minesweepers, aircraft carriers, nuclear submarines – most of the French fleet is gathered here.

Since the sea-lanes are well-protected deep inside a naturally closed harbour, the Romans, Richelieu, Colbert and de Gaulle all decided to use Brest as a naval stronghold. The harbour, a huge stretch of water of 60 sq miles (150 km²), also has excellent look-out posts with delightful views of Sainte-Anne du Portzic, the

Kerbonne garden, the Cours Dajot, Albert-Louppe bridge and the Pointe des Espagnols. Other beauty spots can be visited by motorboat.
(**Vedettes Armoricaines,** ☎ 02 98 44 44 04).

The castle

Musée de la Marine
☎ 02 98 22 12 39
Open daily except Tue. 9.15–noon and 2–6pm.
Entry charge.

Brest castle, a Roman fort built in AD 300, is one of the most beautiful in France. Today it houses the maritime museum. A pocket submarine has been rebuilt and shares pride of place with sailing ships and craft from the South China Sea. There are collections of models, paintings, sculptures and navigation instruments.

Spotcheck

B2

Finistère

Things to do

Trips on a motorboat
Maritime museum
Jeudis du Port
Océanopolis
Short films festival

Within easy reach

*Monts d'Arrée 25 miles (40 km) F, p. 134,
Landévennec 30 miles (50 km.), p. 206
Châteaulin 28½ miles (46 km) SE, p. 208*

Tourist office

Brest: ☎ 02 98 44 13 71

THE WORLD'S END

Horaires d'ouverture
Lundi - Vendredi   11ʰ–1ʰ
Samedi :   15ʰ–1ʰ
Dimanche :   15ʰ–1ʰ

Opening hours
Monday – Friday 11am–1am
Saturday :   3pm–1am
Sunday :   3pm–1am

Restauration rapide de 12ʰ à 14ʰ en semaine

Bar snacks available weekdays between 12 & 2

NIGHTLIFE

The Quartz is a theatre of the avant-garde (☎ 02 98 44 33 77). It has a membership of more than 10,000, and more than 250,000 people attend performances every year. A list of the events is kept up to date at the tourist office (Avenue Georges-Clemenceau, BP 24, ☎ 02 98 44 24 96). The city also holds an annual festival of short films around 15 November, which shows the best French shorts. Since 1995 the Cinémathèque de Bretagne (film library) has been installed in the Quartz Rotunda.

Le Moulin-Blanc, boating and watersports

Le Moulin-Blanc is a busy

marina, and it is the ideal place for a pleasant walk, especially if you stroll along the landing stages to watch the numerous racing ships that are moored there either permanently or temporarily. The Centre Nautique Municipal (watersports centre) is also located in the

marina (☎ 02 98 34 64 64). In the summer the **Jeudis du Port** (Thursdays in the port) event attracts many people. From late afternoon there are free concerts and shows, street theatre, sea shanties and the like to entertain the crowds on the quays and in the adjoining streets (programme available at the tourist office). Le Moulin-Blanc also has a sheltered white, sandy beach.

Recouvrance

Recouvrance is the name of both the largest drawbridge in Europe and of the district with the liveliest nightlife. The girls who patrolled the

pavements on the look-out for sailors have largely disappeared, but the district still has plenty of attractions. The *bar-tabac* on the corner of the Rue Borda must be the only one in Brittany not to close before 6am. From Recouvrance, the Rue de Siam is nearby, and here there are restaurants, cafés, pubs and clubs. One of the best for its choice of beers

and whiskies is **Thalassa** (6 Rue de Siam, ☎ 02 98 44 13 71).

OCÉANOPOLIS

Port de Plaisance du Moulin-Blanc
☎ 02 98 34 40 60
Open from 1 Sept. to 15 June, Mon. 2–5pm, Tue–Fri.: 9.30am–5pm, weekends and public holidays: 9.30am–6pm; from 15 June to 31 Aug.: open daily 9.30am–6pm.
Admission charge.
Océanopolis is Brest's window on the world of science and technology. It has unique and fascinating exhibits covering every aspect of the sea – gales, calm waters, hurricanes. Entire seascapes have been reconstructed in a series of aquaria, containing a total of 110,000 gallons (500,000 litres)! The Breton seascape is explained in detail. There are seals, moray eels, stonefish – anything that lives and moves beneath or on top of the waves in any part of the world is represented here. It is also the world's largest open-air aquarium.

The Saint-Martin quarter

This is a favourite rendezvous for students. If you feel homesick visit the two Irish pubs in the Rue de Glasgow. At the **World's End Pub** you can listen to the Rolling Stones, and at the **Dubliners** it's the Pogues and Sinead O'Connor. Whichever you choose, the beer is excellent. At daybreak, the district once again becomes a bustling wholesale food market.

Silence in
Landerneau...

Trémaouézan

Landivisiau

Landerneau

Moulin de Brézal

La Roche-Maurice

Pencran

Dirinon

This is where salt water mingles with freshwater, and high tide comes in twice a day as far as the Rohan

The Rohan bridge

bridge, one of the last inhabited bridges in Europe, with buildings dating from 1510. This is clearly a fishing port, but Landerneau still has beautiful houses built of gold-coloured stone. There is a French expression *faire du bruit dans Landerneau* 'making a noise in Landerneau', probably originating from the medieval tradition of the hullabaloo, which consisted of drumming on saucepans and cauldrons under the window of a newly married couple.

The Élorn salmon

The river Élorn, a category one river and thus one of the best managed in France, is an angler's paradise, with plenty of trout and recently, even a few salmon. Early in the year, spoons and other artificial lures give the best results. Later on it is better to use bait such as prawns or whipped flies for salmon. The best periods for the summer salmon are from March to July, and in September. If you are a keen angler, you must register with an angling association and get a fishing permit. You will find more detailed information on p. 39 of this guide.

Comptoir des Produits Bretons
☎ 02 98 21 35 93
On the well-known principle of the Irish counters and the Bavarian houses, the Breton counter stocks everything that is produced, created or eaten in the region. It is a very good and affordable idea. You can find it on the Quai

ossuary, which was long used by the inhabitants as a tobacconist! The close at **Dirinon** is dedicated to Sainte Nonne, who took refuge there after being raped by a Gaulish lord in the 5th C., and the close in **La Roche-Maurice** contains a sculpture of Ankou, the messenger of death.

A market with music

What a pleasure it is to go shopping while you listen to **Dan Ar Braz**, **Allan Stivell** and other Breton bands. The inhabitants of Landerneau put this into practice every Saturday market day in summer. It certainly beats canned music in the supermarket! However, the Landerneau market is very special because it is the only one of its kind. It has now moved to the north of the town, but you can still find it by

de Cornouaille, where you will certainly find a gift for 50 F, china for 100 F or even a painting for 1,000 F. The Breton counter also contains a large gallery, in which paintings of Breton life are displayed.

Nearby parish closes

There are four parish closes in the vicinity, of which **Trémaouézan** is the least ornate. The enclosure at **Pencran** has an

following the Rue des Capucins and the Rue Blérit, where Édouard Leclerc, a native of Landerneau and now head of a supermarket chain, opened his first store.

The parish close of Pencran church

Spotcheck
B2

Finistère

Things to do

The harbour festival
Fishing in the river

Within easy reach

Morlaix 22 miles (36 km) NE, p. 132,
Les monts d'Arrée 19 miles (30 km) SE, p. 134.

Tourist office

Landerneau:
☎ 02 98 85 13 09

If you meet him, he will say: 'But, even then it was a supermarket!'

THE HARBOUR FESTIVAL

The Landerneau harbour, situated on the river Élorn, is very dependent on the tides, so it's fun to be there when sand is unloaded from the bulk carriers. They have to work very quickly because they need to go back to Brest before the river is low again. When the tide is high, it is better to have lunch in one of the restaurants located on the Rohan bridge. The water sinks and swirls between the piers of bridge, making its own music. If you are in Landerneau towards the end of July, look out for the Fête du Port (harbour festival). There is lots of entertainment on the quayside, ending in a happy *fest-noz* (traditional Breton night of festivities).

Plougastel-Daoulas
the strawberry town

The Plougastel peninsula contains about 160 small villages dotted over colourful moorland, which is criss-crossed with more than 75 miles (120 km) of footpaths. The paths are especially popular with hikers because they pass through farmland, forest and coastal landscapes. Plougastel is also home to the most beautiful calvary in Brittany. It was erected to commemorate an epidemic of the plague in 1589 and is decorated with more than 80 sculpted figures.

Strawberries

Plougastel is most famous for its strawberry production. The sandy soil is rich in minerals, which give the strawberries their delicious flavour. The skill of the growers is also an important element. Several farms can be visited; list available at the tourist office (6b Place du Calvaire, ☎ 02 98 40 34 98). In Ty Neol, in the Loperhet area, Pierre and Madeleine Rolland invite you to do your own picking along the rows of their strawberry fields. The privilege will cost you 12 F for 2¼ lb (1 kg).

A brief history of the strawberry

Amédée-François Frézier, who commanded the Breton fortifications in Brest in 1740, introduced the strawberry to Plougastel. He had brought with him a few young plants of the famous 'Blanche du Chile' variety from his numerous trips to South America, and he planted a few of them in the hospital gardens. A clever male nurse from Plougastel spirited some specimens away to plant on his own land at Kéraliou. Influential English visitors to the region soon adopted the fruit and began to sing its praises, sending its fame around the world. As a result, plane-loads of Plougastel strawberries still

The Plougastel calvary

A SUNDAY IN PLOUGASTEL

'Arts and Music in the heart of Plougastel' is a Sunday morning performance in the town centre. The traditional celebration has elements of a market, but with an artistic dimension, which is provided by the painters, singers and jugglers, who mix with craftspeople such as potters, basket-makers and rope-makers. They all contribute to the creation of the Sunday fair, which used to be held before mass in the village. The craftspeople give demonstrations of their work. Information is available at the tourist office:
☎ 02 98 40 34 98.

fly out of Brest, with fruit destined for the finest restaurants in the world.

The Albert-Louppe bridge

In the 1930s the Albert-Louppe bridge, which is 3,000 feet (900 m) long, was the only direct link between the peninsula and Brest. Nowadays the bridge is closed to vehicles and so it is an ideal place for hikers or riders to cross the estuary, giving them a magnificent view of the Élorn estuary and Brest harbour. If you want to cross the estuary by car, you have to take the brand new Iroise bridge, which is very close to the Albert-Louppe bridge.

The Albert-Louppe bridge

Daoulas abbey and its garden

Botanical garden
☎ 02 98 25 84 39
Open daily from May to mid-Oct.
Free admission.
The abbey existed in the days of Clovis, c.AD 500, so it is extremely old. The cloister, with its famous columns, dates from the 12th C., but the most impressive part of the building, which is perfectly preserved, is the ablutions basin. All summer long, there are numerous exhibitions in the abbey. A list is available at the tourist office of Daoulas (☎ 02 98 25 84 39). The huge monastery garden contains more than 400 medicinal plants, which are grown in a park planted with 150 species of trees.

This botanical centre is dedicated to disseminating information about these plants, to promoting the development of physic gardens and to enhancing the use of traditional medicines.

The stone route

This ramble, a detailed map of which is available at the tourist office in Plougastel (☎ 02 98 40 34 98), will take you to Kersanton and Logonna. These are the villages from where the stones used to construct all the buildings from the 14th C. onwards were taken. You will also have an opportunity to see the mineral deposits of Lopheret and L'Hôpital-Camfrout.

Roscoff
from privateers to onion-sellers

A harsh-sounding name for a delightful fishing port and centre of agriculture. This small town has preserved its brave spirit and indomitable character, which is imprinted on its narrow streets and the tall frontages of the stone-built ship-owners' houses on the Vieux-Quai, where it is pleasant to linger over morning coffee.

The Exotic Garden on the Île de Batz

A dynamic and prosperous port
Harbour fish market
☎ 02 98 69 79 76

They used to say here 'not three, nor even a hundred Englishmen will frighten me', to demonstrate the courage of the Roscoff privateers as they pursued the ships of His Britannic Majesty. Today, British tourists are welcomed with all the respect due to true lovers of Brittany.

Roscoff is one of the main entry and exit ports for visitors from the UK. Even though the privateers left the quaysides long ago, the atmosphere of the harbour is just as lively and exciting. The **fresh fish market** starts at 6am and is the nerve centre of the town. There is much rushing around with trays full of fish, shellfish and lobsters. The doors of the market are opened to the public at 6.30am (but you must make a reservation a few days in advance). You will enjoy going there to smell the sea-spray and to try to decipher the mystifying code signs used by bidders. In Roscoff, as in Concarneau and Douarnenez, some guided tours are organised and will lead you through this maze and even take you onboard the boats to meet the fishermen.

Johnny Onions
Singer? Football player? No. Here a Johnny is an onion-seller! This is the strange speciality of Roscoff. The story began with Henri Ollivier's brilliant idea. He was not satisfied with trading on the continent, so in 1828 he decided to leave for England to try to sell his onions there. He covered himself with strings of onions and started to sell them door-to-door. He became so successful that soon hundreds of men from Roscoff did the same. The English gave these new hawkers the nickname *Johnny Onions*. Nowadays, a few Johnny Onions carry on the tradition. There is a **museum** in the chapel of Sainte-Anne in the harbour, which tells the tale of the incredible adventures of the Johnny Onion-sellers.

Beaches

There are many beaches around Roscoff. The beach of **Traon-Erch** is absolutely delightful and looks like a

Corsican port. The water is crystal clear blue and green and as transparent as the Mediterranean Sea, but the sand is as fine and glistening as on any Breton beach. The beaches of **Saint-Luc** and the cove of **Perharidy** are much larger, but they tend to become quite crowded.

❀ Île de Batz

There are several daily sailings for the island (the crossing takes 15 minutes), either at high tide from the old harbour or at low tide from the jetty. The ferry companies are called **Compagnie Armein**, ☎ 02 98 61 77 75, and **Compagnie Finistérienne**, ☎ 02 98 61 79 66. The quality of its sandy soil, its microclimate and hard work have all contributed to preserving the reputation of Batz as a market-garden

island. The agricultural tradition is carefully protected: cars are banned and the plots of land are tidily enclosed. Batz is a cultivated oasis in the open sea. However, there are also small creeks on the jagged coast. As soon as you arrive, rent a bicycle at the shop opposite the pier (☎ 02 98 61 77 65) and ride round the island,

The chapel of Sainte-Anne

passing the lighthouse, to the little village where you can take a break and relax on the

Spotcheck
B2

Finistère

Things to do

Fresh fish market in the harbour
The oceanological observatory
The Île de Batz on a bicycle

Within easy reach

*Landerneau, p. 124,
Monts d'Arrée, p. 134.*

Tourist office

Roscoff: ☎ 02 98 61 12 13

THE OCEANOLOGICAL OBSERVATORY

☎ 02 98 29 23 25

Open daily from July to Aug., from 10am to noon and from 1 to 7pm.Closes at 6pm from April to June and from Sept. to Oct. **There are 33 pools containing more than 100 species of fish from all the seas in the world. There are also, many special exhibitions.**

café terrace. Then make for the Georges-Delaselle **Exotic Garden** (☎ 02 98 61 75 65), which is full of handsome specimens of about 1,500 species of plants and shrubs originating from every continent. Once you have toured the garden, it is time for a rest and a swim from one of the small beaches on the way back to the pier.

Saint-Pol-de-Léon
vegetables from the sea

There is a pleasant walk through the old town of Saint-Pol, along the cobbled lanes around the beautiful Chapelle Notre-Dame-du-Kreisker and Pilori's house (Rue du Général-Leclerc), where torture victims were once exposed. This port derives its wealth from its vegetable-growing, which vies with its seaweed production. The surroundings are attractive, especially the Île Callot.

La passe aux Moutons

This causeway is under water at high tide, but at low tide it will take you from Carantec harbour to the Île Callot for a lovely ramble among the dunes and beaches.

The golden belt

This expression indicates the wealth of the Saint-Pol region, Brittany's most important vegetable-growing area. It produces 70% of French artichokes and 90% of its cauliflowers. The best place to buy top-quality vegetables is at the Tuesday morning market, which is set up around the cathedral. The magnificent produce is cheap, and the stallholder's patter is fascinating.

La Couette de Plume: a beautiful view

The best time to come here is when the sun sinks slowly over the dyke that links the Sainte-Anne islet to dry land. The islet is topped by a strange stone called the *couette de plume* (*couette* is a seagull in patois). From the top of this rock there is a magnificent view over the bay. You can walk around the islet and it is entertaining for young

VÊTEMENTS   STERMAN

Spotcheck
B2

Finistère

What to do

Beaches and swimming
lessons
La Couette de Plume walk
Seaweed-tasting
Visiting the Bizien coachworks

Within easy reach

*Landerneau 25 miles
(40 km) SW, p. 124,
Monts d'Arrée 25 miles
(40 km) S, p. 134.*

Tourist office

Saint-Pol:
☎ 02 98 69 05 69

BEACHES

There are magnificent beaches around the Île Callot. The Sainte-Anne beach, supervised and offering swimming lessons, is the busiest. Below the rocks of Krec'h an Drez there is the very beautiful beach of Kersaliou with its white sand and tiny sheltered spots. Near the small harbour of Pempoull the beach of the same name is protected by a sea wall. Around the Sainte-Anne islet the beaches in the little coves are quiet and delightful. You can try a new one every day.

children as a playground has been laid out around the rock.

Algoplus, seaweed-tasting

Rue Sainte-Marie
☎ 02 98 29 13 06
Open Mon. to Fri., 2pm–6pm (4pm off-peak).
Free guided visit.
Sometimes you need to overcome a reluctance to try new and delicious flavours. At **Algoplus** seaweeds are gathered and transformed into cosmetics and into salads, sauces and condiments. Michel and Monique, who established the firm, allow sceptics to discover these new products by visiting the factory. You can watch the collection, cutting, packaging and processing. If you find that sea vegetables are not to your liking, try the cosmetics. Seaweed soap will set you back only 5 F.

Bizien coachworks

Place de l'Europe
☎ 02 98 29 21 00
Open Mon. to Fri.,
9am– noon, 2–5pm,
by appointment only.
Free guided tour.
This name is well-known on all the roads of Europe. Yves Bizien was a blacksmith when, in 1945, he first began to build lorries, thereby turning the family forge into a modern coachworks specialising in heavy vehicles. Before the war the firm produced vegetable trucks that were used for transporting the local produce. A visit to the factory will show you all the stages of production, from the making of huge polyester doors to the decorative paintwork on the side-panels (which often feature landscapes, patterns and even portraits), taking in the cutting machines and assembly lines.

Beautiful Morlaix

The town's sailors, who were excellent navigators, were greatly feared by the English. Their motto was *S'ils te mordent, mords-les* ('If they bite you, bite back'), the second phrase being a play on the name of Morlaix. The Mercredis en Fête (Wednesday festivals), held from 15 July to 15 August in the late afternoon (information at the tourist office, Place des Otages, ☎ 02 98 62 14 94), feature performers of all kinds, including jugglers, comedians and musicians.

In the shadow of the viaduct

The Venelle de la Roche is a narrow, steep passageway that will take you to the upper floor of the two-storey viaduct. The view over the old town and the port is fantastic. The old town also contains the so-called lantern houses, which are unique. Some of them date from the 15th C. The best are the Queen Anne houses at 9 Rue du Mur (☎ 02 98 88 23 26, open daily except Sunday and public holidays, 10am–6pm; off-season by appointment; free admission), and in the Grand-Rue.

The corniche

You do not need to travel to the Pacific islands to find the most beautiful sunsets. People from Morlaix say that a walk at sundown along the Route de la Corniche, by the river Morlaix, is a magnificent experience. If the tide is rising, you will be able to watch the manoeuvres of the sailing ships, weaving gently between beacons and buoys.

Ploujean: on the way to the bay

Only a few miles from Morlaix, the little town of Ploujean retains its typically French country look – the small square, a welcoming bistro and a Breton church. It is also the starting-point for the signposted hike that will take you around the Morlaix bay, a distance of 7½ miles (12 km) from Suscinio manor (GR 34).

Ten beaches in Locquirec

This little village 10½ miles (17 km) to the northeast was once mainly inhabited by fishermen. It is worth visiting to see its splendid sandy beaches, nestling between the cliffs and the rocks. Le Grand Hôtel des Bains, in typical 1930s seaside resort style, was the setting for the French film *Hôtel de la Plage*.

Have a good cigar in Morlaix

Seita, 41 Quai de Léon
☎ **02 98 88 15 32**
Closed from 14 July to 15 Aug. Guided tour by appointment.
Free admission.
Leaves from Java, Sumatra, Central Africa, Latin America... the finest tobacco leaves from around the world end up here in Seita, to be used in the manufacture of the best cigars. You can purchase any of the 300 million Niva or Havanitos cigars that are manufactured each year in the workshops here. Before that, there is a video show to explain in detail why these little cigars are among the most famous in Europe. The factory was opened in 1736 and is still making cigars, chewing tobacco and snuff.

Deux-Rivières Brewery

1 Place de la Madeleine
☎ **02 98 63 41 92**
Guided tour on Mon., Tue. and Wed. at 10.30am, 2pm and 3pm. Off-season by appointment.
Free admission.
The Deux-Rivières Brewery is so proud of its Coreff beer that it sells it only to selected retailers. By no means all the bars of Brittany are allowed to stock it. However, by the end of the visit to this brewery in a former rope factory, you will have earned a bottle of the purest barley beer in the land.

Domaine de Kervéguen Cider

about 12½ miles (20 km) NE. **29620 Guimaëc**
☎ **02 98 67 50 02.**
Open 10.30am–noon and 3–7pm except on Sundays and public holidays or by appointment.
Free admission.
Factories that still operate in the old-fashioned traditional way, like this one does, are very rare. Even the apple trees are maintained with natural methods. The cider is matured in oak casks, just as if it were fine Cognac.

La Cave des Chouchens

16 miles (25 km) E **29650 Plouégat-Moysan**
☎ **02 98 79 21 25**
Chouchen is a fruit and honey-based fermented drink, like mead. You can visit the honey house, the fermentation cellar and the bottling department. Of course, you can taste the *chouchen*, as well as honey made from ivy or blackberry flowers.

Spotcheck
C2

Finistère

Things to do

Brewery visit
Hiking around the bay
Visit to cigar workshop

Within easy reach

Les Monts d'Arrée 12½ m (20 km) S, p. 134,
Huelgoat 18 m (29 km) S, p. 136,
Lannion 22 m (35 km) NE, p. 148.

Tourist office

Morlaix: ☎ **02 98 62 14 94**

Monts d'Arrée
by foot, by bike … or on a donkey

It may seem to be stretching the truth to call them mountains when they do not exceed a height of 1,300 feet (400 m), but the Monts d'Arrée are legendary. Deserted, haunted and enchanted, these hills were once the gates to hell in the Breton imagination. The bare peaks of the Roc'h Tredudon and Roc'h Trévézel, the Vale of Yeun Elez depression and the peat bogs of Saint-Michel-en-Rivoal contribute to giving these hills the title of 'mountains'.

The route through the peaks

Hiking is the best way to discover the Monts d'Arrée, but remember that you are in the mountains. Even though their highest point is only 1150 feet (350 m), the Monts d'Arrée conceal the same dangers as high peaks. It can get extremely cold in winter. If you are hiking, do not stray from the signposted paths and take care that you do not walk into a peat bog. A map showing all trails is available from the Brasparts tourist office. A much easier and more interesting alternative comes from Cahin Cah'âne (Tromarc'h Brasparts, ☎ 02 98 81 40 69, reservations required). Why not hike through the mountains, loading your gear on a **donkey with a packsaddle**. The donkey will even carry your children if they weigh less than 6 stone (40 kg). This makes the whole hike an even more unforgettable experience.

Brennilis

Beavers in Brittany

In 1968 the river Ellez in the Monts d'Arrée was chosen for the reintroduction of the beaver after severe decline in the European beaver population. The society for the study and protection of nature in Brittany organises guided visits to track these famous rodents. You will not be able to see the 40 beavers that now live in the area, because they are still very vulnerable. But you will be shown so many indications of their presence that you will feel as if you had seen them face to face. Information at the nature reserve, SEPNB Monts d'Arrée, 2 Rue du Calvaire, 29410 Le Cloître-Saint-Thégonnec, ☎ 02 98 79 71 98.

Auberge-expo du Youdig: the gates to hell

☎ 02 98 99 62 36
Claude Le Lann will take you to Yeun Elez at 5am, when the sun rises, the animals wake up and the devil goes to bed. He also offers to accompany you on any hiking trip to explain the fauna, flora, history and heritage of

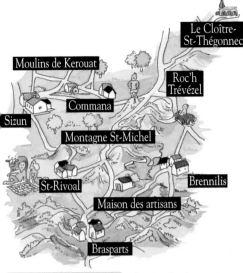

Moulins de Kerouat

Le Cloître-St-Thégonnec

Roc'h Trévézel

Commana

Sizun

Montagne St-Michel

St-Rivoal

Brennilis

Maison des artisans

Brasparts

Spotcheck
B2-C2

Finistère

Things to do

Hiking
The Brennilis beavers
Ecomusée de Commana
Fly fishing

Within easy reach

*Landernau 18 m NW
(30 km), p. 124,
Morlaix 12 m N (20 km),
p. 132,
Châteaulin 20 m SW
(35 km), p. 208.*

Tourist office

Brasparts: ☎ 02 98 81 47 06

✾ LA MAISON DE L'EAU, DE LA RIVIÈRE ET DE LA PÊCHE

Sizun
☎ 02 98 68 86 33
Open daily from 15 June to 15 Sept., 11am–6pm; off-peak, call the museum for opening hours. *Admission charge.*
Water, fish and fishing are important parts of everyday life in Brittany, and their preservation is essential to the continued survival of the region. Water purity, the aquatic food chain and fishing regulations are among the topics covered here. The Maison de la Rivière, with the Parc Régional d'Armorique (☎ 02 98 81 08 88), of which the Monts d'Arrée are part, organises workshops to initiate beginners in the art of fly-fishing. You will learn everything, from fishing techniques to tying your own flies, and the local fishermen will let you into their fishing secrets.

the area. For the evening meal beforehand, his wife, Annick, will make the Breton *kig ha farz*, roast pork with vegetables (900 F per person for the weekend, meals and hikes included).

Kerouat

... and its water mills

Écomusée de Commana
☎ 02 98 68 87 76
Open July–Aug., 11am–7pm.
This tiny hamlet consists of two water-mills, which have been restored to their original 19th-C. condition. The tools, clothing and customs of the miller are reconstructed in detail. Another interesting reconstruction is

Commana, a village containing machinery that recalls the old crafts of the region.

*Travels with a donkey
(see opposite)*

Huelgoat, wood, stone and water

*U*hel-Coat, 'the upper wood', has given its name to one of the largest clearings in the magical forest of Brocéliande, which once spread over the whole region. Huelgoat has been a garrison town since ancient times, and it was fortified under Du Guesclin in the 19th C. Huelgoat owes its prosperity to the discovery of deposits of lead and silver, although the mines are now closed. The granite quarries and tourism have revived the village, which is one of the main 'green tourism' attractions of Brittany.

The lake

The houses of shiny grey granite, a rock found only at Locronan, surround the lake, which is an excellent place for a gentle stroll if you don't feel like going into the forest. You can hire pedalos (information at the Huelgoat tourist office, Place Alphonse-Penven, ☎ 02 98 99 72 32). The lakeside path attracts lots of anglers because there are so many fish in the lake. A few minutes from here, in the Parc de l'Hôpital, you will find more than 800 species of plants in the botanical garden, all of them labelled, including climbing roses from the foothills of the Himalayas and plants from the Andes (Jardin de Huelgoat, ☎ 02 97 99 71 63).

La Rivière d'Argent

The river appears and disappears between huge, slippery, moss-covered, granite blocks. It winds through the forest, disappears again and emerges as a foaming torrent. La Rivière d'Argent (the silver river) is an amazing spectacle in itself. Numerous signposted paths will help you to find your way through the wilderness, towards the *Grotte du Diable* (devil's cave), to the *Ménage de la Vierge* (Virgin's household) and the *Roche Tremblante* (trembling rock). In the heart of this marvellous landscape, at the Moulin du Chaos (in fact, a pile of rocks), there is a free permanent exhibition about the local geology, fauna and flora. A leaflet is available at the tourist office.

Huelgoat honey

5 Route de la Roche-Tremblante
☎ **02 98 99 94 36**
Open 9am–8pm in summer;10am–7pm.
Free admission.
One of the best honeys in the world is made here.

Whether you like it solid or liquid, dark or light, fragrant or flowery, there is plenty of choice in the shop as well as a free tasting at the end of the visit. Before you get there, you can watch the activities of the tireless worker bees as they gather the pollen and even see the fertilisation of the queen bee through a window in one of the

400 hives. But don't worry, you never come into direct contact with the bees.

Huelgoat on horseback

4 miles (6 km) E from Huelgoat
Centre de Loisirs de Kermabilou, La Feuillée
☎ 02 98 99 78 46
Open daily, 9am–8pm.
Admission charge.

This is certainly one of the nicest ways to discover the region and definitely the most authentic. Don't worry if you are not an outstanding horseman or horsewoman – the horses at La Feuillée will be allocated to you according to your ability. Moreover, the bridle paths in the area are quite easy to negotiate. You will enjoy walking or trotting along King Arthur's paths and past the Artus cave. A whole day will cost you 350 F, including meals.

Spotcheck
C2

Finistère

Things to do
The lake path
La Rivière d'Argent
Brittany by caravan
Huelgoat on horseback

Within easy reach
Morlaix 18 miles (29 km) N, p. 132, Châteaulin 22 miles (35 km) SW, p. 208.

Tourist office
Huelgoat: ☎ 02 98 99 72 32

BY CARAVAN IN THE PARC RÉGIONAL D'ARMORIQUE

Caravans and coaches in Brittany
☎ 02 98 99 73 28
End of Mar. to end of Sept. (call for information out of season).
Huelgoat is situated in the Parc Naturel d'Armorique, which contains an extraordinary range of natural curiosities and prehistoric remains. So that you do not miss any of the beauty of the landscape, there is no better way of getting around than a horse-drawn caravan! You can hire one for a week or weekend, for a group or a family. You will be taught how to harness and unharness the horse, and with route maps and guides in your pocket, you can enjoy the countryside in your house on wheels.

Carhaix-Plouguer and Poher, the water country

Vorgium, once the capital of the Gaulish tribe of Osismes, was the crossroads of the west Armorican region. It lay where the road from Roscoff to Lorient met the road from Rennes to Châteaulin, which caused the town to grow rapidly. At the beginning of the 20th C. Carhaix (the towns did not merge until 1956) became the centre of Brittany's rail network. A steam locomotive, a perfectly restored *Mallet 030030* dating from the early 20th C., is on show at the station (☎ 02 98 93 00 01). Carhaix is the ideal place to start if you want to enjoy the beauty of nature to the full.

La Rue de Brizeux

This is the main street, and was built by the Romans. They named it the *Cardo Maximus*, on the north–south axis, as opposed to the Rue Félix-Faure, named the *Decumanus Maximus*, which was on the east–west axis. **La Maison du Sénéchal** in this street is a magnificent example of late medieval architecture.

Hiking in the area

The region offers two very beautiful tours. Maps are available at the tourist office (Rue de Brizeux, ☎ 02 98 93 04 42). The Aqueduct tour – about 3 miles (5 km) long – starts from the small village of **Roscoat** and leads you to the remains of a **Roman aqueduct**, which was once 16 miles (27 km) long. From here there is a magnificent view of the **Montagnes Noires**. The second tour, at 6 miles (10 km), is slightly longer, but it is very pleasant in summer, since the path follows the meanders of the river **Hyères** and in autumn you will see the woods in glorious colours.

Rafting at the Moulin du Roy

Canoe-kayak Club
☎ 02 98 93 30 79
Spend an afternoon whitewater rafting on the fast-flowing waters of the region. This activity is perfectly safe because specialist instructors will accompany you. It will give you an opportunity to discover the river from another viewpoint. If you prefer a smoother ride, try hiring a canoe.

Persivien Leisure Centre

☎ 02 98 93 19 99
How about entertaining the children in the long afternoons? The Persivien centre can take care of them and

THE WATER GARDEN

Maël-Carhaix is 6 miles (10 km) east of Carhaix-Plouguer. In 1992 the little town of Maël-Carhaix decided to take over a marsh, which was situated close to the town. This ugly wasteland was turned into a superb water garden. Written and oral descriptions are provided for more than 300 aquatic plants. Thanks to this original idea, Maël-Carhaix has become one of the main study centres for aquatic botany in Brittany. Waterlilies, reeds and a multitude of other plants and shrubs can be seen blooming in their own natural environment.

allow them to discover nature in an entertaining way. It is run in a similar way to an outdoor activity centre, except that all activities are focused on nature and the environment.

Glomel

Auberge de Saint-Péran

12½ miles (20 km) to the SE of Carhaix
Route de Paule
☎ **02 96 29 60 04**
A wonderful place to spend a weekend, the manor house is situated in a pleasant, leafy park, beside the Nantes canal in Brest. It offers a 3-night, half-board stay at the special price of 525 F. In addition, you will have an opportunity to taste the delicious cold meat products of the region at the **traditional delicatessen** in the inn. However, you do not need to be staying at the inn to buy some of the salami-style sausages or a delicious terrine for about 40 F a kilogramme.

Spotcheck
C3

Finistère

Things to do

Hiking
Rafting at the Moulin du Roy
Water garden at
Maël-Carhaix

With children

Persivien leisure centre

Within easy reach

Guerlédan lake, about 19 miles (30 km) SE, p. 160.

Tourist office

Carhaix-Plouguer:
☎ **02 98 93 04 42**

Callac, donkeys and cycling

The statue of the horse, *Naous*, at the entrance of Callac is a reminder that the village was once home to several stud farms. Today the name of Callac is rather more closely associated with cycling. An international rally takes place here annually in late July, only a few days after the Tour de France has ended. The best cyclists compete, and the race attracts thousands of spectators to the town (information is available at the tourist office in Callac, Place du 9-Avril-1944, ☎ 02 96 45 59 34).

A preserved forest

The Callac district, especially the neighbouring village of **Saint-Servais**, is covered by one of the finest forests in Brittany. **Duault forest** has long been particularly famous as the place where the dukes of Brittany's horses are bred. If you decide to go walking you are sure to come across some megaliths, dolmens or menhirs, which are scattered around the area. The largest and most impressive stone is the Dent de Saint-Servais, near to **Kerbénès**.

The Corong gorge

Starting from the car park reserved for walkers, on the main road from **Saint-Servais** to **Saint-Nicodème**, there is a one-hour walk before you get to the gorge. The signposted path is suitable for all ages and you won't regret taking it as there are stunning views. There are huge, round, moss-covered stones piled one upon the other. Sometimes rushing streams burst through the rocks or alternatively they trickle around and over them. According to legend, the stones are actually getting bigger with time! The whole area is also a well-preserved site of outstanding natural beauty. The wildlife here includes hen harriers, an endangered species of bird of prey in France.

La Verte Vallée

This pleasant lake, which is surrounded by lush green hills, is just waiting for people to come and ride mountain-bikes, hire a pedalo or swim. A picnic area is also available, and there is a signposted nature walk, with signs in both French and Breton, that goes right round the lake. Should you fall in love with the region, you can erect your

tent on a nearby campsite (Camping de la **Verte Vallée**, ☎ 02 96 45 58 50).

Fish leather

Tannerie de Callac
Z.A. de Kerguiniou
☎ **02 96 45 50 68**
Open 9am–noon and 2–6pm, except Mon. morning and Sun.
Free admission.
Fish leather is one of the specialities of Callac. For about 100 F you can buy an unusual salmon-skin purse and a

ling leather belt for 200 F. You will have to spend a little more if you want a decent wallet or a handbag, but the prices remain affordable. You also get an opportunity to watch the various steps of the tanning and manufacturing processes and the careful cutting and sewing of a pair

of fish-leather gloves, which would make a novelty gift.

Bulat-Pestivien
The Breton spaniel

About 6 miles (10 km) E from Callac
Élevage de Cornouaille
☎ **02 96 45 75 62**
Visits only by appointment. *Free admission.*
This hunting dog, which is a favourite with French dog-lovers, originated in Callac in the early 20th C. The beauty and the intelligence of this animal soon charmed not only hunters but others who wanted them as pets. The breeding kennels in Cornouaille are the oldest in France and are regularly visited by dog-lovers who want to know more about the species. Hervé Bourdon, the breeder, says this dog is 'intelligent, good tempered and easy'. A puppy costs about 4,000 F.

Spotcheck
C2

Côtes d'Armor

Things to do

International cycling rally
Walks and sports
Crail donkey sanctuary

Within easy reach

Lannion 27 miles (43 km) N, p. 148,
Guingamp 16 miles (26 km) NE, p. 150.

Tourist office

Callac: ☎ 02 96 45 59 34

❀ **IN DONKEY COUNTRY**
Asinerie du Crail, Saint-Servais
3 miles (5 km) SE from Callac
☎ **02 96 45 94 78**
Guided tours at 10.30am or 2.30pm; off-peak by appointment.
Admission charge.
This typical farm has been turned into a donkey sanctuary and farm. You can make direct contact with the animals since the visitors are allowed into all the fields except those containing the stallions. After this, you will be able to tell the difference between a *grand noir du Berry*, a *baudet de Poitou* and a mule. You can even purchase a little donkey, but be warned – a donkey needs lots of space and constant care and attention.

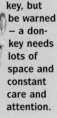

Montagnes Noires
not as black as they sound!

The Montagnes Noires are a natural extension of the Monts d'Arrée but are slightly lower, at between 1,070 and 1,260 feet (326 and 384 m). However, they are just as beautiful, sometimes austere and always shrouded in mystery. The dark forests that probably gave their name to this region have disappeared, although some areas have now been replanted. The Montagnes Noires, and more especially Gourin, were impoverished areas, particularly in the late 19th and early 20th C., and thus many of the emigrants who went to the United States originated from here.

Spézet
Walks in the forest

Spézet, in the heart of the Montagnes Noires, is almost the capital of Breton-speaking Brittany, with its Breton signs and the Breton language festival, which keeps the whole village busy in late May and early June. While you are walking on the narrow, signposted footpaths that crisscross the region, you will come across fountains, chapels, menhirs and bridges, which merge into a landscape of murmuring brooks and moorland, alternating with peat bogs and wild woods. A map of the signposted footpaths is available from the tourist office (☎ 02 98 93 91 18).

Notre-Dame-du-Crann

¾ mile (1 km) from Spézet
Open all year round, 1.30–5pm.
This chapel, which dates from 1535 and is surrounded by

trees, contains an exceptional series of 16th-C. stained-glass windows, which tell the story of Jesus Christ and the Virgin Mary, as well as colourfully portraying the legends of the saints. The rest of the interior is also very attractive. At pardon time, on the Sunday after Pentecost, people come with lumps of butter that have been skilfully carved into religious figures – something that is well worth seeing!

Gourin
Le Roc de Toullaëron

The highest peak in the Montagnes Noires is a few miles north of Gourin. It is 1070 feet (326 m) high and is

worth the climb. Your reward will be a magnificent view According to legend, King Arthur's horse was tied up here for 17 years, which is why 17 sets of horseshoe tracks are carved in the rock.

Châteauneuf-du-Faou
In Paul Sérusier's footsteps

This delightful, quiet village covers the lower slopes of a hill and has an impressive view of the Montagnes Noires. The 19th-C. church contains a chapel with a baptismal font decorated in 1919 by the painter Paul Sérusier (1864–1927) of the Pont-Aven school. Sérusier lived in Châteauneuf for 23 years. There is a good walk along the towpath to the lock and the hamlet of Moustoir, which has a lovely chapel that is commemorated in a nostalgic poem by the Breton Auguste Brizeux. A little to the north, near Pleyben, walk along by the restored railway tracks (information at the Pays du Centre-Finistère, ☎ 02 98 26 82 02).

Saint-Goazec
❀ Park and château of Trévarez

☎ 02 98 26 82 79.
Open daily July–Aug, 11am–7pm; April, May and Sept., 1–6.30pm; open the rest of the year, Sat.–Sun., public and school holidays, 2–6pm.
Admission charge.

In a 210 acre (85 ha) park, surrounding a château built by Marquis de Kerjégu between 1894 and 1906, wooded avenues lead to a horticultural collection unique in Brittany. The gardens are resplendent with camellias, azaleas, hydrangeas, rhododendrons and fuchsias.

Spotcheck
C3

Finistère and Morbihan

Things to do

Walks in the forest
The *crêpe* festival

Within easy reach

*Guerlédan 25 miles (40 km) W, p. 160,
Châteaulin 19 miles (30 km) W, p. 208,
Quimper 22 miles (35 km) SW, p. 220.*

Tourist office

Spézet: ☎ 02 98 93 91 18

A pond and a refreshing fountain make your walk even more pleasant.

GOURIN, CAPITAL OF THE CRÊPE

In the 19th C. Gourin, the capital of the Montagnes Noires, was a major producer of slate, but now it concentrates on animal husbandry and farming. Gourin is famous for its *crêpes* and celebrates this speciality on the third weekend of July in the Tronjolly castle. While older people demonstrate how rye was once threshed with a flail, you can watch them eating *crêpes*. You can also learn how to use the *rozell*, a small, scraper-shaped tool used to spread the batter over the griddle with a twist of the wrist. Breton dancing, music and games are also part of the festival and a good way to burn off calories. Information ☎ 02 97 23 66 33.

Perros-Guirec, a trendy resort

I ts reputation as a trendy resort is well established. Perros (calling it Perros-Guirec will make you sound like a tourist) lives to the rhythm of the summer, the sun, crowded café terraces and nightclubs, which only empty in time for the first swim of the day. If you have never been to Perros, get hold of a long T-shirt, a pair of trainers with the laces untied and some impenetrable designer sunglasses and sit at one of the outdoor cafés that line the Trestraou beach. It's time to relax, you're on holiday!

The beaches

The most famous beach is at **Trestraou**, and although it is north-facing, this white, sandy beach is completely packed, especially around 15 August when the volleyball tournament is held, an event whose reputation is widespread (information from the tourist office, 21 Place de la Mairie). Some people prefer the atmosphere of the **Trestrignel** beach, where swimming is especially safe and is therefore well-suited for children. Between these

The white beach of Trestrignel

two beaches there is the harbour where one leg of the Tour de France à la Voile (yachting race) is held.

Station Voile

Perros is one of seven resorts in Brittany to be awarded the status of *Station Voile* (see pp. 18–19). The sailing centre is open all year round. Whether you prefer dinghies, catamarans, windsurfing, cruising traditional sailing, competition or sports sailing, you can practise them all (information: Plage de Trestraou, ☎ 02 96 23 25 62).

Les Sept-Îles

This is one of the most beautiful bird sanctuaries in Brittany. There are almost 20,000 breeding pairs, including gulls, some of which have wingspans of almost 5 feet (1.5 m) and fly

at more than 45 mph (70 kph). There are also gannets, guillemots, razorbills and the stormy petrel, (one of the smallest seabirds in the world), which you can watch through binoculars at dusk. Three ferry companies organise regular trips to the islands. Booking is recommended and can be made either at the harbour station or the tourist office.

THE TRENDY TOUR

After an afternoon relaxing on the Trestraou beach, come to the terrace of the Britannia (19 Boulevard de la Mer, ☎ 02 96 91 01 10), which faces south, so that you can enjoy the last rays of the sun. When you have dined at, say, the Vieux Gréements, in the harbour (☎ 02 96 91 14 99), visit the most famous casino on the north coast (☎ 02 96 23 20 51) and spend a few francs at the gaming tables (there is a strict dress code) or try your luck at the one-arm bandits. Lucky or not, your next stop should be at Clem's, near the casino, for a lively atmosphere and a wide range of Mexican beers (the *Tequilabière* is delicious, but give your car keys to someone else). After 1am, follow the crowd and choose the night-club that takes your fancy. There are three of them on the beach!

The festival city

In early July a festival of comic strips is held in the town. The aim, which is almost achieved, is to compete with the similar event at Saint-Malo, and is getting busier every year (20,000 visitors in 1996). Three of the cartoonists who are responsible for the increasing reputation of the festival – Loisel, Vicomte and Krahen – are from Perros. In early August, the **Festival de la Cité des Hortensias** (festival of the city of hydrangeas) is a good opportunity to see a parade of Bretons dressed in traditional costume in the flower-decked town and to enjoy *festou-noz* celebrations, which usually end in the small hours. To find out more about these two events, pick up a leaflet at the tourist office.

Spotcheck
C1

Côtes d'Armor

Things to do
Beaches, volleyball and sailing
Bird sanctuary
Festivals in Perros

Within easy reach
Paimpol 22 miles (35 km) E, p. 156.

Tourist office
Perros-Guirec:
☎ 02 96 23 21 15

✾ Wax museum
Port de Plaisance
☎ 02 96 91 23 45
Open daily, except Mon. mornings, 1 May, 30 Oct. and school holidays, in Feb. and April 10am–6.30pm. *Admission charge.* Numerous battles have taken place in this area, including the Ligue War, Brittany Succession War, the rebellion of the Chouans against the Revolution and the Revolutionary war. The museum contains reconstructions of these battles, and there are other realistic, lifesize representations of episodes from Breton history.

Côte de Granit Rose

Ploumanac'h

Trégastel

Perros-Guirec

Le Castel

Île Milliau

Trébeurden

An elephant,
a bell, even
Napoleon's
tricorn hat, these are just
some of the fantastic
shapes that you can make
out in the rocks along
this coast are endlessly
fascinating. The Pink Granite Coast starts at Perros-Guirec and ends at
Trébeurden. Although it is pink rather than gold, the coast is an absolute treasure. Discover it on foot – there is no need to hurry – and in the late afternoon sit on a rock and wait for sunset. The view is a feast for the eyes. This
section of the coast will soothe your soul, calm your mind and lift your spirits.

Walking in the Traouïëro Valley

This valley is a magical
world of huge granite
blocks, which are balanced
precariously on each other.
On your 3-hour walk,
which begins at the tide-
mill of Ploumanac'h-
Trégastel, you will find
some explanations of the
geological origin of the
valley and will begin to

understand how the micro-
climate here has produced
some very special plants. If
you still want to know why
the rocks are round and

pink, you can find more
information if you visit the
Maison du Littoral
(☎ 02 96 91 62 97, open
daily, July–Aug., 3–6pm).

Trégastel
The energy resort

There is another wide expanse of sand on the beaches of Coz-Pors and Grève Blanche. If the weather is cold or wet then you can enjoy fountains, geysers, slides and diving boards, all at a temperature of 82°F (28 °C). The **Forum de Trégastel** consists of several indoor pools and is accessible directly from the beach of Coz-Pors. If you prefer more active sports, then try the sea-kayaking. After just a few hours of training, you will be able to paddle your way through the shallow waters, accompanied by an instructor, who will show you the wonders of the coast (Base Nautique, 39 Rue de la Grève-Rose, ☎ 02 96 23 45 05, Mar.–Nov.).

Trébeurden
Discovering the flora

This is another beautiful resort, but it is not all there is to see on the Côte de Granit Rose. At low tide you can walk to the **Île Milliau**, which has almost 50 acres (20 ha) of moorland, rocks, cliffs and fine sand. Further out to sea is **Molène**, a rock topped by a large sand dune. There are regular sailings from Trébeurden to Milliau, in the company of

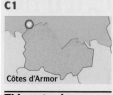

a specialist guide. You will be able to find more than 250 plant species (information at the tourist office, ☎ 02 96 23 51 64). The Île Milliau is covered in megaliths, and make sure you visit the **covered avenue**, which is easily accessible but beautiful and mysterious.

Le Castel
A magical place

This is a good destination for ramblers. A small footpath circles the peninsula, where wild moor alternates with rocks beaten by the wind and surf. Even if it is not as famous as the Rochers Sculptés de Rothéneuf (sculpted rocks), Le Castel has a very fine rock resembling a human profile. However, unlike the rocks of Rothéneuf, this one called Le Père (the father), has been carved only by time and wind.

Quellen
The marshes

It took thousands of years to create this dune, which has left behind a marshy lagoon that was soon covered in quicksands and reeds. Horses are sometimes allowed to roam freely in the area, playing their part in the natural management of the land. The area looks rather like the Camargue in the south of France, although the horses there are truly wild. The marsh is also inhabited by nesting birds, such as ducks, snipe and warblers. Some low footbridges have been built to let you explore deep into this unique Brittany wetland without getting wet.

Spotcheck
C1

Côtes d'Armor

Things to do

Discover the coast
Learn to sea-kayak
Sea excursions

Within easy reach

Morlaix 28 miles (45 km) SW, p. 132,
Paimpol 28 miles (45 km) E. p. 156.

Tourist office

La Maison du Littoral:
☎ 02 96 91 62 97

PLOUMANAC'H:
LAND OF SAND AND ROCK
Magnificent beaches, where fine, white sand contrasts with the round, pink rocks, stretch away into the translucent, calm blue water. The castle on the Costaérès islet is part of the backdrop. Ploumanac'h is like a dream, but you will need food for the body as well as the soul, so visit the restaurant called Le Phare (39 Rue Saint-Guirec, ☎ 02 96 91 41 19),which serves a hearty Breton *cotriade* with potatoes.

Lannion
A marriage of old and new

In the Breton language *lann* means 'religious community' or 'monastery', and Ion was a Welsh monk who was exiled to Brittany. The two words gave a name to one of the most charming towns in Brittany, with some fine, half-timbered houses. But Lannion is also a town at the leading edge of technology: on 11 July 1962 at 12.47am the dish on the Radôme received the first images broadcast live via satellite from the United States. Lannion is also to be the home of a training camp for the Olympic Games.

Village of Yaudet
☎ 02 96 48 35 98
or ☎ 02 96 46 41 00
Guided tour Mon. and
Fri. at 2.30pm in high
season. *Admission charge.*
The Vikings forced the inhabitants of Lannion to return inland, and the town was originally on the site of the village of Yaudet, an area littered with menhirs and dolmens. Other remains indicate the existence of a moderately important medieval centre. There is a well-preserved barracks overlooking the Léguer, a reminder that there was a garrison in the town in the 18th C.

The Valley of the Léguer
A good family walk could start from the Quai de la Corderie in Lannion and lead to Yaudet by following the leafy banks of the river Léguer. The walk lasts for about an hour. At low tide the Léguer will reveal the numerous wrecks, some of them extremely old, that litter the bed of the river. Around one of its loops, you may also disturb the numerous birds that come to feed on the mudflats. If you want to continue this walk along the river further inland, go on a guided walk with the Centre d'Initiation at Belle-Isle-en-Terre. The ramble will enable you to discover the wildlife of the wetlands and ponds in the district. Special tours focusing on a theme, such as otters or salmon, will take you into the heart of the countryside (☎ 02 96 43 08 39).

The white-water stadium
Did you know that France's canoeing teams, which did so well at the Atlanta Olympics in 1996, came to train in Lannion in the great white-water stadium? This technological wonder is also open to the general public, and there are plenty of courses organised for all levels of experience, in inflatable and non-inflatable craft and kayaks.

Breton whisky

Warenghem Bretagne, Route de Guingamp
☎ **02 96 37 00 08**
Open daily except
Sun. and Mon.
morning, 8am–noon
and 1.30–6pm
Free admission.
The Bretons have many
things in common with
their counterparts in
Wales and Ireland,
including food and
drink. Warenghem is
a real Breton malt
whisky, which is aged
for three years. It has
become very popular.
The black-and-white
label is reminiscent of
the colours of Brittany,
and it costs no more
than any other good
bottle of whisky
(around 70 F).
After visiting the
factory, enjoy a
whisky-tasting
session during
which you can
also try the
pommeau
(sparking
apple wine)
and the *fine
de Bretagne*
(brandy) in
the factory
shop.

There is even white-water
rafting! You will have the
time of your life, but remember that it is essential to book

in advance by phone. The
number is ☎ 02 96 37 43 90
mornings and ☎ 02 96 23
54 80 afternoons.

Pleumeur-Bodou
Capital of tele-communications

Site de Cosmopolis,
Musée des
Télécommunications
and Radôme
*6 miles (10 km) NW from
Lannion*
☎ **02 96 46 63 80**
Open daily except Sat.
and Sun., Oct.–Mar.,
1.30–5.30pm; April,
May, June and Sept.
daily 10–6pm (except
Sat. in April); July–Aug.,
daily 10am–7pm.
Admission charge.
Pierre Marzin, Secretary
of State for Research in
the 1960s, who was a native
of Lannion, decided in

Spotcheck
C2

Côtes d'Armor

Things to do

Discovering nature
Introduction to canoeing
Son-et-lumière at the Musée
des Télécommunications
Visit to a whisky factory

Within easy reach
*Morlaix 21 m SW (35 km),
p. 132,
Callac 27 m S (43 km),
p. 140,
Paimpol 20 m E (33 km),
p. 156.*

Tourist office
Lannion : ☎ **02 96 46 41 00**

1962 that the Centre
National d'Études des
Télécommunications
(national centre for tele-
communication studies)
should be set up not far
from Pleumeur-Bodou. This
event is now celebrated in a
son-et-lumière show (performances several times daily),
and there is running com-
mentary in the Musée des
Télécommunications.
Newer technology is also
represented in the form
of artificial intelligence,
ISDN and so on. The
centre has seven themed
displays and is fun for all
the family. It is a popular
outing for French schools.
The huge Radôme geode,
which stands on the moor,
is a fascinating sight and
attracts photographers from
all over the world.

Come on Guingamp!

Why is this city so charming? Perhaps it's because of the cobbled streets and the tall granite houses. Or the public park with its paths edged with flowers and the last bandstand in Brittany? Or is it the Plomée fountain in the town centre? Is it the steps of Saint-Jacques and Trotrieux beneath the fortified wall? All these features make the town worth a visit, but what is really important about Guingamp and what makes the whole population move from the town to the Roudourou stadium every Saturday is a black-and-white football.

Football crazy

First they were in the local league, then in the third, then the second, and finally the first division (the premier league). Guingamp has climbed the rungs of the football ladder and is now on a par with such wealthy teams as Paris-St Germain and Monaco, whose budgets are tenfold that of Guingamp. This outstanding success for a town with only 8,000 inhabitants is all due to one man – Noël Le Graët, who has been chairman of the club for many years. A Breton by birth, Le Graët has fought like a lion to make the club champions of French football.

The **Roudourou Stadium** has twice as many seats as the number of inhabitants of Guingamp! All this has done wonders for the reputation of this little town.

The town of camellias

Association Caméllia, Rue Hyacinthe-Cheval
☎ 02 96 43 71 35
Visits only by prior telephone appointment.
In the early 1990s Fanch Le Moal, a horticulturalist, created a new variety of camellia, which he named 'Ville de Guingamp', an idea given to him by the actress Marlène Jobert. The **Fanch garden** contains as many as 500 named cultivars. You are unlikely to leave without taking a few stems. You can even dry the leaves and use them to make a refreshing cup of tea!

Shady banks of the river Trieux

Saint-Loup

The most important festival in the town is held every year in mid-August and lasts for a whole week, during which you will see traditional dances from all over the region and Breton wrestling tournaments. The show continues in the evenings, with street theatre and concerts in the cafés in the Place du Centre. Towards the end of the week, the national dance champion is chosen, and he is honoured with much rejoicing and plenty of *galette-saucisse* (sausage in a buckwheat crêpe) and cider. Be warned: during this week there are no vacancies within 15 miles (20 km) of the town. Should you have to go to Guingcamp at the last minute, a list of guest houses is available at the tourist office (Place du Champ-au-Roy, ☎ 02 96 43 73 89). There is plenty of good-quality accomodation in the area.

The river Trieux

The river banks are ideal for pleasant walks beside the water and through the villages of the region. Head for the Ponts-Saint-Michel, then take your time strolling to the Place du Centre and the Rue du Grand-Trotrieux. If you talk to the many anglers you will find on the way, you will learn how to buy a one-day fishing license which will enable you to fish in the clear waters of the river Trieux. Tackle is sold at (or can be hired from) the hunting and tackle shop, 25 Rue des Ponts-Saint-Michel. A day's fishing will cost about 200 F.

THE KNIGHTS' PARDON

This pardon takes place every year in late June at Saint-Péver, a few miles south of Guingamp. Information at the Mairie (town hall), 1 Rue Lanrodec, ☎ 02 96 21 42 48. After the mass and the procession, pedestrians and riders gather for the blessing of the horses, which involves immersing the animals in a small pond near the chapel. The mood is different in the evening. The knights have been pardoned – until next year.

their livers. Foie gras is a speciality of the Ferme Huet, which also sells free-range poultry. Should you spot the capon you wish to eat for the next Christmas and New Year celebrations, you can reserve it in the summer and it will be sent to you once it is ready. A capon costs about 150 F a 2¼ lb (1 kg).

Foie gras and poultry
Ferme Huet, Pabu
☎ 02 96 21 03 13
Brittany produces foie gras, and the geese of the Guingamp region are famous for the quality of

In Guingamp the traditional dance is the dérobée, an Italian dance brought back by Napoléon's soldiers, the Grognards

Tréguier, welcome to the *rias*

The capital of the region once known as Trégor is a sleepy little town beside a sea inlet of the type known as a *ria*, whose banks are are ideal for rambles and hikes. From the harbour, continue along the quay towards the Saint-Laurent chapel. You will pass the villages of La Montagne and Kerautret and reach the banks of the river Jaudy, which you can follow to Pointe Jaune, which lies on a bend in the *ria*. A little further on, there is a spot with a panoramic view of the mouth of the Jaudy. If you take the same path back, count the public wash-houses that you pass on the way – there are dozens of them!

Revolutionaries, but its fortunes were revived in the 19th C. thanks to its trade in fruit and vegetables. A **pardon** is offered to **Saint Yves** every third Sunday in May in the superb cathedral that is dedicated to him. More than 10,000 people come to the town to celebrate the Christian festival. The younger generation usually continue to celebrate late into the night, at which point the festival is no longer religious.

Les Mercredis de Tréguier

On Wednesday evenings entertainments are organised at the Place des Halles and Place du Martray featuring Celtic music and local snack foods, such as *galettes-saucisses* (a sausage in a buckwheat pancake), Breton pastries and cider. If you know Brittany at all, you will realise that there is a Place du Martray in almost every town of more than 2,000 inhabitants. That is because the name comes from 'martyr', and it is the public square in which executions were held.

Plougrescant
The *Marie-Georgette*
4 miles (7 km) NW of Tréguier
This old ship used to carry the mail to the inhabitants of the Île de Batz. The *Marie-Georgette* has now been converted into a pleasure boat-cum-fishing vessel. It will take you out to sea so that you can

Tugdual and Yves
Tugdual is one of the seven original saints of Brittany. The town of Tréguier was founded at his behest in the 6th C., and it soon became the capital of Trégor. It was invaded by the Normans and persecuted by the French

try your hand at catching mackerel and pull up a few crab-pots. This is a good introduction to the two types of traditional Breton fishing, for mackerel and shellfish. To make a booking ☎ 02 96 92 51 03 or, better still, speak to the owner of the **Ar Vag** in **Plougrescant**.

The hell of Plougrescant and the paradise of Port-Blanc

An inlet in the coastline at the mouth of the Jaudy estuary is known as Baie d'Enfer (Hell Bay). When it is stormy there are dreadful roaring noises in the rock formations of the bay, and according to popular belief, the noises are made by the souls of the damned, who were trapped and tortured in the flames of hell. Woe betide the fisherman who sailed into the bay as the dead would clutch at the boat, causing it to capsize. The Bretons used to compare this bay to the adjoining coast of Port-Blanc, where the sea was much calmer, by saying: *Ifern Plougouskant ha baradoz Porz-Gwen* (the hell of Plougrescant and the paradise of Port-Blanc).

Port-Blanc
A sea view
6 miles (9 km) NE of Tréguier
This tiny port is a good place to come to enjoy the last rays of the sun and think about the ships that used to arrive here from England carrying the war-chest to be used to pay for the battles against the kings of France, who tried to subjugate Brittany in the 12th C. Port-Blanc has become a favourite resort among holiday-makers from Guingamp, St Brieuc, Rennes and even Paris. But, fortunately, it remains an unspoiled fishing port, huddled around its chapel.

Pleubian
Centre d'Études et de Valorisation des Algues (CEVA)
7 miles (12 km) NE of Tréguier
Presqu'île de Pen-Lan
☎ 02 96 22 93 50
Guided tour, Mon.–Fri. at 3.30pm, open to the public July–Aug.
Admission charge.
Seaweeds have a surprising number of uses. They can be made into food and cosmetics, used in polishes, photographic film and even in soft furnishing fabrics. Learn all about them at the CEVA, a research centre at Pleubian, which is constantly looking for new industrial applications for seaweed and promoting their use in as many ways as possible. This is the only seaweed research centre of its kind in Europe. Visitors can see displays and a promotional film about its work.

Spotcheck
D1

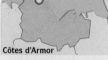

Côtes d'Armor

Things to do
The Wednesdays of Tréguier
The kite festival
Sea fishing
Learn about seaweed

Within easy reach
Île de Bréat 13 miles (21 km) NE, p. 154, Paimpol 9 miles (15 km) E, p. 156.

Tourist office
Tréguier: ☎ 02 96 92 30 19

LES PASSAGERS DU VENT
14 Rue de Bazile
☎ 02 96 22 93 16
If you want to learn to fly a kite, how to handle it skilfully and where to find the wind to make it fly, the Passagers du Vent (wind travellers) association will be glad to help you. This club, whose members practise their hobby on the Sillon de Talbert, a 2 mile (3.5 km) headland swept by sea breezes, organises French and Breton kite-flying tournaments and other competitions, such as the Open de Lutèce. The kite festival (Fête du Cerf Volant), held every year in July or August, is a big crowd-puller. Watching the beautiful flying kites and the skill of their owners in handling them makes for a memorable day out for all the family.

Bréhat
the colourful island

Your first thought on landing on the island is that you are in a Mediterranean garden – flowers, cacti, pines and palm trees surround sunny terraces.

The island has a sheltered cove, which benefits from the microclimate. If you want to take a walk around this lovely island, take the first footpath on the left. Go to Goareva and, if you feel energetic enough, climb the hill. Far out to sea, what appears to be a huge snake sliding into the water is the Sillon de Talbert, a geological formation of pebbles that roll against each other and cause the massive structure of the peninsula to move. Cars are not allowed on Bréhat.

A crowded place

Le Bourg, the main town, has a small square, narrow streets and a tiny church with a granite belfry. Unfortunately, the town is packed to bursting in the summer. It is the most visited island in northern Brittany, with 400,000 visitors a year, mostly in the high season, so if you took the precaution of packing a picnic basket, well done! It is worth visiting the town just to admire the collection of decorative plates at the **Restaurant des Pêcheurs**.

The Corderie cove

The best way to leave Le Bourg is from the Corderie cove. A short 18th-C. bridge, known as the Pont ar Prat or the Vauban bridge, after its engineer, links the two parts of the island together. The Corderie is on your left after you cross the bridge. There is a cobbled pier at which a few small dinghies, belonging to yachts anchored in the cove, tie up at high tide. As the cove is particularly sheltered and difficult to get to, it was once a favourite hideout for privateers. The shore is also lined with elegant villas.

The Rosédo lighthouse

Once you are on the Île Nord, you will find a pleasant beach on the left. It is just the spot for a picnic, for there is shelter from the wind and it is south-facing. On your right, the Rosédo lighthouse is part of a 12-light system along the northern Goëlo coast and the Arcouest headland.

The bustling town centre in Le Bourg on Bréhat

Spotcheck

D1

Côtes d'Armor

Things to do

Walks and sea trips

Within easy reach

Tréguier 13 miles (21 km) SW, p. 152.

Tourist office

Bréhat: ☎ 02 96 20 04 15

Sailing around the archipelago

Bréhat island is surrounded by lots of small islets. What could be more delightful than zigzagging between the rocks on an old sailing ship with its brass fittings and fragrant wood panelling? That is just what the *Vieux-Copain*, a tuna boat that is listed as an historical monument, enables you to do. Several trips are available, lasting for one or more days. You can choose whether to help sail her, and you can board from the islands or mainland. For full details contact Serge Le Joliff, who will do his best to organise the trip of your dreams. (☎ 02 96 20 59 30).

The northern part of the island

Continue your walk from the Rosédo lighthouse along the coast. The landscape changes, as the hydrangeas and eucalyptus trees give way to a moorland covered with short

grass, gorse, broom and bracken. A few pine trees give some height to this coast, which appears to be flattened by the wind and sea. In this part of the island, only a few houses

battle against the elements. To the right lie the ruins of the former **Léproserie de Saint-Riom**, a leper colony. In front of you is the pink granite **Paon lighthouse**, which looks too frail to withstand the waves, but that is just an impression.

Port-Clos

To return to the landing-stage you will have to go back over the bridge, although you can avoid Le Bourg. If you arrive early to catch the boat, enjoy the view from one of the three terraces of the hotel. Spending a night on the island is a very chic thing to do. At the **Hôtel Bellevue** you can expect to pay about 450 F per person, including meals (lots of seafood). Have a last look at the piers of Port-Clos and at the many birds of the islands, both seabirds and land birds – gulls, cormorants, blackbirds, crows and magpies.

THE FLOWER ISLAND

A ship will take you to Port-Clos. On your way to Le Bourg you will pass sub-tropical landscapes of hydrangeas, fig trees and even eucalyptus. Bréhat is called the island of flowers for two reasons. The first is its microclimate. The second refers to its inhabitants. Tough privateers and brave fishermen, the people of Bréhat were plant collectors and brought back many exotic trees, shrubs and seedlings, which have adapted to the climate, at least in the southern part of the island.

Paimpol
home of the 'Icelanders'

The 'Icelanders' were the fishermen of Paimpol who sailed to Iceland to fish for cod. The blackened wooden lintels over the doors of the houses record the names of 2,000 sailors who were lost at sea while cod-fishing off distant Newfoundland. The story of Paimpol and the lives of its inhabitants are more closely linked with deep-sea fishing, which flourished in the 19th C., than those of any other Breton port, even Saint-Malo and Cancale. Fishing made the fortunes of many, but was the despair of many more.

The cliffs of Plouha

A tour of the town

The town hall and the church reveal a great deal about the life of a small town. In Paimpol both these buildings are in the same street – Rue Pierre-Feutren – and are worth visiting. The church of **Notre-Dame-de-Bonne-Nouvelle**

(Our Lady of the Gospel) is still filled with the memory of the many pardons that were celebrated before each departure in search of the great fish shoals off Iceland

Engraving on the altar of Paimpol church

and Newfoundland. Inside, the altar is engraved with fishing scenes. The **town hall**, which is almost next door, is one of the most lavish buildings on the island and is the former home of a ship-owner. As you take the Rue Labenne down to the harbour, you will pass the old cod-drying factory, which has been turned into the **Musée de la Mer** maritime museum; ☎ 02 96 22 02 19, 1 April–30 Sept. and school holidays, 10.30am–1pm and 3–7pm. Admission charge).

Marché au Cadran

This wholesale market in Paimpol is one at which the bidding automatically decreases. This simply means that the prices are reduced automatically if the growers offering their produce for sale do not manage to get rid of all their stock. So the best time to go is when the market is ending, at about 10.45am. The market is held daily, from 9am to 11am, behind the station. The wholesale buyers from cooperatives throughout the region come here to get fruit and vegetables, but they'll be happy to make room for you. Don't leave without buying a little box of **coco beans**, the famous dried beans from Paimplon, which keep extremely well.

Beauport abbey

The abbey is a Norman structure, but stands on Breton soil. The beauty of its Gothic columns are evocative of the wealth of the monks who lived in the abbey in the 12th C. The magnificence of the architecture and its wild setting will impress even those who are not enthusiastic about looking at piles of old stones.

Arcouest Point

The GR 34 footpath passes the Pointe de l'Arcouest (Arcouest point), a good place to look out over the **Goëlo Coast**. This is also the place to

catch a ferry for the island of Bréhat (hourly departures from 8.30am). In July and August, tide permitting, you can also take half-day **mini-cruises** to the Trieux estuary (timetables vary, 100 F per person). **Vedettes de Bréhat**, ☎ 02 96 55 79 50.

Plouha

An incredible view

12 miles (20 km) SE of Paimpol

At 330 feet (100m), these are the highest cliffs in Brittany. The best place to see the view is from the footpath leading from the Pointe du Minard. A pleasant walk of about three hours will take the most energetic to the Pointe de Plouézec across heathland. It is a good idea to take a pair of binoculars so that you can watch the antics of the birds nesting on the cliff face. You will have a magnificent view of Bréhat and other islands in the archipelago. If

Spotcheck
D1

Côtes d'Armor

Things to do

Maritime museum
Marché au Cadran
Hiking and mini-cruises

Within easy reach

Lannion 20 miles (33 km) W, p. 148,
Guingamp 22 miles (35 km) S, p. 150,
Tréguier 9 miles (15 km) W, p. 152.

Tourist office

Paimpol: ☎ 02 96 20 83 16

you want to get a feel for what life was like in Paimpol in its heyday, read *Fishermen of Iceland* (1886) by Pierre Loti, who lived in the town.

HARNESS RACING AROUND PAIMPOL

Off-road harness racing in a horse-drawn cart called a *marathon* is practised on the moors of Lancerf, along the banks of the rivers Trieux and Leff. It can be a hair-raising ride: the route includes narrow paths and fords. Information: ACECA, Claude Hervé, ☎ 02 96 55 90 58.

Around Saint-Quay and Binic, entertainment for night and day

When the monk Ké landed in Kertugal cove, he was beaten up by local women, who were convinced that he was the Devil himself! Left for dead, he prayed to the Virgin, who produced a healing spring for him that enabled him to impose his rule on his erstwhile attackers. The miraculous fountain is still there, in the town centre of Saint-Quay-Portrieux, which has become one of the most attractive resorts in the region. By day there is sun and sand, and by night the town comes alive with the whirring and clanking of the 80 fruit machines in the casino!

The Casino beach

The beaches

There are five beaches in the resort, all of them well sheltered from the wind and safe for bathing. The **Casino** beach is closest to the outdoor tables of the cafés. There is a children's seawater swimming pool between the Casino and the **Châtelet** beach. There are also the beaches of the **Grève Noire**, with its dark-coloured sand, the **Comtesse** beach, which has a lovely view of the Ile de la Comtesse, and the **Plage du Port**. Even at low tide, the walk to the sea is not a long one because the beaches are wide and the tide does not go out far.

Binic

In winter, when the wind and the drizzle sweep over the deserted quay, there is not a soul to be seen. The whistling of the wind in the halyards makes the inviting warmth of the few cafés that are open doubly inviting. In summer the scene changes completely. The café terraces are packed, there is music everywhere, the sun beats down ... but Binic remains just as delightful, whether you are in its narrow lanes or at the Quai de Courcy, where the shops are. Binic is the water-sports centre of the *département* (Rue de Bellevue, ☎ 02 96 73 76 80), and offers various activities such as catamaraning, windsurfing, scuba-diving and sea kayaking.

The deep-water yacht harbour

The marina is one of the most up-to-date in Brittany. It only opened in 1991 and has berths

A HIKE ALONG THE GR 34 FOOTPATH

The GR 34 hiking trail runs from the new harbour of Saint-Quay westwards to the Pointe du Sémaphore. The harbour master's office, built in 1860, is still in operation and overlooks the sea about 100 yards (100 m) from the little village. Immediately next to it, an elaborate indicator board shows you just where you are in the bay and mentions places of interest. The trail then turns south, towards Kercadoret, offering more views of the countryside. A little further on, past the villages of Keirouet and Saint-Maurice, the path climbs gradually to Étables-sur-Mer, a small family resort with two good beaches (Les Godelins and Le Moulin) and a public park, which is also listed as a protected nature reserve, thanks to its masses of flowers.

for 1,000 ships of all sizes. In summer take a stroll along its piers, between the yachts, each as beautiful, comfortable and luxurious as the last. The *Rapaz*, a magnificent 60-feet (18-m) long schooner, panelled with rare woods (iroko and mahogany), is also moored in the harbour and undertakes excursions (reservations required) to Cap Fréhel and the Trieux estuary (information ☎ 02 96 33 57 61). If you are not quite as adventurous, just while away the time on the terrace of the **Westland** (new harbour, ☎ 02 96 70 48 81) where they sell the very best ice cream in town.

Nightlife

There is a French saying: *abondance de biens ne nuit pas* ('you can never have too much of a good thing'). So, if you came here for fun, you have lots of places to choose from between Saint-Quay and Binic (Étables tends to close down at 10pm). In the late afternoon you can visit the **casino** (6 Boulevard du Général-de-Gaulle, Saint-Quay, ☎ 02 96 70 40 36), which has a sea view. If the one-armed bandits deliver the loot, why not try an apéritif at the **Clipperton Club** (Quai de Courcy, Binic, ☎ 02 96 73 60 45). The house cocktail costs 30 F and loud jazz is played. If you want to move on, return to Saint-Quay and find **L'Espadon** (Chemin des Douaniers,

Spotcheck
D2

Côtes d'Armor

Things to do

Beaches and water-sports
Sea trips on a schooner
Hikes

Things to do with children

Seawater pool

Within easy reach

Guingamp 16 miles (26 km) SW, p. 150, Saint-Brieuc 12 miles (20 km) S, p. 164.

Tourist office

Saint-Quay: ☎ 02 96 70 40 64

L'Espadon in Saint-Quay

☎ 02 96 70 38 20), where you will find thousands of people listening to music from Quebec and drinking unusual beers. Is it 2am already? It's time for the techno fans to make for **Le Radeau** (5 Avenue Foch, Binic, ☎ 02 96 73 61 54; 60 F a drink). Everyone else will prefer to patronise the **Étrier**, a real 'beach club' (3b Place de la Plage, Saint-Quay, ☎ 02 96 70 99 08; 60 F a drink). If you want to start all over again, you'll have to wait until 2pm for the casino to reopen.

Lac de Guerlédan
inland water-sports

The lake, forest, deep gorges, narrow valleys and rushing torrents are all more typical of the foothills of the Pyrenees than of Brittany. In 1923 an engineer from Pontivy decided to change the course of the river Blavet and dam the mass of water that now forms the largest lake in Brittany. He submerged 17 locks and built a dam 155 feet (46 m) high and 660 feet (201 m) wide, in the certain knowledge that the area would become a prime tourist destination, as indeed has proved to be the case.

Relaxing at the lakeside
☎ 02 96 28 51 41
The rustic landscape and forest are favourite places for walkers, ramblers, mountain-bikers and horse-riders, and there are many signposted paths to follow. The lake is also popular with water-sports enthusiasts, and the water-sports centre is open all year round. There are dinghies and rowing boats as well as pedalos, water-skiing and kayaking. At the lakeside there are look-outs, outdoor cafés and other amenities where parents or the less active can enjoy the view without expending too much energy.

Poulancre gorge
When the sun shines, this spot looks like a scene in the Cévennes. When there is a light grey mist, the landscape becomes mysterious and somewhat unreal, and you might think that at any moment Merlin, Morgan-le-Fay or Viviane will appear since this was, according to the Breton version of the Arthurian legend, their favourite haunt. The wildlife is so rich that it attracts the experts, but anyone can enjoy the magnificent forest environment. A footpath follows the course of the Poulancre, which has cut

The reservoir at Guerlédan covers about 7½ sq miles

Forges-des-Salles, one of the oldest metal-working factories in Brittany

its deep bed in the rocks, making it look like a canyon in the western United States.

A full basket

Venison terrine is an unusual dish with the strong flavour of game, and you are unlikely to find it anywhere except the **Auberge des Cerfs de Kerfulus** (☎ 02 97 39 68 99). If venison reminds you of Bambi and you can't bear to eat it, there are plenty of other delicious regional dishes – veal, pigeon, *kig ha farz* and

BIKING TO ROSTRENEN

About 12½ miles (20 km) west of the lake, this ancient citadel, a historic site, is the start and finish point for a cycling tour around one of the most beautiful parts of Brittany. A winding track will take you into the valley of the Daoulas, whose sheer shale escarpments, gorse and heather look almost alpine. The route then takes you to the ancient Cistercian abbey of Bon-Repos, where the Blavet meets the Daoulas, before reaching the lake shores. More information at the Comité Départemental de Cyclotourisme: ☎ 02 96 43 76 67.

laez gwell – available from the **Ferme-auberge de Cléguerec** (☎ 02 97 38 06 14), or **goat's** cheese from Lescouet-Gouarec (☎ 02 96 24 86 44).

Saint-Aignan
❋ Musée de l'Électricité

About 1¼ miles (2 km) SE of the lake
☎ **02 97 27 51 39**
Open daily 1 May–15 Sept., 10am–noon and 3–6pm.
Admission charge.
The building of the Guerlédan dam, the story of the first electrical household appliances and the invention of the X-ray – the **Musée de l'Électricité** (electricity museum) is a great source of information about this basic utility, which we use all the time without really thinking about where it comes from. This museum of electrical power is packed with anecdotes, extraordinary inventions and incredible machinery from the early days of electrical power. The Guerlédan power station, which supplies electricity to the whole region, was the obvious place to put the museum.

Forges-des-Salles
The Iron Age

About 1¼ miles (2 km) W of the lake
☎ **02 96 24 90 12**
Open daily, July–Aug. 2–6pm, April–June; Sept.–Oct. weekends only.
A short footpath leads through the forest from the lake to the **Forges-des-Salles**. These ironworks are evidence of the region's golden age, when the ironworks of the forest fed the furnaces of the Rohan family, the local gentry, and supplied the king's army with canon and the local

Spotcheck
D3

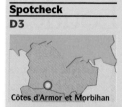

Côtes d'Armor et Morbihan

What to do

Hiking, biking, horse-riding
Water sports
Poulancre gorge
Electricity museum

Within easy reach

Guingamp about 28 miles (45 km) N, p. 150
Saint-Brieuc about 28 miles (45 km) N.E, p. 164
Pontivy about 12 miles (20 km) S, p. 244.

Tourist office

Guerlédan:
☎ 02 96 28 51 41

peasants with farm implements. The forge provided work for the whole region and did not start its inevitable decline until the mid-19th C., when deposits were found in eastern France. The village has now been reconstructed, with its workmen's cottages, the château with the espaliered trees in its grounds and other features of 19th-C. life, so you can see history brought to life.

Loudéac full of surprises

Loudéac is a surprisingly busy place. There are lots of fairs, displays of local crafts, horse races and fly-fishing competitions, and it is the European headquarters of the association of towns that hold Passion plays. It is one of the historic trading centres of Brittany. The local peasantry would flock to the town to exchange their wares for manufactured goods. Most of the fairs have now gone, but the tradition survives in the hospitable nature of the town's inhabitants. The surrounding countryside is still rich farmland, which is dotted with grain silos and specialises in the rearing of chickens and pigs.

Ateliers Michel and René Allot
Making and restoring furniture, Zone des Parpareux
☎ 02 96 28 18 69
Open daily except Sat. afternoon and Sun. 9am–noon and 2–7pm.
Free guided tour.
The hundreds of items of craft furniture piled at the entrance to this workshop will give you a foretaste of the skill and artistry of these two brothers, who handle tenon-saws, chisels and planes like artists handle palettes and paintbrushes. In the workshop you can watch craftsmen shaping and turning pieces of wood, which they turn into stylish furniture. Then it is the job of the varnishers and upholsterers. There is an atmosphere of dedication and skill in this craft factory, which has the pervasive feeling of a job well done.

Fête du Cheval
The race meeting has been held annually since 1936. This is when horses are treated like kings in Loudéac. The breeders curry-comb, brush and polish their mounts, which will be taking part in the steeplechasing (Société Hippique Rurale, ☎ 02 96 28 35 71).

The gamblers of Loudéac
More money is bet on horses at Loudéac than anywhere else in western France. Races are held regularly on the racecourse, which is famous throughout France and regularly attracts several thousand

race-goers. The races are held in spring and a racing calendar can be obtained from the tourist office (Place du Champ-de-Foire, ☎ 02 96 28 25 17). The most famous race is held during Easter weekend, when more than two million francs are gambled on the horses.

La Chèze

Musée Régional des Métiers

6 miles (10 km) SE of Loudéac
Rue du Moulin
☎ 02 96 26 63 16
Open daily except Tue. high season, 10am–noon and 2–6pm; off-peak, 2–6pm. The regional craft museum is among the most

beautiful museums in Brittany. It tells, in an amusing and captivating way, how workers used to live. Groups of children can even enjoy a treasure hunt while they find out what slate-miners, printers, saddlers and carpenters did and how they worked. The museum also holds contemporary craft exhibitions.

Ploeuc-sur-Lié

The wings of the Côtes d'Armor

16 miles (25 km) N of Loudéac
Avel-Dro, Mairie de Ploeuc-sur-Lié
☎ 02 96 64 22 00
Avel-Dro, about 20 miles (30 km) north of Loudéac, has a paragliding and hang-gliding school, which holds courses for all levels. It will teach complete beginners who are staying in the area for a few days or offer advanced courses for those who have some familiarity with the sport. For those who are in the neighbourhood for a short stay only, an initiation flight is available in a two-man hang-glider, which you share with an instructor. This is an excellent way to become acquainted with this high-altitude sport.

Spotcheck
D3

Côtes d'Armor

Things to do
Regional craft museum
Visit a biscuit factory
Fête du Cheval and racing
Hang-gliding courses

Within easy reach
Saint-Brieuc 25 miles (40 km) N, p. 164,
Lamballe 25 miles (40 km) NE, p. 168,
Pontivy 14 miles (22 km) SW, p. 244.

Tourist office
Loudéac: ☎ 02 96 28 25 17

COMPAGNIE BISCUITIÈRE (BISCUIT FACTORY)

Route de Rennes, Zone des Parpareux, Loudéac
☎ 02 96 66 00 12
Open Mon.–Fri., 9am–noon and 1.30–6pm.
Free admission.
Punchs, a local type of Breton biscuit, are made here. Inside the shop a glass display window allows you to look into the factory and see how these biscuits are made. At a bargain price, a decorated 1¼ lb (600 g) tin box decorated with Breton landscapes or characters costs 35 F. Another biscuit factory to visit is the Biscuiterie de Ker Cadélac (Route de Pontivy, Rue Enaud, ☎ 02 96 28 66 55), where you will be offered delicious *palets au beurre* (butter biscuits).

Saint-Brieuc and its bay

Maison de la Baie
Site de l'Étoile, Hillion
☎ 02 96 32 27 98
July–August 9am–7pm
(Sun. 2–7pm), out of
season 9am–12.30pm
and 1.30–6pm
(Sun. 2–6pm).
Admission charge.
This museum has exhibits
about sailing life and the
natural treasures of the Saint-
Brieuc bay. There is an
exceptional view and lots of
video shows and exhibitions
about the wildlife in the bay.
The star attraction of the
Maison de la Baie is the
Marinarium, a fascinating
demonstration of the ecology
of the coastal environment.

The beaches
The closest beaches to Saint-
Brieuc are at Plérin-sur-Mer.
They are very busy at high
season and provide various
activities under the name **Cap
Armor** (☎ 02 96 74 68 79,
in July and August). The
programme includes beach
volley-ball, archery, sand-
yachting, sea trips, pony-
trekking and rock-climbing.
The village of Plérin is on
the hillside facing Le Léguer,
the port of Saint-Brieuc,
which is dominated by an
impressive viaduct.

The town deserves a one-day visit although it
does not have a great reputation as a tourist
attraction. The old town centre is based
around the cathedral of Saint-Étienne. But if you
don't have much time to spend in Saint-Brieuc, go
and 'do the Saint-Gui', as they say. The Rue
Saint-Guillaume is a busy, cobbled pedestrian
shopping precinct. It is much more fun shopping
here than standing in a queue at the Carrefour
hypermarket, and you will have time
to sit and
relax on
one of the
many café
terraces.

The salt pans
**Langueux, SE exit
from Saint-Brieuc**
☎ 02 96 62 25 50
The bay of Saint-Brieuc has
been producing salt for
centuries. Around Langueux
there were as many as 47 salt
pans, which have left their
mark on the landscape. The
method used for drying out the
salt using fire is explained in a
permanent exhibition.

Yffiniac
The Bernard Hinault race
4 miles (7 km) E of Saint Brieuc

Bernard Hinault, one of the greatest French cycling champions of recent years, was born and still lives in Yffiniac. A major cycle race named after him is held here just before the summer every year. It attracts champion cyclists from all over the country. However, cyclists also use the track for practice throughout the year, both in competition and as part of the cycling tour, which is a special feature of this area.

Plédran
In the woods
5 miles (8 km) S of Saint-Brieuc

Overlooking the bay of Yffiniac, about ten minutes from Saint-Brieuc, the **Plédran wood** is a good place to explore on foot, on horseback or on mountain-bike, using the signposted pathways. There are family activities, a strenuous walk, a chequered bowling green and a play area for children. It all makes for a great day out for the family.

Quintin
The town with two châteaux
About 12 miles (20 km) SW of Saint-Brieuc
☎ 02 96 74 94 79
Open daily, 15 June–15 Sept., 10.30am–12.30pm and 1.30–6.30pm; out of season open Sat. and Sun. 2.30–5pm.

This little town, only the size of a village, happens to have not one but two of the proudest châteaux in the region. They stand in the same grounds, right in the town centre. Quintin also has a rich cultural life, which culminates in the November celebrations of the Fête de Saint-Martin (Martinmas) and the Festival des Chanteurs de Rue (street singers' festival).

Spotcheck
D2

Côtes d'Armor

Things to do

Maison de la Baie and the Marinarium
Night riding across the bay
Trips into the Plédran wood
Beaches, sailing and sports
Visit the two châteaux

Within easy reach

Guingamp 17½ miles (28 km) NW, p. 150, Saint-Quay about 12½ miles (20 km) N, p. 158, Guerlédan about 28 miles (45 km) SW, p. 160.

Tourist office

Saint-Brieuc:
☎ 02 96 33 32 50

NIGHT-TIME RIDING ACROSS THE BAY

This is an unique and amazing experience for riders, some of whom come from a long way away for the adventure. It is organised by the Association des Cavaliers d'Extérieur des Côtes d'Armor and is possible only when there is a full moon and when low tide occurs around midnight. Are you tempted? If you are an experienced rider, telephone ☎ 02 96 74 98 19 (answering machine message: ☎ 02 96 74 68 05) to find out the date when the right conditions will apply. Even if you can't make the date but love horses, telephone anyway. At night-time, the horses walk or trot but the Association also organises daytime gallops across the bay. For riders and spectators, the sight of nearly 200 horses thundering across the sands is an impressive one.

Pléneuf-Val-André

a popular resort

Pléneuf is one of the most popular resorts on the Côtes d'Armor. Its huge sea-wall and endless beach are comparable to those of Dinard. The promenade leads to the Pointe de Pléneuf, which overlooks the bay of Saint-Brieuc, opposite the bird sanctuary on the Île du Verdelet. Pléneuf is a resort favoured by wealthier holiday-makers, who can afford luxury villas, and by yacht-owners, so it has some of the best nightlife on the Brittany coast, centring around the casino. Pléneuf is also a major shopping centre, especially in the tourist season.

Sports in Pléneuf-Val-André

Pléneuf-Val-André is one of the *Station Voile* sailing ports. It can, therefore, offer every type of activity connected with sailing and yachting, including lessons and an introduction to the maritime environment for children (École Française de Voile, ☎ 02 96 72 95 28). There is also training for regattas for more experienced yachtsmen and women (Yacht Club du Val-André, ☎ 02 96 72 21 68).

On land, but not very far from the sea, golfers can practise their swing on a 3¾ mile (6 km) golf course beside the beaches (Golf Club du Val d'Armor, ☎ 02 96 63 01 12).

La Malle du Capitaine

Rue Winston-Churchill
☎ **02 96 63 09 75**
Close to the sea-wall, this shop is a real treasure chest. A handsome sea-chest costs about 3,000 F. Consider it a summer investment!

Along the coast

Between Cap Fréhel and Pléneuf there are many places that deserve a visit, beginning with Sables-d'Or-les-Pins,

whose poetic name is indicative of the tranquillity of this tiny seaside resort. Its many supporters claim that its huge beach, covered with golden sand, is the finest in Brittany. In fact, the beach is artificial, the work of developers who launched the resort in the 1920s! Les Sables also has a casino that, like the resort, is small but charming. Plurien is slightly set back from the sea and has a tiny chapel whose beams are inlaid with scallop shells, the sign of the pilgrims who made the arduous trip to the shrine

of St James at Compostela. The island of Saint-Michel, out in the bay, can be reached on foot at low water, but don't get caught out by the incoming tide!

Dahouët

A peaceful port

1 ¼ miles (2 km) W of Pléneuf

This little fishing port nestles in the estuary of the Flora, where yachtsmen tend to moor as much for the shelter it provides as for the picturesque port, with its granite jetties and the few trawlers that still use it. The resort of Val-André a little further on so delighted a French actress that she changed her name accordingly, which is why she is now called Charlotte Valandrey!

Saint-Alban

La Crêperie

1 ¾ miles (3 km) S of Pléneuf

Z.A. Le Poirier
☎ 02 96 32 98 06
Open daily, July–Aug.
Mornings, out of season, by arrangement.
Free admission.

Brittany has several thousand *crêperies*, of course, but this is not a pancake restaurant, it is a *crêpe* factory. **M. and Mme Girardot** invite the public to come and see what they do. You can watch the assembly line for these delicious Breton *crêpes*, from measuring the ingredients and mixing the batter, right up to the tasting, without which no visit would be complete. *Crêpes* (thin wheat flour pancakes, usually sweet) and *galettes* (buckwheat pancakes, usually savoury) are an ancient Breton tradition and are delicious. Each manufacturer has its own 'little something', which it adds to make all the difference between one brand and another, and these are always a trade secret! The little village of Saint-Alban is also very pleasant. Its granite houses are built in the traditional local style.

Spotcheck
E2

Côtes d'Armor

Things to do

Sailing and golfing lessons
Rambling and scuba-diving
Visit to a crêpe factory

Within easy reach

*Cap Fréhel 15½ miles (25 km) NE, p. 172,
Saint-Cast 19 miles (30 km) E, p. 174.*

Tourist office

Pléneuf-Val-André:
☎ 02 96 72 20 55

SCALLOPS AND DIVING
Erquy, 5½ miles (9 km) NE of Pléneuf
Scallop-fishing accounts for the livelihood of most of the 3,000 inhabitants of this village. However, the fat years of the 1970s are gone. The trawlers now go out for only two hours a day, four days a week, and only from November to March. If you are unable to watch the return of the boats, followed by a cloud of screeching gulls, take a little excursion to the formidable peaks of the Cap d'Erquy and the surrounding moorland, which is reminiscent of that of Cap Fréhel. There is a delightful signposted path, which is easy walking for young and old, unless you prefer to explore the depths in search of wrecks in the bay of Saint-Brieuc. (For scuba-diving, equipment hire and lessons, information is obtainable from Label Bretagne Plongée,
☎ 02 96 72 49 67.)

Lamballe
the heart of Penthièvre

The person responsible for Lamballe's original prosperity was Jeanne de Penthièvre, and in the 15th C. it was the capital of the district that bore her name. But the ambition of another family, the Montforts, robbed Jeanne of her achievement. Lamballe was defeated and was subsequently attacked during the Wars of Religion. It suffered once more from the forces of the French Revolution in 1792. Its only hope was to become a trading centre, and it did so with great success, specialising in leather and processed foods, especially after the opening of the Paris–Guingamp rail link.

A stroll through Lamballe

La Tête Noire
☎ 02 96 50 88 74
Lamballe has successfully combined ancient and modern. The proof lies two steps from the Place du Martray. **La Tête Noire** is a delightful bistro, dating from the 15th C., with a double entrance, diamond-pane windows and a tavern attached, which is patronised by the local teenagers. Lamballe is worth a detour just for La Tête Noire, but take advantage of the stop to visit the collegiate church of Notre-Dame-de-la-Grande-Puissance, as the starting point for a pleasant walk around the château.

The executioner's house ... and Mathurin Méheut

The executioner's house is now the tourist office! Presumably the executioner officiated in the Place du Martray, where public executions were performed. This is a magnificent, 14th-C., half-timbered house with a pointed roof, one of the best preserved in Brittany. The **Musée Mathurin-Méheut**, which is on the first floor, contains some 5,000 of the painter's works. This is the largest collection of water-

colours and drawings by the artist who came from Lamballe and whose work can be seen in the great museums of the world. Mathurin Méheut (1882–1958) made a point of depicting Breton daily life through the traditional occupations of the inhabitants.

At the crossroads

Several tours and rambles pass through Lamballe. You can choose to go on foot (GR de Pays 086), by bicycle (route available from the Comité Départemental de Cyclotourisme, ☎ 02 96 42 98 66, after 6.30pm) or on horseback

(Association des Cavaliers d'Extérieur des Côtes d'Armor, ☎ 02 96 73 12 38).

Moncontour
Hilltop village
6 miles (10 km) SW of Lamballe
Tourist office
☎ 02 96 73 50 50
Moncontour perches on a rocky peak, and is one of the loveliest villages in Brittany. The 11th-C. ramparts, narrow passageways and shops with quaint signs, inspired by medieval inn signs, form the backdrop to a medieval reconstruction held every August, which attracts many visitors. The surrounding countryside is covered with hiking trails.

Jugon-les-Lacs
A moment of relaxation
10 miles (16 km) SE of Lamballe
Life in this village centres around the lake. In summer it is a typical resort, with a beach, bathing, sailing dinghies and rambles. All this is in a picturesque setting because Jugon is an ancient fortified town, which was designed to defend the Dinan-Lamballe

road. The lake is artificial, created from local streams, which were rerouted 800 years ago. This large stretch of water was originally designed to deter invaders, but today it is the kingdom of the pedalo and

the pleasure boat. There is also windsurfing and yachting.

Spotcheck
E2

Côtes d'Armor

Things to do

Riding and visits to stud farm
Hiking and mountain-biking
Medieval show at Moncontour

Within easy reach

Loudéac, 25 miles (40 km) SW, p. 162, Saint-Cast, 18¾ miles (30 km) NE, p. 174, Dinan, 25 miles (40 km) E.), p. 182.

Tourist office

Lamballe : ☎ 02 96 31 05 38

THE STUD FARM

Club Hippique, Lamballe
☎ 02 96 31 00 40
or ☎ 02 96 31 37 95
This is the second most important stud farm in France. There are stables, a training ground, a garage for horse-drawn vehicles, a saddlery, a forge and a tack room, which are open to the public if you book first. There is also a riding school, and you can learn how to look after the 120 animals that live here permanently. The cosy atmosphere, the stone buildings, the handsome stallions and powerful draught horses are symbols of the wealth of the region. Three important months in the stud year are January, when the stallions are presented; early August, when the Concours Hippique National (national horse championships) are held at the stud farm; and late September, when the Fête du Cheval is held in the town and at the farm.

La Côte d'Émeraude

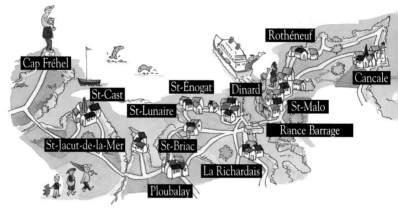

From the Cancale rock to the cliffs of Cap Fréhel, the Côte d'Émeraude (Emerald Coast) consists of alternating sunny coves and inlets and steep rocky headlands. The GR 34 footpath, formerly used by customs officers, hugs the coastline and is an excellent hiking trail. Local guides are available at the tourist offices of the various resorts. These maps, which point out all the local attractions, were created by Maurice Réauté, who also organised the first signposted trails in France. You might even meet him on your ramble between Saint-Malo and Saint-Cast.

Le Montmarin

Le Montmarin, near La Richardais, is one of the few ship-owners' mansions (known in this part of the world as *malouinières*) on the left bank of the river Rance. The roof is designed like the upturned hull of a ship, a creation that people considered sheer folly when it was first built. It is not open to the public.

Saint-Lunaire
Sand for the karts

The most beautiful women in Brittany are said to come from Saint-Lunaire. Will you meet them in the pews of the little Romanesque church that points towards Jerusalem? Or on one of the four beaches of the seaside resort? The **Grand-Plage** is a sheltered beach; the **Fosse-aux-Vaults** is less crowded because the access path is longer; **Port-Blanc** is close to the village of Saint-Éno-gat, and the **Longchamps** beach is rather exposed to the wind. From September to June, after the tourists have removed their towels and sunshades, this beach is dedicated to the sport of sand-yachting or sand-karting. All along the Côte d'Émeraude the sand is firm enough for this unusual sport (Yacht Club de Saint-Lunaire, ☎ 02 99 46 37 91).

THE RANCE DAM

The Rance tidal power station is a unique construction producing more than 600 million kWh of electricity a year, sufficient for a town of 250,000 inhabitants. If you want to visit the power station, you will have to book in advance (☎ 02 99 16 37 14). The wide range of powerful tides in the Rance estuary caused French engineers to plan the construction in the early 1960s. The power station was opened by President Charles de Gaulle in 1967, and it is the most popular site of scientific interest in France. Inside, the operators responsible for supervising the 24 generators ride around on bikes! A new visitors' tour was inaugurated in 1996 and includes a tour of the amazing machine room along a signposted route and a slide show. The power station operates on the established principle of the tide-mill, plus a few technical improvements. By bridging the river between Saint Malo and Dinard, the dam has brought together two towns that were previously locked in bitter rivalry. Drivers should be warned that traffic across the dam is heavy and potentially dangerous, so police checks are frequent.

A little further on, the **Décollé headland** is famous for the panoramic view over the whole coast – and for **La Chaumière**, a well-known nightclub.

Saint-Briac

Dinard golf course

The village is slightly smaller than Saint-Lunaire but it is just as lively. The painters Auguste Renoir, Paul Signac and Henri Rivière did much to make it a favourite resort of artists in the late 19th C., almost a Pont-Aven in miniature. The famous Dinard golf club is actually here among the dunes of Saint-Briac. The sheltered **Salinette** beach is popular, but the loveliest beach is that of **Port-Hue** as it has spectacular views over the Agot and the **Dame-Jouanne** islands.

Spotcheck
E2-F2

Côtes d'Armor and Ille-et-Vilaine

Things to do

Hiking along the coast
Golf and sand-karting
Visit to the Rance dam

Within easy reach

*Saint-Brieuc, p. 164,
Dinan, p. 182,
Mont St Michel, p. 190.*

Tourist office

Côte d'Armor Tourisme:
☎ 02 96 62 72 00

Ploubalay

Water tower
Restaurant du Château d'Eau

The water tower at Ploubalay provides the best view of the region, and it is also a good place to eat because it has a restaurant built on the top of it. The restaurant serves local dishes, which are predominantly seafood. Another good place to eat has opened in Ploubalay, and it is one of the best-housed in France in a French stately home. The **Josse** company, on the road to Dinard, can be visited on application. The workshop uses ancient materials, such as tiles, sandstone and wood, to create beautiful objects, many of which adorn the local residences.

Cap Fréhel
moorland, pink sandstone cliffs and fine sand

Cap Fréhel

Pléhérel

Plévenon

La Latte Fo

Fréhel

Fresnaye Bay

Port-à-la-Duc

Matignon

M ore than 200 feet (60 m) of rocky cliffs overlook the restless sea. The red and yellow moor and the dark rocks provide Cap Fréhel with an almost surreal desert aspect. Legend has it that the long amaranth streaks that make the cape iridescent are traces of the blood of an Irish missionary. At the foot of the cape, a stone, said to have been thrown there by Gargantua, is called the *Amas du cap* (the cape pile). Another tall, narrow stone is known as Gargantua's walking-stick!

The Fréhel lighthouse
☎ 02 96 41 40 03
Open daily, ask the warden.
Free admission.
The lighthouse is a world-famous landmark overlooking the English Channel and towering almost 330 feet (100 m) above it. It can be

seen for 70 miles (110 km), making it one of the most powerful lighthouses in France. The first lighthouse using ecliptic signals was erected here in the mid-19th C., but it was destroyed by the Germans in World War II. A new one was erected in 1950. If you climb up the 140 steps at nightfall in clear weather, you can see the flash of the Corbière lighthouse, on Jersey in the Channel Islands, to the north.

Fresnaye bay
At low tide Fresnaye bay is one of the largest mudflats in France. It is safer to walk here than in the bay of Mont-Saint-Michel, and you

can even venture out as far as the famous mussel beds. Fishing for shellfish is a popular activity, and the clams are especially tasty in this region. At one end of the bay, a marker buoy marks the shipwreck of the *Laplace*, a frigate that sank in 1950 after a forgotten World War II mine exploded.

La Latte Fort
☎ 02 96 41 40 31
Open every day from Easter to Sept., 10am–12.30pm and 2.30–6.30pm; off peak on Sat. Sun. and in the school holidays, 2.30–5.30pm.
Admission charge.
Kirk Douglas himself said he

was impressed with the rugged savagery of the coast, when he came here to work on the film *The Vikings* with Tony Curtis. The Goyon-Matignon family built the fortress 700 years ago. The castle has an impregnable keep and massive fortifications, which have resisted

The villages

Fréhel and Plévenon are two small picturesque, inland villages, which become very busy during the Fréhel carnival and the Fête de la Mer (sea festival) at Plévenon (crafts, oyster-tastings, etc). Pléhérel, near Pléneuf, has one of the loveliest sandy coves in the region. Port-à-la-Duc, in the middle of Fresnaye bay, is a fishing village with a stone sea-wall on which it is pleasant to stroll.

From Matignon to Monaco

Although Caroline, Albert and Stéphanie of Monaco have never visited the place, it was a lord of Matignon

Spotcheck
E2

Côtes d'Armor

Things to do

Visit to the Fréhel lighthouse
Walk in Fresnaye bay
Walk in Frémur
Bird sanctuary

Within easy reach

Pléneuf-Val-André 15 miles (25 km) SW, p. 166.

Tourist office

Fréhel Cape:
☎ 02 96 41 53 81

every attempted attack. If you peer down at the rocks below, you will soon understand why!

Walking by the Frémur

The Frémur is a small river running between green fields from the back of the bay. It can be reached by the GR 34 path. You can ramble or hike along the course of the river to the Château de Vaurouault through lovely farmland, meadows and heathland. Once at the château caution is advised: according to legend, a ghost walks the ramparts. The ghost is said only to appear to cuckolds, however, which may or may not be a reassuring or an endearing character trait on its part.

who, by marrying a Grimaldi, became prince of Monaco in 1731. He thus linked the destiny of Monaco with that of a village on Cap Fréhel. It was also Goyon-Matignon's town house in Paris, the Hôtel Matignon, that is now the official residence of the prime minister of France. Claude Casissian, the brilliant hoaxer and gate-crasher, was also born in Matignon in 1926.

BIRD SANCTUARY

At the foot of Cap Fréhel, the Fauconnière sanctuary owes its name to the fact that, in the past, it was a favourite nesting place for falcons. Today, the bird sanctuary is one of the most beautiful in Brittany. On a sunny day, it is pleasant to watch shags, oyster-catchers, and sea-gulls with a wingspan of up to 5 feet (1.5 m) diving and gliding on thermals or see gannets plunge more than 33 feet (10 m) into the waves. Down below, guillemots and puffins dive into the water. Take a pair of binoculars with you. The view is amazing, especially during the nesting season, which varies from one species to another. There are guided tours every day from June to Sept. Information from the Syndicat des Caps, ☎ 02 96 41 50 83.

Saint-Cast
and its seven beaches

long with its neighbour, Dinard, Saint-Cast became a popular resort in the early 19th C. when enthusiasm for taking the sea air swept the country. The French government first decreed that firms should give their employees paid holidays in 1936, which meant that seaside holidays were no longer the sole preserve of the wealthy. As a result, Saint-Cast, originally something of an elitist resort, now happily caters for everyone.

Guildo

Just a few minutes from Saint-Cast, the little port of Guildo has berths for the coasters that carry construction wood around the north coast. The unloading is interesting to watch. The port is dominated by the **Château**

du Guildo, which was the backdrop for the amorous liaison between Gilles de

Bretagne and Françoise de Dinan in the 15th C. There is an expression, *courir le guilledou* (running the guilledou), which dates from Gilles' debaucherous time at Guildo.

L'île des Ébihens

A stroll by the sea

3 miles (5 km) E of Saint-Cast (on foot)
This is a privately owned island between Saint-Cast and Saint-Jacut, but its magnificent white beaches are accessible at low tide. Be careful that you are not caught unawares by the incoming tide. In the 1980s

an ancient Gaulish (Coriosolite) village was discovered on the island.

Plancoët

Water for mountain-biking

10½ miles (17 km) S of Saint-Cast

One of the best French mineral waters comes from a local spring. At a time when some other spring waters are coming under scrutiny for nitrate

content, pesticide residues and so on, the water of Plancoët is a yardstick for reliability – zero nitrates, but enough vitamins to give the locals their healthy complexions and the energy they need to compete for the international mountain-biking trophy. This gruelling 44 mile (70 km) off-road race between Plancoët and Saint-Jacut is held every July. Naturally, it attracts large crowds, so take care while watching it.

Plédéliac

Barley beer and troubadours

15½ miles (25 km) SW of Saint-Cast

Ferme-auberge de Belouze

☎ 02 96 34 14 55

At dinner time, turn inland and make for the imposing ruins of the Château de la Hunaudaye. Nearby, at the **Ferme-auberge de la Belouze**, a lovely 15th-C. farmhouse, a young couple have opened a real medieval banqueting hall. For about 100 F you will be served a medieval feast based on game, accompanied by the traditional Breton barley beer (*cervoise*). On some evenings, troubadours, jesters and jugglers entertain the guests while they are eating. The farmhouse inn also offers accommodation, so you can drink barley beer to your heart's content and sleep it off on the premises.

Spotcheck
E2

Côtes d'Armor

Things to do

International mountain-biking trophy
Festival of the sea at Saint-Jacut
Swimming and walking at low tide

Within easy reach

*Piéneuf-Val-André, p. 166,
Lamballe, p. 168,
Dinan, p. 182.*

Tourist office

Saint-Cast:
☎ 02 96 41 81 52

SAINT-JACUT, A WORLD APART

8 miles (13 km) E of Saint-Cast

The people of Saint-Jacut consider themselves to be islanders, and this explains why they had their own 'language', which they spoke until the 1960s. In early June a big Fête de la Mer (sea festival) is held here, when various craft and fishing vessels parade and there is plenty of seafood to eat, to the accompaniment of Breton and Celtic folk music, which has become so popular again. Information: Côtes d'Armor Tourisme, ☎ 02 96 62 72 00. Saint-Jacut, which is really a peninsula, has no fewer than 11 beaches. At low tide this is a prime place to fish for cockles, but it is not so good for bathing because the sea goes out a long way.

Dinard
a favourite British resort

On summer evenings at midnight the town loses its rather genteel, British feel, which made it such a popular resort with the English middle classes. The casino, the entrance to the Plage de l'Écluse and the café terraces on the edge of town resound to techno-music, and the drink is beer rather than tea. The Croisette, the Newport and the Petit Casino are the places to start a nightclub crawl to Saint-Lunaire, Pleurtuit or Saint-Briac. At daybreak the resort becomes an English enclave again.

An Englishwoman made its name

A beautiful Englishwoman fell in love with Dinard and its climate in the 19th C. and succeeded in doing what her fellow countrymen had failed to do by force a hundred times over the course of three centuries. Mrs Faber conquered Dinard and imprinted it forever with the mark of the English upper classes, who had hitherto favoured Normandy. On her recommendation, several British families settled here, building seaside villas, including the Villa Eugénie. This now houses the **Musée du Site Balnéaire** (seaside resort museum), the Maison du Prince Noir (house of the Black Prince), a trinitarian priory on the beach that bears his name, and the Villa Monplaisir, now the town hall. The first tennis club in France was opened here in 1879. Next came a golf club, then an Anglican church – and Dinard was born.

Saint-Énogat, and the sand is just as fine. The beach at Dinard is also famous for its striped beach shelters. They can be rented for about 40 F a half-day or 1,000 F a month.

Sea-fishing or a trip on the Rance

Emeraude Lines
☎ 02 99 40 48 40
Trips start in the early mornings to the Îles Chaussey, to the Pointe du Grouin and to Cap Fréhel. Once onboard ship, you will be supplied with a fishing line to catch the big fish that makes for a great holiday photograph. A less strenuous option would be to go for a simple sea trip

The beaches
Service des Bains
☎ 02 99 46 18 12
The beach of **Écluse** no longer charges 1.20 F for bathing, reduced rates for children and servants, but the beach remains elegant and fashionable. There is more of a family atmosphere on the beaches of **Prieuré** and

THE MARKET

Held on Tuesday, Thursday and Saturday mornings. Dinard's market is one of the most flourishing in Brittany. There is a wonderful array of local delicacies, seafood and fish, of course, as well as *andouille* (chitterling sausage), black puddings, pâté and *galettes* – all at reasonable prices. It is also a paradise for bargain hunters of all types. Reduced clothing and second-hand goods stalls sell their wares, and it is not unusual to unearth a few items by one of the great names in ready-to-wear designer clothing at bargain prices.

along the Rance. This trip is offered by the same shipping company.

Walks

Between the Plage de l'Écluse and the Prieuré, the Promenade du Clair-de-lune hugs the coastline below the houses of the Bric-à-Brac district, which was named by an English buyer visiting a villa on the Pointe du Moulinet. This side catches the morning sun. On the other side, the Promenade de la Malouine leads to the Plage de Saint-Énogat, where the villas are more baroque. If your walk takes you as far as Port-Blanc, take the **painters' path** leading to Cap Fréhel. It is signposted with reproductions of works by Zuber, Isabey and Picasso.

The British film festival
☎ 02 99 88 19 04

Apart from the traditional and ultra-smart **Concours Hippique** (gymkhana) in August and the lush golf course next to Les Longchamps, Dinard ties an extra knot of friendship every year by holding a British film festival in early October. Sean

Spotcheck
E2

Ille-et-Vilaine

Things to do

Bathing, sea trips and golf
Sea-fishing
British film festival
Dinard market

Within easy reach

Dinan 14 miles (23 km) S, p. 182
Cancale 12 miles (20 km) E, p. 192.

Tourist office

Dinard: ☎ 02 99 46 94 12

Connery, Jacqueline Bisset and Hugh Grant have been celebrity guests. There are lectures, autographing sessions and discussions. Don't miss the statue of Alfred Hitchcock in the town centre, with crows perching on his arms.

Neither French nor Breton –

Saint-Malo!

I n 1590 Saint-Malo, a Roman Catholic city, refused to allow Henri de Navarre, a Protestant, to accede to the throne of France. The city proclaimed its independence, declaring itself to be a republic, and it was not reintegrated into France until 1594. This story displays the independent and pioneering spirit of the Malouins and Malouines – as the citizens of Saint-Malo are known. They are proud, free, haughty and powerful. Sailors from the city are buried all over the world: in Valparaiso, Mauritius, San Francisco, Maracaibo and Saint-Pierre. Its sons brought back gold from Peru. Duguay-Trouin and Surcouf held Rio to ransom and raided the British colonies in India. The explorers Cartier and Charcot won Canada and the Antarctic for France. The 19th-C. historian, Michelet once said of the town's inhabitants: 'These people daily perform deeds more daring than those of Columbus.'

Within the walls

The walled city is a closed world, whose cobbled streets are almost entirely devoted to tourism. There are hosts of restaurants of all sizes, cafés and, of course, the tall mansions, which bear witness to the glorious past of the city. The Hôtel White, home of the

The Saint-Vincent gate was cut into the ramparts in 1709

duchess Anne, the cathedral of Saint-Vincent and the Rue de la Pie-qui-Boit are all evidence of the city's rich heritage. These survived the bombs of World War II or have been rebuilt exactly as they once were. A guide to these sights is available from the tourist office. The walk continues with a tour of the ramparts (guided tours, starting at the Fort National, are available from the tourist office).

The terraces of the Place Chateaubriand

This is the largest open space inside the walled city. On one side there are the ramparts and the castle, and on the other are the stone houses whose ground floors are all occupied by the large terraces of cafés, the best-known of which is the **Hôtel de l'Univers** (☎ 02 99 40 89 52). The locals are justly proud of this tiny inn. It is like stepping back into an ancient dockside tavern. The wood panelling, souvenirs from ships and leather stools are reminders of the briny and trips to exotic islands. The walls are covered with engravings, drawings and photographs recalling events in the life of the city. In late afternoon, the terrace of the **Hôtel de France et de Chateaubriand** (☎ 02 99 56 66 52) remains in the sun for the longest.

The bookshop Môle

In festive mood

Saint-Malo holds an annual festival of comic strips on the Quai des Bulles in late October (information at the tourist office). Another event, the Festival Étonnants Voyageurs (a travel show), could have been held in one of the other towns along the coast, such as Brest, Lorient or even Gourin (the Bretons are such prolific travellers), but it must be admitted that it was made for Saint Malo. Every year, between the National Fort and the Quai Duguay-Trouin, the festival attracts thousands of visitors on the same quest for excitement and adventure. The theme changes every year – the United States, the Far East, Latin America. There are exhibitions of photographs, displays of foreign cultures, interviews and lectures with travel writers and many other events. All these combine to make the three days in May an unforgettable experience.

Saint-Malo by night

If you want to win or lose a few 10 F pieces in a welcoming atmosphere visit the **Casino** (opposite the Plage de l'Éventail, ☎ 02 99 40 64 00). If that is not to your taste, try the **Angelus Bis,** (3, Rue des Cordiers ☎ 02 99 79 32 04). This bar also has a dance floor, but it is so tiny that it can be deafening. **Cunningham's Bar** (☎ 02 99 81 48 08) in the port of Bas-Sablons has two large, wood-panelled rooms with a decor that is both sea-faring and British. If you want to sound as if you are a local, just tell people you are going to the 'Cunni'. The place for dancing in Saint-Malo is **L'Escalier**, at La Buzardière,

| **Spotcheck** |
| **E2** |

Ille-et-Vilaine

| **Things to do** |

The festivals
Sailing and water-sports
Sea trips
The Aquarium
Visiting the naval dockyard
Saint-Malo by night

| **Within easy reach** |

Dinan, p. 182,
Cancale, p. 192,
Dol-de-Bretagne, p. 194.

| **Tourist office** |

Saint-Malo:
☎ 02 99 40 64 48

(☎ 02 99 81 65 56) just outside the town.

The sculpted rocks of Rothéneuf

Rue des Rochers Sculptés
☎ **02 99 56 97 64**
In the 19th C. a certain Abbé Fourré decided to tell the history of the Rothéneuf family by sculpting the rocks on a headland. Unfortunately, the faces are being slowly

Rothéneuf's head sculpted from natural rock

eroded, but they are still remarkable and are an extraordinary example of rock sculptures. The resort of Rothéneuf itself has some of the loveliest beaches in the

The bar of the Hôtel de L'Univers

The Hôtel du Centre in Rothéneuf is the best place for an apéritif at the end of the day

During the hurricane of 1987, part of the sea-wall itself, which extends as far as the Rochebonne slipway, was destroyed. The houses in this area are stone-built and have some lovely detailing and carving. This is one of the places that the people of Saint-Malo themselves like best. From 15 September to 15 June, sailboarders skim over the inshore waters. For more information,

contact the Surf School, ☎ 02 99 40 07 47.

Fort National and the beaches

Perhaps because it is west-facing, the beach of the **Môle** is a favourite with the locals, but the **Plage de Bon-Secours**, to its right, is just as good and retains enough water at low tide to enable children to swim. The **Grande Plage de l'Éventail**, just below the Fort, also has its devotees. At low tide the beach is fully exposed right up to the fort, making it possible to walk there. There are lots of rock-pools, which are good for shrimping and for shellfish, so it is a good idea to wear non-slip shoes.

MARINE FLEA MARKET

Rue Trichet
☎ **02 99 81 37 07**
Pieces of marine junk, ropes, sailing jackets, lengths of iron chain, clothing, compasses – it's all here and it's all cheap. But you won't find a polished sea-chest or stick barometer: this is strictly the cheaper end of the trade.

Saint-Malo, Station Voile

In Saint-Malo there are plenty of opportunities for practising water-sports, from water-skiing, surfboarding, jet-skiing, sea-kayaking or rowing in a dinghy. There are several yacht clubs and water-sports centres, a list of which is available from the tourist office.

The marine baths
☎ 02 99 40 75 75

The bracing air is an invitation to take some healthy exercise. The **Centre de Thalassothérapie de Saint-Malo**, a seawater spa, offers an 'aquatonic' programme that is unique in France, as well as special retraining programmes designed for sportsmen and sportswomen.

The port of Bas-Sablons

This is a marina with berths for 1,200 boats along its pontoons. It is a pleasant place

region. There is the **Nicet** (you have to walk down 100 steps), the **Val** and best of all the **Havre du Lupin**, a tiny, well-protected cove, surrounded by five beautiful beaches. Rothéneuf is also the place to pay homage to Jacques Cartier, who discovered Canada in 1435. The **Manoir-musée** (☎ 02 99 40 97 73), a museum dedicated to Cartier, is inside the manor house in which he was born and where he died.

❀ The Sillon beach

This is the huge white, sandy ridge, that links Saint-Malo to the mainland (*sillon* means furrow or ridge). At high tide and in stormy weather the waves cover this sandbank completely and even crash onto the road.

The beach of Bon-Secours, at the foot of the ramparts

for a stroll, and you can walk out to the landing-stages to have a look at the boats, which range from small craft to luxury yachts.

Solidor Tower

The tower stands on the Saint-Servan slipway. Like the château, it was built in the late 14th C. by Jean IV, not to protect the people of Saint-Malo but to keep a watch on them. It houses the **Musée du Long Cours et des Cap-Horniers** (museum of long hauls and Cape Horn seafarers; ☎ 02 99 40 71 58). The nearby port of Saint-Servan, with its wooden terraces, is a pleasant place to visit.

Grand Aquarium

Z. I. La Madeleine
☎ 02 99 21 19 02

This aquarium was only built in the 1990s, and its declared ambition is to vie for importance with Océanopolis in Brest. The exhibition halls are organised by theme and ecological environment. There are fish from all over the world to delight the visitor. There is a Mediterranean tank, an Atlantic tank and a tropical fish tank. The special shark pen is particularly impressive. There is also a reconstruction of a wreck, seen from an underwater perspective. The cinema shows three-dimensional films, which

are fascinating, and lectures and special events on the theme of the sea are organised on a regular basis. The Aquarium has a shop that, in addition to the normal museum items, sells cosmetics, soaps and bath-salts made from seaweed.

Naval dockyard

34 Quai Garnier-du-Fougeray
☎ 02 99 40 17 55
Open Mon.–Fri.
Free admission, by appointment only.

This is where the high-speed boat was built that completes the run from Corsica to the French mainland in less than three hours. The guided tour starts in the drawing office where the designs are created. You then visit the huge shipbuilding yards and follow the whole process, from the germ of an idea to the bottle of champagne smashed against the side of the ship to launch it down the slipway and off on its maiden voyage.

SAILINGS TO THE CHANNEL ISLANDS AND SEA TRIPS

Gare Maritime Émeraude Lines
☎ 02 99 40 48 40;
Condor,
☎ 02 99 56 42 99
Saint-Malo is very close to Jersey, Guernsey and Sark – closer, in fact, than the English mainland! Boats leave from the Gare Maritime, Cale de la Bourse. There are frequent sailings and you can choose whether to stay there for half a day, a day or a weekend. Jersey is full of duty-free shops, but Guernsey is more unspoiled. Sark is like something out of the past, with its tiny port, high cliffs and glorious green vegetation. And, of course, everyone speaks English. *Le Renard*, a replica of Surcouf's privateering ship, is used for various types of cruises. Contact *Le Renard*
☎ 02 99 40 53 10.

Dinan, Jewel of the Rance

Neither time nor the English have been able to subjugate the proud city of Bertrand du Guesclin, who won back so much French territory from the English. Dinan, at the head of the Rance estuary, is the best-preserved medieval town in Brittany. It is also a hive of activity, as shown by the many little craft shops in the ancient houses with their overhanging upper storeys, where the roofs almost touch to form a nave over the narrow lanes of the old town.

The old town

This is the soul of Dinan. In the Rue de la Poissonnerie and the Rue de l'Horloge the corbelled, half-timbered houses, with their overhanging upper storeys, were the work of naval carpenters and look something like the fo'c'sles of ships of the king's fleet. In the Place des Cordeliers there is a Franciscan monastery, which was founded in 1241. The weekly street market is held on Thursday mornings in the Place du Champ-Clos and the Place Du-Guesclin.

The château and the ramparts

☎ 02 96 39 45 20
Open daily, 1 June–15 Oct., 10am–6.30pm; 16 March–31 May and 16 Oct.–15 Nov., 10am–noon and 2–6pm; 16 Nov.–31 Dec. and 7 Feb.–15 March, 1.30–5.30pm.
Admission charge.

Built in the late 14th C. by Estienne Le Fur, the architect of the Solidor Tower in Saint-Malo, this impregnable fortress was also a stately home. The walk around the ramparts, whose first stones were laid in the 13th C., starts from here. The fortress also contains a museum (☎ 02 96 39 45 20, same opening times as the château, admission charge), which traces the history of the town through its various rooms, from the first lord of Dinan, who took up residence in about the year 1000, until the arrival of the railways in the late 19th C. A whole section of the museum is

Place des Cordeliers

devoted to the painters who worked in the region, from Dagnan-Bouveret to Corot, and including Méheut.

Shopping

If you want to know the meaning of a strange carving on one of the houses, go and ask the owner of the antiquarian bookshop in the Place Saint-Sauveur, whose cellar of treasures is full to bursting with books, drawings, paintings and lithographs. (**Serge Davy Livres Anciens**, 4 Place Saint-Sauveur, ☎ 02 96 39 63 00.) The Rue de Jerzual and the Rue du Petit-Port are inhabited by artists and craftspeople. There are silk paintings, carvings and woodwork, pottery and hand-woven fabrics. These little shops, almost hidden by the elaborate porches or behind façades of tall windows, are full of originality and character, so do go inside.

The harbour

The Rue du Jerzual leads straight to the harbour. It was once busy and bustling, connected with trade from Saint-Malo, from where the coasters would arrive laden with salt and spices. In exchange, Dinan was the port for canvas and linens. The little bridge over the Rance has not changed since the 15th C. Nowadays, it is a particularly lively spot on summer evenings, just right for a drink by the harbour before you guide your boat up the Ille-et-Rance canal, the Vilaine or the Nantes–Brest canal (boat hire: Crown Blue Line, ☎ 02 99 34 60 11). Alternatively, you may prefer a short excursion of between 45 and 60 minutes up the Rance (Émeraude Lines, Port de Dinan, ☎ 02 96 39 18 04).

The banks of the Rance

The Rance is a deep, wide estuary, which runs through a series of narrow valleys, whose tops are covered with woodland. The roofs of mansions built by the notables of the region peep through the trees. The river banks are favourite places for hiking and walking and the locals are

SAINT-SULIAC

Right bank, 12 miles (20 km) N of Dinan
This is a village that has been preserved to look exactly as it did in the 19th C. It is so authentic that it was used as a location for many scenes in the French film *Grand Banc*, an adventure film about Newfoundland. The little port, with tall shale houses in the steeply sloping lanes, have retained the atmosphere of a little village, which regularly saw its sons sail away to the icy shores of Canada. The sheltered lake is particularly recommended for those who want to learn to sail (École de Voile, 02 99 58 48 80). A lobster dinner at an affordable price can be had at La Grève, ☎ 02 99 58 33 83, in the harbour facing the setting sun over the Rance – a wonderful visual and gastronomic experience.

Things to do

Boat trips
Walks beside the Rance
Fête des Remparts

Within easy reach

Lamballe, p. 168,
Dinard, p. 176,
Dol-de-Bretagne, p. 194.

Tourist office

Dinan: ☎ 02 96 39 75 40

fond of walking to the meadows of Lehon, which were written about by Roger Vercel. Further upstream, the tow path will take you to the picturesque lock of La Hisse.

Fête des Remparts

Dinan revives its past on the first weekend in August every second year, at the **Fête des Remparts**, during which troubadours, showmen with dancing bears and knights in shining armour mix with the crowds in the streets. This is the biggest medieval pageant in Europe.

Combourg
in the footsteps of a giant

This is where François-René de Chateaubriand, one of the greatest French writers, wrote his *Mémoires d'outre-tombe*. The soul of the author still hovers over this medieval city, which is dominated by the majesty of the imposing residence in which the writer spent two years as a young man. The town's devotion to its hero, its architectural heritage and the delightful surrounding countryside make Combourg a romantic place to stay.

CHATEAUBRIAND
1768-1848

The château
☎ 02 99 73 22 95
Open daily except Tue.
1 Apr.–30 Oct.,
2pm–5pm; July–Aug.,
daily 11am–12.30pm
and 1.30–5.30pm.
Admission charge.
The château has a tower at each of its four corners, enclosing a narrow courtyard. The building is topped with a parapet walk and has machicolations, so it is a veritable fortress. The first stones of the Château de Combourg were laid in the 11th C., but it was not until the 18th C. that it was acquired by Chateaubriand's father. Most of the interior decoration is from the 19th C., although there are a few items of 16th-C. furniture. It is still owned by the family.

The grounds and their romantic foliage
'You ought to paint all this…' The story goes that these words were spoken to Chateaubriand by his sister Lucile, referring to the castle grounds, and it was this that made the young François-René first take up his pen. Of course, the park is not as large as it was in the 18th C., but it has retained its romantic charm. A short stroll down its broad avenues, lined with oaks and sweet chestnuts, will evoke the atmosphere experienced by the young Vicomte de Chateaubriand.

The old town
Small granite houses line the network of lanes and tiny squares. The town first grew around the church before the château was built in the 11th C. and the **Rue de l'Abbaye** is the most typical and still contains the vestiges of a priory church. There are a few imposing buildings, such as Maison de la Lanterne in the Rue des Princes, and the house of the Knights Templar in the Place du Marché, which are interspersed with antique shops for which the town has acquired a reputation.

L'Écrivain Restaurant
Opposite the church
☎ 02 99 73 01 61
Closed Thursdays.
A traditional hostelry in the town centre. Its red mullet with cooked oysters and salt breast of duck have given M. Menier a well-deserved reputation. Furthermore, the surroundings are picturesque and the prices reasonable (menus begin at 70 F).

A café in the Rue des Princes

Spotcheck
F2

Ille-et-Vilaine

Things to do

Route des Châteaux
Walking and mountain-biking

Things to do with children

Cobac Parc

Within easy reach

Baie du Mont, p. 188,
Dol-de-Bretagne, p. 194,
Rennes, p. 196.

Tourist office

Combourg:
☎ 02 99 73 13 93

LANHELIN: CHILDREN'S PARADISE

Cobac Parc, Route de Pleugueneuc
About 6 miles (10 km) NW of Combourg
☎ 02 99 73 80 16
After the gloominess of the castle, you can change the mood by driving to Lanhelin and Cobac Parc, a delight for children. Attractions include a little train, a model village and an aviary.

François-René, Vicomte de Chateaubriand

Route des Châteaux

Combourg is the most famous of the local châteaux, but there are many more in the district. At Meillac, for example, the Manoir de la Hautière and the Château du Breil are open to visitors, but the best of all is the **Château de Lanrigan**, whose French Renaissance lines and decoration are reminiscent of the châteaux of the Loire. And since the road leads there, travel on to the lovely little

town of Saint-Léger-des-Prés, whose parish close and 16th-C. church are typical of Brittany. Why not round off the day with a visit to a **cabinet-maker's workshop**, one which specialises in the restoration of local wooden buildings is **Atelier de Pierre-Yves Lancelot,** Saint-Léger-des-Prés, ☎ 02 99 73 65 65.

World of water

The region is full of rills, rivulets and streams, which make the many possible hikes all the more pleasant. Or try a hike or mountain-bike ride to the **Etang de Boulet**, a 9 mile (14 km) round trip (route available from La Maison de la Randonnée, ☎ 02 99 67 42 21), or walk along the paths leading to the little village of Dingé for a ramble beside streams and pools. For the less active or the more romantic, there is a short walk of about an hour around the lake at Combourg. The abundant birdlife will remind you of the

passage in which Chateaubriand describes the lake and its 'feathered caravan of water-fowl, teal, kingfishers and snipe'. In fact, Chateaubriand spent only two years of his life at Combourg, and this was supposed to be in exile. Chateaubriand's room was in the Tour du Chat (cat tower), which was said to be haunted by a former owner, but don't worry, it's not scary!

The 16th-C. Château de Lanrigan

Around Tinténiac

Tinténiac is the heart of the *département* of Ille-et-Vilaine, and it is one of a series of picturesque villages in the vicinity whose inhabitants' lives are governed by the course of the river Vilaine, tourism and the various festivals and fairs, which preserve the traditions of the region. This is an agricultural district, which produces delicious food, all of which can be tasted at the local farms, many of which have now been turned into inns.

The ramble to the 11 locks

The second Rance dam

This dam is less impressive and high-tech than the big Rance tidal dam between Saint-Malo and Dinard. However, the Rophemel barrage is a good place to go for a ramble. It was built in 1937 and is wedged between deep green and rocky gullies. It was

built to dam a lake about 6 miles (10 km) wide and supplies electricity to the whole Rennes area.

Tinténiac

Along the canal
(Tourist office)
Musée de l'Outil et des Métiers,
5 Quai de la Donac
☎ 02 99 68 09 62
Open daily,
1 July–30 Sept., 10am–noon and 2.30–6.30pm.
Admission charge.
This little town beside the Ille-et-Rance canal has preserved the memories of ancient occupations that were once practised in the countryside. The museum of trades and tools on the Quai de la Donac is an Ali Baba's cave

for those who love old tools – implements used by cobblers, harness-makers, clog-makers and coopers are displayed. The museum, a model of its kind, is housed in a former grain store.

Cycling along the Ille-et-Rance canal

One of the best ways to see the surrounding countryside is by bicycle. Cycling tours are organised from Tinténiac and pass the Château de Montmuran, after taking the path beside the Ille-et-Rance canal. Information is available from the Comité Départemental de Cyclotourisme:
☎ 02 99 54 67 54.

Guitté
The fair

Tinténiac has a modern museum to celebrate occupations that have now disappeared. Guitté, a little community of 500 inhabitants, is another place that has managed to retain 'the soul of times past'. Every year in early August it holds the **Rencontres des Artisans d'Art et des Produits du Terroir**, a major crafts fair. Ceramicists, potters, hand-loom weavers and basket-makers come to set up stall in the fairground. There are also sellers of pork products, grains, foie gras, cattle-breeders and fishermen, all of them witnesses to a Breton way of life that has not only a past but also a great future.

Hédé
The locks

From the time a small pleasure boat sails up to the first Hédé lock, it will take all afternoon for it to get through them all. In fact, it will have to go through as many as 11 lock-gates! The sight of the boats rising and falling to the rhythm of the heavy gates as they open and close is popular with strollers along the towpath of the Vilaine. The unfortunate lock-keeper

is kept busy from dawn until dusk on summer days. The difference in the water level from the first to the last lock is an astonishing 90 ft (27 m). Hédé, which stands on a hill overlooking the river, is a bustling village which holds a **Festival de Café-théâtre**, a theatre and music festival, in mid-August.

Québriac
Zooloisirs

At the exit from Tinténiac on the Rennes Road
☎ **02 99 68 10 22**
Open April–Sept.
Free admission.
This is a large leisure park enjoyed by young and old. There is a children's play area and children's zoo, as well as fauna and flora of the region and exotic birds. The flower garden contains thousands of roses, which are a fragrant and visual delight when they are in bloom. There are also plenty of places to eat and drink and to buy souvenirs, and most people take a picnic and spend the whole day here.

A typically charming Breton street in Guitté

Spotcheck
F2-F3

Ille-et-Vilaine

Things to do

Museum of trades and tools
Craft fair at Guitté
A cycling tour in the country
Walking to the Hédé locks

Things to do with children

Zooloisirs at Québriac

Within easy reach

*Dol-de-Bretagne, p. 194,
Rennes, p. 196.*

Tourist office

Tinténiac: ☎ **02 99 68 09 62**

BÉCHEREL, BOOK CAPITAL OF FRANCE

☎ **02 99 66 80 55**
Ten years ago, 12 passionate booksellers decided to turn Bécherel into a book town. Since the town now has 12 bookshops, a bindery and three art galleries, serving fewer than 1,000 inhabitants, they appear to have succeeded. A **book fair** is held on the first Sunday of every month, and this brings together all the antiquarian book-dealers in western France. It so happens that Bécherel is one of the prettiest towns in France.

Mont-Saint-Michel Bay

a jewel in a casket

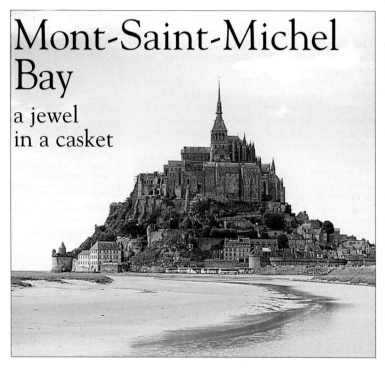

The bay itself, in which is reflected the intricate silhouette of the abbey, is not as well-known as it deserves to be. It is said to be lifeless and soulless – it is certainly flat, but it is never boring. When the sun sets over the Cancale rock, which faces the Mount, it reveals its contours in relief and the colours are a revelation to the walkers and sightseers who stroll along the beach to reach the little village of Saint-Benoît, where they might sample oysters on the terrace of one of the two or three little restaurants. If you know how to watch it, you will find the bay enchanting. For instance, you might spy some of the last few seals on the coast of France, which live between Les Hermelles and Tombelaine.

Mont-Saint-Michel
☎ 02 33 60 14 14
Unaccompanied or guided tour.
Mont-Saint-Michel is the eighth wonder of the world, included in the list of UNESCO World Heritage Sites and an important tourist destination for both French and international tourism. In fact, among the hordes of tourists, sunhats on their heads and cameras slung around their necks, it is difficult to sense the soul of the monks who worked so hard to build this magnificent abbey 1,200 years ago. Avoid 15 August if you can, and try to visit the Mount on a Monday in September, when it is likely to be least crowded. Start with the Grand-Rue. This main street is the inevitable succession of souvenir shops, cafés and restaurants, such as the **Restaurant de la Mère Poulard** (☎ 02 33 60 14 01), which is famous for its omelettes (menu from 90 F) and its butter biscuits (*galettes au beurre*; 49 F for a 12 oz (350 g) box). The Grand-Rue is nevertheless full of interesting medieval architecture, with roofs that seem to touch each other across the narrow street, cobblestones and turretted houses, such as the **Maison de**

la Truie-qui-File, towards the end of the street near the abbey. The abbey itself was built in the 10th C. and will be the highlight of your visit. It is a truly magnificent sight, and what is more, it took only 16 years to create this masterpiece of Gothic art.

Couesnon is visible at low tide. Granville can be seen in the east, and in the west, when the weather is fine, you can see the bay of Cancale and the Pointe du Grouin. In the north stands the Tombelaine Rock, which consists of the same type of

Spotcheck
F2

Ille-et-Vilaine

Things to do

Maritime museum
A walk across the bay
Learn sand-yachting

Within easy reach

Dinard, p. 176,
Saint-Malo, p. 178,
Dinan, p. 182.

Tourist office

Mont-Saint-Michel:
☎ 02 33 60 14 14

himself that the saint was not a saint and that his dream was just a nightmare. But St Michael returned at night to demand that the abbey be built. Faced with such persistence, Aubert recognised the divine origin of the apparition and set to work. Finally, the Mount, which had been called Mont-Tombe and was a refuge for a few hermits, was transformed into the Mont-Saint-Michel and began to attract pilgrims from all over the world.

The ramparts

The view is magnificent from the parapet walk around the ramparts. On the side facing the bay, the Cours du

granite as that which the Mount is made of. The soil in the bay is made of softer shale, which explains how the Mount and the Tombelaine Rock were able to resist erosion. The entrances to the ramparts are on either side of the Grand-Rue.

History and legend

In the year of grace 708, the Archangel Michael appeared in a dream to Aubert, Bishop of Avranches, and asked him to build a basilica. Faced with such a hard task, Aubert decided to persuade

The biggest tide in Europe

When the tide rushes in around the Mount, it can attain a depth of almost 50 feet (15 m). If you want to understand why the tide here has the widest range of any in Europe, visit the **Musée Maritime** (open 9am–5pm in season, ☎ 02 33 60 14 09).

LA MÈRE POULARD

SALT MARSH LAMB

This lamb has the best flavour in the world because the ewes feed on the grasses of the salt marsh in the bay, which are covered at high tide by sea-water and are thus salty. The little streams that irrigate the area are called *criches*. In spring it is not unusual to see the ewes sleeping on the dikes, beside the water-meadows. The label *gigot de pré salé* had been abused so often that breeders got together and created a quality label. This label is a guarantee that the lamb followed its mother to feed on the vegetation of the salt marsh from the age of three weeks and did so for 230 days a year. Each year, in the first weekend in July, Courtils, which is 6 miles (9 km) from the Mount, holds the Fête du Pré Salé. The programme includes an open-air mass, a trip in a little train and an outdoor barbecue – with lamb on the menu, of course!

Here you will learn how the tide works and about the sand-dredging works around the Mount, which cost 600 million francs!

The crazy Couesnon

The river Couesnon marks the boundary between Brittany and Normandy and, as the saying goes, 'through its folly, put the Mount in Normandy'. The capricious but lovely watercourse winds from the Fougères region to Mont-Saint-Michel. Between the Château de la Ville-Olivier and the Mézière windmill, the GR 39 follows the course of the Couesnon, a ramble lasting about three hours across a verdant valley, passing old granite quarries and welcoming villages. Information at the Fougères tourist office (☎ 02 99 94 12 20) or the Pontorson tourist office (☎ 02 33 60 20 65).

On the Hermelles Bank

Filling a basket with oysters, mussels and cockles will cost you only 20 F. But you will have to catch them yourself on the Hermelles Bank, right in the middle of the bay. The bank is a 240 acre (100 ha) reef, almost 7 feet (2 m) high, created and maintained by a colony of marine worms. It is the largest reef of its kind in Europe.

Cherrueix and its beach

This is one of the prettiest villages on the coast. The church has a bell-tower and it has three windmills by the sea wall. The main road, which hugs the bay, does not run through Cherrueix, and this is probably why the village has remained unspoilt. The sand of the beach is firm, so sand-yachting is a popular sport. An international competition is held on the third weekend in August. Cherrueix is one of the few places in Brittany where this sport is practised all year round (Noroît Club, ☎ 02 99 48 83 01). If you want to learn how to do it, and spend a pleasant and bracing mini-holiday, go on a sand-yachting weekend with Loisirs Accueil (☎ 02 99 78 47 51), which offers a package, including accommodation and four hours of training.

❀ A GUIDED TOUR OF THE BAY

Le Vivier-sur-Mer
☎ 02 99 48 84 38
Admission charge.
Walking across the bay alone is a very risky business and is not advisable. The tide is said to come in 'at the speed of a galloping horse'. Furthermore, the bay is full of soft mud and quicksands. The Centre d'Animation de la Baie offers guided walks. The guides know the bay extremely well and are familiar with the marine environment, its riches and its dangers. And, as for the 'galloping horse', there are several riding stables, which offer opportunities for riding and pony-trekking in this unique setting (Ferme Équestre de Riskop, ☎ 02 99 80 21 25; Aux Amis du Cheval, ☎ 02 99 89 16 87).

A Mount, but no longer an island

Human beings and nature are both to blame. as the Mount is gradually re-attaching itself to the mainland. For centuries,

humans have been trying to reclaim the land around it, building dykes and seawalls where sheep can graze. In the 19th C. it was decided that it would be a good idea to be able to get to the Mont-Saint-Michel by tram, so the tongue of land covered with water at high tide was drained. The tram disappeared after World War I but not its foundations. Today, the Mount is only completely cut off during very high tides. Nature has also played a part in this process, because sediment is constantly being deposited at the foot of the dyke, thus causing it gradually to become silted up. Several solutions have been considered for keeping the Mount in its splendid isolation, including straightforward plans to remove the dyke altogether and replace it with a footbridge or a tunnel.

Cancale
the pearl in the oyster

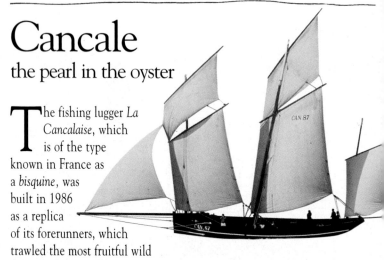

The fishing lugger *La Cancalaise*, which is of the type known in France as a *bisquine*, was built in 1986 as a replica of its forerunners, which trawled the most fruitful wild oyster-beds in France. *La Cancalaise* is a tall ship (a sailing ship), manned by volunteers, and is a symbol of the pride and tradition of the town. *La Cancalaise* is also the word for a woman from Cancale, one whom neither the vicissitudes of life nor the storms of Newfoundland could subjugate. You can take a sea voyage on *La Cancalaise* between April and October (☎ 02 99 89 77 87).

Cancale

If you have the good fortune to approach Cancale by the corniche, the coast road, just as the sun is setting and when the tide is high, you will begin to understand the magic of this ancient fishing port. You will be able to see over the little harbour, called La Houle, (in the sea-lanes of which a few trawlers still linger), and the two jetties, which shelter ships from the west wind. Down below there is a hive of activity: the stalls are overflowing with oysters and

the café terraces are teeming with patrons. François Mitterrand's favourite café, the **Armada**, is right at the end of the harbour.

An oyster museum
Musée de l'Huître et du Coquillage
☎ 02 99 89 69 99
Admission charge.
If you want to learn all there is to know about the oyster, the queen of Cancale, this is the place. A guide will welcome you and explain the differences between the various types of oyster and why the tides are so important in their

cultivation. There is a film about the work of an oyster-farmer and an explanation of how the oyster grows and develops. You will then be totally prepared for a guided tour of the works. Before leaving, have a look at the 1,500 types of shell in the museum.

A circle of creeks

Not far from Cancale, **Port-Mer**, **Port-Pican** and **Port-Briac** there is a succession of sunny, sheltered creeks opposite the Fort des Rimains. The fort stands on an islet, and it successfully withstood several attacks by the English. Today it belongs to the famous Parisian master baker, Eugène Poilâne. On the Port-Mer dyke, there are several pleasant cafés, which are full to overflowing at apéritif time. The beaches of **Verger** and **La Touesse** and **Du-Guesclin** cove, towards Saint-Malo, are also very busy during the tourist season.

Café in the harbour of La Houle

A coastline to explore on foot

The GR 34 runs between Saint-Malo and Cancale and is accessible to all. It hugs the magnificent coastline, rising and dipping at the headlands, coves and sand dunes. If you leave in the morning from the Pointe du Meinga, you will easily reach Cancale by late afternoon. Your route will take you past heathland, pine trees, beaches and rocks, and you will also pass the château owned by Léo Ferré at **Du-Guesclin cove**, the Verger chapel and, finally, the semaphore signal at the Pointe du Grouin, from which there is a magnificent view over the whole Emerald Coast.

saint-Coulomb
Beaches and *malouinières*
2½ miles (4 km) W of Cancale

From this little village you can go on a tour of the local *malouinières*, the ship-owners' homes. La Fosse-Hingant and Le Lupin are among the best. Saint-Coulomb also has one of the most beautiful beaches in Brittany, Les Chevrets cove.

When the tide goes out, take a picnic and spend the day at the Petit Chevret beach. It has a low, rounded headland from which you can view the many rocks and islets that are scattered along the coast.

Spotcheck
F2

Ille-et-Vilaine

Things to do

Sea trips
Visit the oyster museum
The coastal footpath

Within easy reach

Dinard, p. 176,
Saint-Malo, p. 178.

Tourist office

Cancale: ☎ 02 99 89 63 72

OYSTER-TASTING

On the Quai Saint-Thomas, right at the end of La Houle harbour, oyster-farmers have installed little stands for their baskets, which are full of all kinds of oyster. This is an opportunity for the producer to sell direct to the consumer at a price starting at 16 F for a dozen medium-sized specimens. To complete the experience, you may be able to find somewhere to perch on the quayside with a plateful of open oysters in front of you. They even supply you with fresh lemons. Go on — give them a try!

Port-Mer creek between Cancale and the Pointe du Grouin

Dol-de-Bretagne
the heart of the marshes

William the Conqueror, King John and, before them, the Franks and Normans tried and often succeeded in ransacking Dol-de-Bretagne. The status of this bishopric, which was created by Nominoé, the first king of Brittany in the 9th C., caused many to covet its wealth. The French Revolution and the royalist rebellion of the Chouans left 15,000 dead and started the city's decline. It was not until the railway arrived in the 19th C. that tourism revived the fortunes of the city of St Samson, one of the saints who brought the Gospel to Brittany.

Grande Rue des Stuarts
According to Victor Hugo: 'Dol is not a town … it is a street.' Yes, but what a street! It looks like the nave of a Gothic church, with its arcaded or half-timbered houses, its uneven cobble-stones and its mansions, including the 13th-C. **Maison des Petits-Palets**. The Grande Rue des Stuarts is the town's shopping and tourist centre.

The cathedral, a majestic pachyderm
The massive bulk of the cathedral of Saint-Samson is due largely to the time it took to build – five centuries, starting from the 12th C. It thus includes a mixture of styles from Romanesque to Gothic, as well as being multi-functional as the southern part served to defend the town.

The north tower was unfinished because of lack of funds and throws the whole building out of balance. Inside, the proportions are more harmonious.

Mont Dol
The 215 feet (65 m) high Mont Dol was surrounded by water until the sea receded in the 13th C., and it still dominates this region of marshland. It is topped by the **Notre-Dame** tower, which continues to attract pilgrims.

This is also one end of the GR 34, which starts from the cathedral steps. There are two ways to get to the summit: by way of the little road that winds up its flanks or via the straight, vertical line of the cliffs on the south and west, which are covered in pitons and are very popular with rock-climbers. A guide is available at Point 35, ☎ 02 99 79 35 35.

Carfentin

The Champ Dolent menhir
1¼ miles (2 km) S of Dol-de-Bretagne
Legend has it that 'the end of the world will have come when the menhir has finished sinking into the earth'. Despite the grain of truth in this – the marshy ground is causing it to sink gradually – it

will still be safe to picnic here in several thousand years' time. At 31 feet (9.5 m) high with a circumference of 29 feet (8.7 m), this is the biggest menhir in Brittany. It is a mystery how it was transported and raised in 500 BC.

Landal
The eagles of Brittany
7½ miles (12 km) SE of Dol-de-Bretagne
Château de Landal
Free admission.
The Château de Landal (*top photo*) may look sturdy and picturesque, but little remains of the first fortress which was built here in the 12th C. Its avenue of oaks, deep moats, imposing precinct and five towers were restored in the 19th C., and it must look now very much as it did in its heyday. It is in this magnificent setting that eagles are now being bred. An exhibition is held featuring the king of the birds of prey every day from April to November inside the ramparts. (☎ 02 99 80 10 15).

Saint-Méloir
A craft village
10½ miles (17 km) NW of Dol-de-Bretagne
This little inland village decided to renew its links with the tradition of local crafts. The potters, basket-makers and glass-blowers have their workshops and display their handiwork there. Each item is unique because it is entirely handmade. Prices start at around 30 F, but you will have to pay 50 F for a good piece of pottery or a little glass vase and about 100 F for a willow mackerel basket. Once upon a time, these crafts were very widespread – there were up to 80 basketweavers in Saint-Méloir – and now they are being given a new lease of life thanks to tourism. Glassworks, ☎ 02 99 89 18 10. Pottery ☎ 02 99 89 23 28.

Spotcheck
F2

Ille-et-Vilaine

What to do
The eagle show

What to do with the children
Roza Parc

Within easy reach
Saint-Malo, p. 178,
Dinan, p. 182,
Combourg, p. 184.

Tourist office
Dol-de-Bretagne:
☎ 02 99 48 15 37

ROZA PARC
Roz-sur-Couesnon
12 miles (20 km) E of Dol-de-Bretagne
☎ 02 99 80 28 47
Admission charge.
This is one of the few leisure parks for children in the region. It has a karting track and, a ski run, and there are carriage rides and mini-golf. It is also the site of a museum of mankind. The village stands on a hill overlooking the bay.

Rennes
the regional capital

Église St-Mélaine

Brittany's parliament

Place des Lices

Town Hall

Theatre

Musée de Bretagne
Musée des Beaux-Arts

National Theatre of Brittany

Every time a magazine produces a league table of the quality of life in the major towns of France, Rennes tops the list. You will soon understand why. Rennes is an important commercial crossroads, as well as a dynamic cultural centre and a university city, which is as busy at night as it is during the day, and everything is done with a sense of creativity that is often avant-garde. It is also a centre of science and technology and an architectural masterpiece. In short, it has everything to offer.

Place Sainte-Anne

Taking the street on the left leading from the Place Hoche, you will come to the little Place Sainte-Anne. The street leading from it is the busy **Rue Saint-Michel**, which is full of cafés and chic boutiques. No. 13 Place Saint-Michel, the **Auberge des Barrilières**, is the oldest house in the city, built in 1580.

❋ Brittany's parliament

The Parlement de Bretagne was built in the 17th C. and was one of the most important historic buildings in the region. It was damaged by fire in 1994 but was reopened in September 1999, thanks to the hard work of artists and craftsmen who worked on its restoration. It was rededicated

during the Rennes festival and is once again open to the public (information from the tourist office). The Rue Saint-Georges, which leads from the parliament, is lined with attractive half-timbered houses, which are mostly cafés and restaurants. Rennes was short of stone when it was first built and so made use of the wood from the neighbouring forests for building materials. The Place Hoche, near the Place du Parlement, leads into the Rue Saint-Mélaine, one of the oldest streets in Rennes. If you feel like a snack, you are close to one of the best bakeries in town, the Boulangerie Hoche (17 Rue Hoche, ☎ 02 99 63 61 01).

The garden of Thabor

The main entrance to the garden is next to the church of Saint-Mélaine. There is a waterfall, a grotto, avenues of trees, as well as flowers, shrubs, groves and arbours, all laid out

delightfully to offer the stroller colour, fragrance and repose. The park was once the garden of an abbey. It extends over an area of about 24 acres (10 ha) in the town centre.

Le Musée Breton

20 Quai Émile-Zola
☎ 02 99 28 55 84
Daily except Tue.
10am–noon and 2–6pm.
Admission charge.
The museum is not just for exhibitions. It also regularly organises discussions and lectures on historic and cultural themes (☎ 02 99 79 01 98). This is a good way of enabling you to get to know what daily life in Brittany is like, from the original inhabitants to modern times. And since you are here, why not combine it with a visit to the **Musée des Beaux-Arts** (fine art museum), which is in the same building?

Lunchtime already!

The locals eat lunch at the pavement tables of the little restaurants in the old town. The best places for lunch are in the Rues Saint-Georges, Saint-Melaine and Vasselot, Place des Lices and Place Sainte-Anne.

Rennes by night

By day and by night Rue Saint-Michel, Place des Lices, Rue Saint-George and Rue de Nemours make Rennes a hive of activity. From May onwards the café terraces are full to bursting, even at 2am! As there is so much choice of where to go, here are a few pointers. La Banque (5 Allée Rallier-du-Baty, ☎ 02 99 78 13 13), English decor, and Le Chantier (Bas des Lices, ☎ 02 99 31 58 18), rough and ready decor as the

name implies, are fashionable bars patronised mainly by young people. For guaranteed atmosphere there are Le Barantic (☎ 02 99 79 29 24), Le Green Pub (☎ 02 99 79 28 85) and the Saint-Michel (☎ 02 99 79 71 25), all three in the Rue Saint-Michel. For the early hours of the morning, there are the Café Méliès (13 Quai Lamennais, ☎ 02 99 79 26 86), Le Bentley (27 Rue de la Monnaie, ☎ 02 99 31 57 64), which is more intimate, and, of course, Bob Pub (12 Rue de la Parcheminerie, ☎ 02 99 79 53 05). For billiards, snooker and pool there is Le Muséum (12 Rue Duhamel, ☎ 02 99 35 14 02), and for jazz-lovers, Le Dejazey (54 Rue Saint-Malo, ☎ 02 99 38 70 72). There are less discotheques, but L'Espace (45 Boulevard de la Tour-d'Auvergne, ☎ 02 99 30 21 95) and the Pub Satori (3 Rue Liothaud, ☎ 02 99 33 90 52) are a couple of the most popular ones.

Les Trans

This festival, which was started in the mid-1970s, has become a legend. The **Transmusicales de Rennes** (known in French as *Les Trans*) are among the best music festivals of their type in the world. Étienne Daho, Nirvana, Niagara, Noir Désir and Stéphane Eicher were all discovered here. In early December the streets of Rennes are thronging, the venues are full, and there is

always plenty of new talent waiting to be discovered. An experience not to be missed (information from tourist office ☎ 02 99 67 11 11).

Travelogues

Madrid, Rome and the suburbs have already served as themes for this film festival, which is unique and manages to attract more and more people every year. **Travelling** is a festival of travelogues organised by the students of Rennes II University (☎ 02 99 14 11 47).

The International Fair

The fair is held in mid-March and brings hundreds of exhibitors to Rennes. They bring with them everything, from household appliances to travel aids, including food, drink and automotive products. It is the most important trade

show in western France (information from the tourist office).

OUEST-FRANCE: FRANCE'S PREMIER DAILY NEWSPAPER

Z. I. Chantepie
☎ 02 99 32 60 00
Evenings, by appointment (8–10 months in advance).
This is the largest daily newspaper in France (p. 73) and a major employer in the city of Rennes. *Ouest-France* **was the first French newspaper to adopt the new, ultra-sophisticated printing and production technology. You can visit the facilities and are sure to be impressed by the giant rolls of paper, which are used to feed the enormous presses that run at top speed.**

Market in the Place des Lices

Every Saturday morning there is a market in the Place des Lices, and it is one of the largest markets in France. If you are there on a Saturday, the flower market in the upper part of the square should not be missed. The colours and fragrances can be yours for a very low price. If you are there on a weekday and want a treat, try the delicious chocolate at Kergoff (12 Place des Lices, ☎ 02 99 78 17 12).

Special offers in Rennes

The package scheme known as 'Weekend in Rennes' has been running for several years. If you are thinking of visiting Brittany ask for the list of participating hotels. Make a reservation for

The Au Boulingrain crêperie, Rue Saint-Mélaine

one night at one of these hotels and, once you are there, fill in the special form that you take to the tourist office at the Nemours Bridge (☎ 02 99 67 11 11). You will be given a little gift and your second hotel night will be free. Valid at weekends only.

Noyal-sur-Vilaine: a Ricard or nothing at all

Ricard Factory, Route de Paris
☎ 02 99 04 16 16
Tue. and Thur., by appointment only.
Free admission.

The Rennes region has a local production unit for pastis, the famous aniseed-flavoured aperitif. Detailed explanations and the secrets of how it is made are revealed – not all of them, of course! – including what it is that makes Ricard different from all the other brands of pastis, for example the packaging. You can [watch the] bottling [...] will be [...] [vi]deo, which [...] [l]ong and [...] [hi]story of the [Ri]card group. [...] [e]xit there is the [...] free tasting.

ATIMCO, Combourg

[...]OMBÉES [...] NUIT

[...]ty lights up in [...] July to welcome [...]s, artists, actors, [...]s, story-tellers, [...]rs, poets, mime [...]s and troubadours. [...] [perf]ormers and public [...] [alo]ng the streets, [...] [thea]tres and halls for [...] festival whose [...] [nam]e means 'nightfall' [...] [to]urist office [...] [02] 99 67 11 11).

Citroën factories at Chartres-de-Bretagne

☎ 02 99 86 31 31
Open Mon.–Fri.; closed in Aug.
Free admission.

The Citroën factories, which lie along the bypass that leads to Nantes, are open to the public. There are visits to the assembly lines, which show how the parts are assembled, and you can see the paint-shop and an exhibition of photographs.

Around Rennes

Rennes is surrounded by woods. A short stroll in the forest of Saint-Sulpice is the perfect way to spend a Sunday afternoon. Take the Fougères road and at Mi-Forêt turn left and follow the road to Saint-Sulpice where there is a ruined abbey. Although it cannot be visited, the ruins are very picturesque. From here, lots of footpaths are marked and signposted and make for easy walking for the whole family. Route maps and booklets about the area's attractions are available from the Rennes tourist office and will guide you along the various paths and help you recognise the species of flora and fauna, which in these mixed woods include beech, birch and oak trees.

EARLY MORNING COFFEE

For a really early morning coffee, before 7am, try the area around the railway station. Otherwise, the Café de la Place, Place Sainte-Anne, opens early (☎ 02 99 78 31 03), and will get your day off to a good start. Close by is the picturesque Café Breton, (14 Rue Nantaise, ☎ 02 99 30 74 95), which is another option. After 9am all the establishments in the upper Place des Lices open their doors. But if you like lots of space, the Piccadilly (Place de la Mairie, ☎ 02 99 78 17 17) is the biggest and best-known café-restaurant in Rennes.

A café in the Place Sainte-Anne

Fougères
guardian of a glorious past

Perched on a rocky promontory overlooking a green valley, Fougères has retained the grandeur of its glorious past, which includes outstanding feats of bravery and an association with great writers. Fougères was one of the strongholds of the Chouans, who opposed the French Revolution, and the town inspired Victor Hugo, Honoré de Balzac and Gustave Flaubert. In the early 20th C., Fougères had a thriving boot and shoe industry. Today, the town is justly proud of its huge medieval fortress and its farming and livestock.

by 13 towers. Access is by a bridge over the Nançon, whose marshes served as a moat.

The old town
After visiting the château, see the 11th-C. church of Saint-Sulpice, which was rebuilt in the 15th C., then make your way to the Place du Marchix, which is surrounded by 16th-C. wooden buildings. In the Middle Ages a cattle market was held here by the banks of the Nançon, and this was also the district of the dyers and tanners. On your way up the Rue Nationale look out for the **Musée Emmanuel de la Villéon** (1858–1944), which displays paintings of the Breton countryside by this local Impressionist artist.

The château
☎ 02 99 99 79 59
Open daily 15 June–15 Sept., 9am–7pm; 1 April–15 June, 9.30am–noon and 2–6pm; the rest of the year 10am–noon and 2–5pm. Closed in Jan. *Admission charge.*
The Château de Fougères was an outpost of medieval Brittany and one of the largest and best-preserved strongholds in Europe. It was built between the 12th and 15th C. and consists of a series of fortified enclosures flanked

The Château de Fougères

The shoemaker's art

In the early 20th C. there were nearly 100 factories and thousands of workers in the footwear industry in Fougères. The industry gradually declined but is returning today in the form of three main enterprises specialising in top-of-the-range women's shoes: **Narcy** (☎ 02 99 94 49 36), **J. B. Martin**, which produces 600,000 pairs a year, and **Minelli** (CPCO). The latter two factories can be visited all year round by first telephoning the tourist office, 1 Place Aristide Briand, ☎ 02 99 94 12 20.

PARC FLORAL DE HAUTE BRETAGNE

Le Chatellier
6 miles (10 km) NW of Fougères
Open from 20 March to 11 Nov., Sun. and public holidays; 10 July to 21 Aug., 10am-6pm, 2pm-6pm out of season.
☎ 02 99 95 48 32.
This park consists of 10 magnificent gardens. There is a Persian garden, a Greco-Roman city with its Mediterranean plants, and the city of Knossos, covered in camelias. As for the 7 others, you will have to discover their themes for yourself. You will also get ideas for your own garden. Plants are for sale and the gardens are open all year round.

The tourist office also organises visits to 37 other local industries, including granite quarries and duck-rearing farms.

The Aumaillerie market and auction

Route d'Alençon
☎ 02 99 99 25 50
Open to the public on Fri. morning.
Admission charge.
The cattle market on the outskirts of Fougères sells calves, cows and bulls using the same methods that have been working efficiently for decades. You will need to get up early (about 5am) to watch the auctioneer in action. Thousands of beasts are on offer at one of the largest cattle markets and auctions in France. Although some transactions have been computerised, there is no substitute for the fascinating gestures and whispered consultations.

The forest of Fougères

A few miles from Fougères a range of hills offers many opportunities for walks and rambles. There are also

bridle paths and mountain-bike trails. There are many different paths, a number of which lead past dolmens and megaliths, around thickets and rivers and even allow you to take a rest beside a silvery lake. The most popular hiking trails are those of **Pierre Courcoulée**, marked out in yellow, and the **Vieux Châteaux**, indicated in blue.

Vitré
a culinary town

What is the first thing to do when you arrive in Vitré? See the castle and visit the old town? Look at craft workshops and go for walks? There's plenty of time for that! The first thing you should do when you arrive in Vitré is to take a table at the Chêne Vert (☎ 02 99 75 00 58) or at the Pichet (☎ 02 99 75 24 09) and order a *roulade Sévigné*. A delicious blend of guinea-fowl, walnut, knuckle of ham, egg, russet apple and baby vegetables, it is a delectable, digestible savoury, and very affordable. The *roulade* was created here 15 years ago, a product of the fertile imagination of four talented cooks from Vitré. Since then the *roulade* has become the culinary symbol of the town. The recipe is available at the tourist office (Place Saint-Yves, ☎ 02 99 75 04 46).

The château

This was one of the most beautiful of the citadels dedicated to the defence of the Marches, the gateway to Brittany. The building was begun in the 11th C and the three towers are topped with conical roofs. Inside, the museum (☎ 02 99 75 04 54) is of special interest because of its famous cabinet of curiosities, which was created by a local man, Arthur de la Borderie, in the 19th C.

A short walk through the town

Vitré is a medieval town with largely intact ramparts, cobbled streets, half-timbered houses and handsome 17th-C. mansions belonging to the seafarers who made Vitré's fortune in the early 17th C.

The **Rue de la Beaudraie** is a pleasant place for a stroll, because of the charm, grace and even magnificence of some of its houses. Every style is represented, from the earliest Romanesque to Flamboyant Gothic, and including small Baroque workmen's cottages in the **Rue de la Poterie**. In the northwestern corner of the town, the 15th-C. machicolated Brindolle Tower is part of the ramparts. You can take a guided tours of the town, but the best idea is to take part in one of the nighttime tours organised by the tourist office. The brightly lit façades will reveal secrets that are strangely concealed during the day.

Mme de Sévigné's tour of the region

The full name of the author of the famous *Letters* was Marie de Rabutin-Chantal, until she married a certain Henri de Sévigné, owner of the **Château des Rochers-Sévigné**. There is a special tour, which is almost 60 miles (about 100 km) long, to the lovely mansions in which she lived, the Rochers-Sévigné Château, **Bel-Air** and **Bois-Cornillé**. Near to Rochers-Sévigné the lake at Valière offers a wonderful walk from the mill at Haie to La Ferronnière.

Setting off on the right foot

Noël France, 6 Avenue d'Helmstedt
☎ 02 99 75 70 36
Retail sales Mon.–Fri., 9am–noon and 1.15–6.15pm. Sat. all day 9am–6.15pm. The Noel company is a major shoe and

*Château des Rochers-Sévigné
(below and above)*

sportswear manufacturer in the region. The local factory outlet offers some excellent prices on its makes of hiking boots, children's shoes and other items made in the factory, as well as brand-names of other manufacturers, including Sledgers, Impertinente and Line 7. A large range of Umbro sweatshirts and tracksuits is available, all of which are in the latest styles.

THE GR 34 FOOTPATH

Vitré is the starting point for this long trail, which passes quite near Fougères before reaching the coast at the Bay of Mont-Saint-Michel, which it runs around, almost without losing sight of the Mount.

Spotcheck
G3

Ille-et-Vilaine

Things to do
Guided tour of the town
Mme de Sévigné tour
Starting point of the GR 34

Within easy reach
*Combourg 35 miles (56 km) NW, p. 184,
Châteaubriant 30 miles (50 km) SW, p. 304.*

Tourist office
Vitré: ☎ 02 99 75 04 46

I scream, you scream ...
**Les Délices du Valplessis,
5 Rue de Plagué**
☎ 02 99 74 58 80
Factory shop, open Wed.–Sat. 10am–1pm and 1.30– 6.15pm. Closes on Sat. at 5pm.

The Délices du Valplessis is the third largest ice cream manufacturer in France, with an ultra-modern factory (which cannot be visited). It can produce up to 62,000 choc-ices and 30,000 cones an hour. Quite impressive! The shop stocks a wide range of cakes, sundaes and other iced desserts at very good prices. Bring insulated bags so that you can take lots home with you.

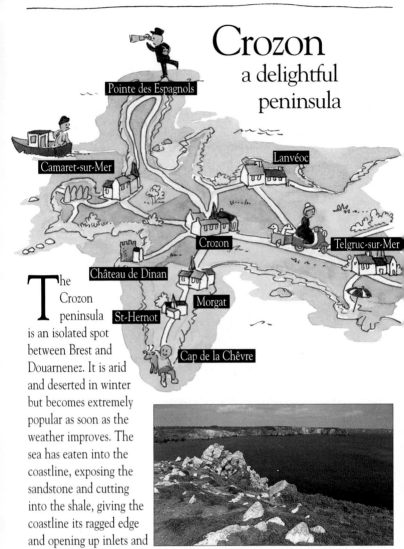

Crozon
a delightful peninsula

Pointe des Espagnols

Camaret-sur-Mer

Lanvéoc

Crozon

Telgruc-sur-Mer

Château de Dinan

Morgat

St-Hernot

Cap de la Chêvre

The Crozon peninsula is an isolated spot between Brest and Douarnenez. It is arid and deserted in winter but becomes extremely popular as soon as the weather improves. The sea has eaten into the coastline, exposing the sandstone and cutting into the shale, giving the coastline its ragged edge and opening up inlets and coves. This makes it a paradise for rock-climbers and windsurfers, but it is also a very pleasant place in which to laze about in the sun.

Little village

Crozon is at the heart of the peninsula, and two places to visit in the village are the **Church of Saint-Pierre** and the workshop, where a range of craft items and jewellery called **Grains de Couleurs** is made (opposite the sign for Morgat, ☎ 02 98 26 20 50). Yves-Marie, a painter, decorates the objects, while Myriam creates Venetian, baroque and faceted mirrors. Each piece is original, and they are making a good name for themselves. This is the time to 'discover' their work.

Lanvéoc

Pretty town

2½ miles (4 km) N of Crozon

A good place to stop for a midday meal is the Hôtel-Restaurant de la Rade, in the centre of the village of Lanvéoc. For 100 F you will be served a meal consisting of a variety of seafood. That is rare enough to deserve a mention, but Lanvéoc also has a very pleasant little sheltered beach where you can bathe.

Camaret
Small fishing port
6 miles (10 km) W of Crozon

If you only have a few hours to spend here, you could do worse than to stroll around the harbour. Its pleasant bistros are particularly active at night, but the café terraces are a good place to linger in the afternoons, and in the morning you can sit and watch the activity in this former crayfish port, which has been largely converted to other types of fishing. The Vauban tower is one of the best-preserved of the

CAP DE LA CHÈVRE

This headland is one of the best places in the whole of Brittany from which to watch the sunset. Stop, sit down and watch the red disc floating in its yellow, then orange, then indigo halo and gradually sinking into the sea to light up America. You feel that you are at the world's end. The Cap de la Chèvre has many hiking and rambling paths, which are suitable for all ages. It is an important and well-known navigation point for sailors, who keep well clear of it because of the submerged rocks. It is also a surfers' paradise on days when the breakers are at their longest and highest.

small forts that were built along the coast on the orders of Louis XIV. Carry on walking as far as the Point de Camaret. There is a boatyard there where the boat-builder plies his trade in the open air. He is used to visitors and will be happy to answer any questions about his craft.

Morgat
A trendy seafront
2½ miles (4 km) SW of Crozon

Morgat has a very long seafront. It is popular as both a family resort and with young watersports enthusiasts. Young and not so young mix happily on the various restaurant terraces, where they lunch between tanning or surfboarding sessions. If you are the sort of person who would like to try some of these water-sports but don't dare, go to **Point Passion**, Plage de Morgat (☎ 02 98 26 24 90). You will get safe and reassuring instruction on how to handle a catamaran or a surfboard. Morgat also has some of the loveliest caves in Brittany, of which the best is the **Grotte de l'Autel**, accessible by boat (tourist office, ☎ 02 98 27 07 92).

Spotcheck
B3

Finistère

Things to do
Hiking
Learn to sail

Within easy reach
Douarnenez 29 miles (46 km) SE , p. 214.

Tourist office
Crozon : ☎ 02 98 27 07 92

Nearby
The Pointe des Espagnols

You will need to return to Crozon in order to reach the northern arm of the cross formed by the peninsula, called the Pointe des Espagnols. In the late 16th C. the Spaniards came to help the Liguers who fought Henri I, and forced the local people to build the almost impregnable fort that stands at the tip of the headland. This is one of the key points of the Brest coastline. If you look to the right you will see Île Longue, which is one of the nerve centres of the French national defence network and an atomic submarine base. You can ask to visit it, although it is unlikely permission will be given.

Landévennec
and the Ménez-Hom

The new Térénez bridge has spanned the Aulne since 1952

The garden of Landévennec

You would think you were in a Mexican garden. The extraordinary mildness of the climate of Landévennec allows a number of sub-tropical plants to grow all over the town, including in the abbey garden (*photo p. 207 top*), which contains several palm-trees and bay trees, which cannot be found anywhere else in Brittany. In the north of the town, at the **Poullier du Loch**, a few rare species of campion have taken root. Take a stroll deep among the plants and you will discover the wonderful fragrance of bog-myrtle. This is a rare wild plant and must not be picked.

Upstream along the Aulne

From Landévennec you will walk in a huge circle between the river and the forest before you reach the **Térénez bridge**. This bridge over the Aulne was built in 1927 to shorten the time taken to travel between the Crozon peninsula and Brest – before that a huge detour to Châteaulin had to be made. The bridge was destroyed in the war and

This quiet little town, sheltered by a number of hills, lies on the final meander of the river Aulne before it reaches the coast at Brest. The climate here is particularly mild, and the atmosphere is peaceful. This is probably what St Guénolé was considering when he founded one of the oldest abbeys in Brittany in the 5th C. The restored part of the abbey still houses a religious order, and you are invited to attend the daily prayers, the times of which are displayed at the entrance to the church. The order of monks is well integrated into the modern world because they even maintain a camping ground in the ruins. They also have a shop where they sell fruit preserves, which they make themselves and which are delicious.

KERMARZIN FARM

☎ **02 98 27 35 85**
Open daily April–Oct.,
10am–7pm; off-peak,
10am–noon and 2–7pm.
This farm on the little
road that runs from
Landévennec to Argol,
near the forest of the
estate, is a very attrac-
tive wood and stone
building, which houses a
museum celebrating the
traditional Breton drink.
You will learn everything
there is to know about
cider here, including the
apple varieties used to
make it, the harvesting,
the pressing, the fermen-
tation and how it
matures in the barrels.
And when the cider is
drawn you can drink it,
accompanied by a few
crêpes, because the
estate also has its own
crêperie. If you book in
advance you will be
treated to a magnificent
feast of local dishes,
including *kig ha farz*. In
summer visit the
orchards – they will take
you there in a romantic
horse-drawn carriage!

was rebuilt in 1952. You will
need to cross it before you
reach the boat cemetery of
Landévennec, where the huge
immobile hulks in the blue
water have a surreal air about
them. The view as the sun
sets over the round islet of
Tibidy is incredible.

Ramble to Ménez-Hom

This is one of the peaks of the
Armorican range. Although it
is only 1,100 feet (330 m)
high, its desolate air and the
strange power it exerts are
quite unearthly. Ménez-Hom
was once a Celtic holy place.
From here you can see over
the whole of the Crozon
peninsula and the bay of
Douarnenez and, in the
north, the wide curves of the
River Aulne and the Monts
d'Arrée; between them there
are the coast and the city of
Brest. In the south you can
see as far as **Locronan**, justly
recognised as one of the
prettiest villages in France.

Spotcheck
B3

Finistère

Things to do

The Landévennec garden
Ramble to Ménez-Hom
Visit to the Kermarzin farm

Within easy reach

Brest 30 miles (50 km),
p. 120,
Monts d'Arrée 30 miles
(50 km) E, p. 134.

Tourist offices

Crozon: ☎ 02 98 27 07 92
Châteaulin:
☎ 02 98 86 02 11

Guides will take you on a
hike, and can be contacted
through the tourist offices
of Crozon (☎ 02 98
27 07 92) and Châteaulin
(☎ 02 98 86 02 11). It is a
nice easy walk for all ages.

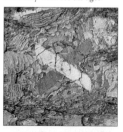

Châteaulin
and the Aulne valley

Châteaulin nestles in a wide meander of the Aulne and at first sight does not appear to have much of interest to offer. This quiet little town, which stretches along the two shady riverside quays, nevertheless has certain attractions. The first of these is the deep, green valley that lies all around it. The town is also a favourite stop for salmon fishers and cyclists, for whom it holds a grand prix race. It is the headquarters of Doux, Europe's largest exporter of poultry, and there are other food industries here as well.

The town on foot
Châteaulin has few places of interest, but a walk through the town will soon show you what a peaceful place it is. Thursday is market day, and the **Quartier des Halles,** where the market is held, is quite lively. After strolling along the stone-built embankments of the Aulne, walk up to the 15th- and 16th-C. **Chapel of Notre-Dame**. It stands in a lovely setting on a hillside, surrounded by old houses, which climb the hill to the ruined château.

On board the *Rumengol*
You can sail down the Aulne from Châteaulin to Brest on board an ancient sand-carrying sailing barge 73 feet (22 m) long. The boat was restored in 1990, and now the *Notre-Dame-Rumengol* is used as an unusual cruising barge from Châteaulin between mid-June and late August. There are several trips, and timetables vary depending on

Chapel of Notre-Dame at Châteaulin

the tides. The round trip lasts 4½ hours (for information ☎ 02 98 86 02 11).

Port-Launay
A quaint village
The village of Port-Launay, once the port for Châteaulin, stands on another meander of the Aulne and is typical of Brittany. Its low houses follow the line of the river, against a lush, verdant background. A few miles to the northwest is the chapel of Saint-Sébastien, a fairly modest but interesting

Spotcheck
B3

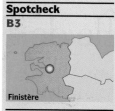

Finistère

Things to do

Down the Aulne by sailing barge
Rambling along the Aulne

Within easy reach

*Brest 29 miles (46 km)
NW, p. 120,
Monts d'Arrée 16 miles
(25 km) NE, p 134,
Quimper 19 miles (30 km)
S, p. 220,
Locronan 12 miles
(19 km) SW, p. 218.*

Tourist office

Châteaulin:
☎ 02 98 86 02 11

building, it was built in the heart of the countryside in the 16th C. in the hope of warding off the plague.

Pont-Coblant
Rambling beside the Aulne

The hardiest ramblers should take the route to Port-Coblant out of Châteaulin, following the towpath beside the Aulne. The walk is about 12½ miles (20 km) long and passes ten locks. It is a wonderful way to discover this beautiful valley. Pont-Coblant, the destination, is a tiny hamlet, whose resident population is barely more than 500 people, although it is a popular spot with holiday-makers. It is surrounded by slate quarries, one of which has been covered over and closed with a grille to serve as a shelter and refuge for bats, a mammal that is fast disappearing from the European countryside due to intensive farming and urbanisation.

Pleyben
The calvary

2½ miles (4 km) N of Pont-Coblant

Pleyben is famous mainly for its *galettes* (buckwheat pancakes) and its calvary, one of the most impressive of such religious sculptures in Brittany. It was built in 1555 next to a side door of the church. It consists of a huge pedestal, pierced with triumphal arches and topped by various scenes from the life of Christ. The figures are depicted in astonishing detail and some wear 16th-C. Breton costume.

SALMON FISHING

Châteaulin has always been the capital of salmon fishing in France, and the fish even features prominently in the town's coat of arms.

The salmon population has declined in recent years because of a deterioration in water quality, but the trout and salmon populations are again increasing, thanks to the various environmental associations. Young salmon once more leap upriver to breed and lay their eggs in March and April. Fishing with a rod and line using a spoon, a fly or a devon (a plastic lure) is allowed below the locks for about 100 yards (100 m), where the fish leap out of the water at the weirs. Inquire at the tourist office about a fishing licence.

The Pont-Coblant lock

Île de Sein
like 'a flat plate lying on the water...

KENTOC'N NERVEL

LE SOLDAT
QUI NE SE RECONNAIT PAS VAINCU
A TOUJOURS RAISON

... with enough pepper (courage) to blot out the sun'. This is how the poet Georges Perros described the Île de Sein. The island looks totally unlike the other islands off Brittany, and one is almost afraid to go there and disturb the environment. Throughout history, its inhabitants, who number only 350 or so out of season, have distinguished themselves by their courage. They earn their livelihood by fishing and from growing potatoes, and they are extremely tenacious, if only to resist the elements. This makes them all the prouder to be *Sénans*, the French name for Sein islanders.

How to get there

The **Penn ar Bed** company has daily sailings from Audierne from September to June (9.30am) and three sailings a day in July and August (9am, 11.30am and 4.50pm). Prices: 122 F for an adult and 67 F for a child. The trip takes about an hour, (☎ 02 98 70 02 37). In season, **Biniou** launches also make the trip every day. Inquire at 8 Rue Racine, Audierne, ☎ 02 98 70 21 15. It is also possible to get there from Douarnenez.

The port and the village

The island has only one village, in which the houses huddle together for protection from the violent storms. There are no cars on the island and no traffic lights, and the only concession to vehicular traffic is a few delivery tricycles which carry barrels through the narrow streets. The public buildings, which meet the needs of the local population, consist of a few *crêperies*, a few shops, a hotel-restaurant, a medical centre and a school. Sein has no water source, so here, as on many of the islands, use it sparingly.

Topography of the island

Seen from the air, the island looks like a huge crab's pincer, swept by the waves. It is only 1¼ miles (2 km) long and ½ mile (800 m) wide. The highest point on the island is only 19 feet (6 m) above sea level! This explains why Sein has been flooded by the sea so often, forcing the inhabitants to take refuge on the roofs of their houses and even in the bell-tower. Hardly anything grows on the island. There are no trees or shrubs, and only a few vegetables survive, protected by low stone walls. Yet the landscape has its own inimitable charm.

The church of Saint-Gwénolé

Each stone of the church, which was built between 1898 and 1901, was transported individually on the heads of the local women from the port where it was unloaded. This is perfect justification for the Latin inscription over the entrance, which reads: 'By the power of God and the sweat of the people.' Inside the church there is a votive offering by English sailors who were saved from shipwreck in 1918 by a wedding party, which, headed by the bride and groom, did not hesitate to brave the breakers to come to their rescue.

'A QUARTER OF FRANCE'

This historic phrase, uttered by General de Gaulle, has passed into French history. On 6 July 1940 the General assembled the first 600 Free French volunteers who had been able to make it across the channel to London. He discovered that no fewer than 150 of them came from the Île de Sein. In fact, all the islanders had come. 'The Île de Sein is thus a quarter of France,' exclaimed General de Gaulle. In 1960 he personally dedicated the monument to the Free French fighters of the island and was struck by the inscription *Kentoc'h mervel*, 'rather die'.

| Spotcheck |
| A3 |

Finistère

Things to do

Walking around the island

Tourist office

Audierne: ☎ 02 98 70 12 20

The chapel of Saint-Corentin

This chapel at the western end of the island was restored by the rector himself, who recovered stones from other ruins. The ancient statue of the bishop and patron saint of the chapel, which has now disappeared, was reputed to be able to influence the weather to obtain favourable winds. All that was required was to turn its crosier in the required direction. If that didn't work, the bishop was covered in guano!

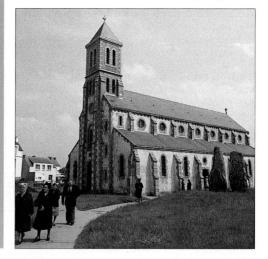

Pointe du Raz and Cap Sizun

Brittany's wild west

St-They

Audierne

Pointe du Raz

Plogoff

Pont-Croix

The western tip of Brittany is a wild and mythical place, whose beauty is admired by the

tourists who flock here from all over Europe. Each of the rocks, overlooked by the high, windswept cliffs, has a name. In good weather the Île de Sein can be seen from the statue of Notre-Dame-des-Trépassés, which overlooks the sea. The Pointe du Raz, made famous by its appearance on post-war French stamps, is a national site of scientific interest and one of the world's truly wild places.

Return to nature

The Pointe du Raz became the victim of its own success. It was trampled upon by visitors and ravaged by wild winter storms. The Conservatoire du Littoral, a coastal conservation body, therefore launched an initiative to preserve the site. A huge parking lot and shopping centre were demolished, and a unique experiment in replanting the moorland was undertaken which took several years. Sadly, nothing is perfect, and the charming little Hôtel de l'Iroise, which stood like a lone sentinel on the moors, was also sacrificed.

La Maison du Site

☎ 02 98 70 67 18
Open 9.30am–7.30pm, in season.
Price: 100 F for 1–4 people, then 25 F for each additional person.
At the entry to the Pointe du Raz, the **Maison du Site**, in the heart of the new shopping complex, is an information centre that offers guided tours of the whole Pointe du Raz area. The lovely walk is preceded by an illustrated talk about the area, which lasts for about two hours. You will need sturdy footwear for

La Vieille lighthouse off the Pointe du Raz

climbing the rocks, and you ought not be too afraid of heights!

Plogoff
Route to the Pointe du Raz
☎ 02 98 70 37 48
Open July–Aug., 8am–7pm. Other times, 8am–noon and 2–6pm. *Free admission.*

CAP SIZUN RESERVE
☎ 02 98 70 13 53
Open 1 April–30 June and Sept.–Oct., 10am–noon and 2–6pm; July–Aug., 10am–6pm, and hikes organised Mon. and Thurs. to explore the site (9am–noon).
This is one of Europe's most famous nature reserves, which harbours important colonies of migratory and nesting birds. It can be visited along a signposted path on a clifftop 230 feet (70 m) high. The reserve covers approximately 100 acres (40 ha). The best time to see it is between 15 April and 15 June.

Plogoff is famous throughout France for the fierce campaign, conducted between 1976 and 1981, against the proposed siting of a nuclear power station nearby. It is now a peaceful village at the far end of the Raz headland. The low stone walls that protect the plots of land from the wind are built from the very stones that were used as projectiles by the population in their battle with the forces of law and order!

The Pointe du Van and Bay des Trépassés
The Van headland and the bay are not as popular with tourists but are no less attractive. Van has a lovely little 17th-C. chapel, the chapel of Saint-They, which seems to cling miraculously to the cliffside. The Bay des Trépassés (trespass bay) has a fine, curving beach of pebbles and sand, and the lost city of Ys is said to lie in the waters of the bay. At low tide, caves in the rocks are exposed, and these can be explored.

Pont-Croix
Pont-Croix should be visited for its architecture, especially the 13th-C. collegiate church of Notre-Dame-de-Roscudon. The spire, which also serves as a bell tower, was the model for the spires of the cathedral at Quimper. A few ancient, narrow

Spotcheck
A3

Finistère

Things to do
Walks and guided tours
Cap Sizun Reserve
Visit to a biscuit factory

Tourist office
La Maison du Site:
☎ 02 98 70 67 18

streets, lined with lovely medieval houses, surround the cathedral. There is a pleasant walk down to the river, with steps leading down the steep main road, the Grand-Rue.

❀ Biscuits from the Pointe du Raz
Route from the Pointe du Raz, Plogoff
☎ 02 98 70 37 48
Open July–Aug., 8am–7pm; the rest of the year 8am–noon and 2–6pm. *Free admission.*
For many French people, the typical Breton delicacy is a butter biscuit (*galette pur beurre*). If you like these biscuits visit the Pointe du Raz biscuit factory, where you can watch Breton butter biscuits and other cakes and biscuits being made. The visit ends with a tasting, of course, and you can buy the factory's products from its own shop.

Douarnenez
from fishing to pleasure boats

Old riggers and working ships lie side by side in the harbour museum of Port-Rhu

D ouarnenez nestles in the back of the bay that bears its name. Its little streets still echo to the sounds of the glorious past of its sardine fishermen, who made its fortune in the early 20th C. The town has three harbours – a marina, a museum harbour and a fishing harbour. It was once the sixth largest fishing port in France, but after serious problems in the fishing sector, it concentrated more on its other industry, canning.

catches of mackerel, monkfish, cod and plaice are sold off. To attend the auction, contact the tourist office, 2, Rue du Docteur-Mével, ☎ 02 98 92 13 35. Guided tours of the port are also organised every Monday and Wednesday, from 1 July to 31 Aug.

The fishing harbour
The Douarnenez fishing port offers a unique opportunity to experience what daily life is like for fishermen. Fish are unloaded at the quayside from 11pm and this goes on all night. The fish auction begins at 6am, when the

The Cobreco canneries
Tourist office of Douarnenez
☎ 02 98 92 12 35
Sat. only, 10am–noon (after booking at the tourist office).
Free admission.

This is one of the largest canneries in Douarnenez, and it specialises in luxury foods based on tuna and scallops. Visits to the ultra-modern facilities are allowed only in June and July, and the factory owner himself provides the commentary. At the end of the visit, there is a shop (which is open all week) where you can buy the produce at bargain prices.

Tréboul
Tréboul and Ploaré were once separate villages, but they are now part of Douarnenez. Tréboul is linked to the town by a large metal bridge, which allows vehicles to cross the estuary of Port-Rhu, and by a footbridge, which offers the possibility of a pleasant walk. There is a little seaside resort

The chapel of Sainte-Hélène

along the beautiful beach of **Sables-Blancs.** Tréboul cove is the site of the marina and a water-sports centre, which is open to anyone aged between 4 and 77.

The *Chasse-Marée*
**L'Abri du Marin,
Rue Henri-Barbusse
☎ 02 98 92 09 19**
Open Mon.–Fri. 9am–noon and 1.30–6pm.
The *Chasse-Marée* is a publication about traditional Breton life. The headquarters, just above the port, has a specialist bookshop from which several publications about traditional Breton crafts and customs are available. They also organise a festival of old ships and boats in August, at which there are Celtic songs, dancing and folk music.
For information:
☎ 02 98 92 29 27.

The harbour museum
**Place de l'Enfer
☎ 02 98 92 65 20**
Open 15 June–30 Sept. 10am–7pm; off-peak 10am–12.30pm and 2–6pm.
Admission charge.
The Port (musée) is a must. There are 60 traditional types of craft, all at full size, which are housed on two floors of an old cannery. About 20 traditional fishing boats are also tied up at the quay of the old renovated port, to which there is still free access. There are even some craftsmen who will demonstrate the old crafts, including a marine blacksmith, and there are presentations about seafaring occupations.

Tréboul-Douarnenez sea-water centre
**BP 4, Tréboul, 29 175 Douarnenez CEDEX
☎ 02 98 74 47 47**
The Tréboul-Douarnenez seawater treatment centre is approved and certified for the treatment of patients who have been in accidents. It has a rehabilitation centre, which specialises in orthopaedics and sports rehabilitation. The centre treats patients who are suffering from the serious after-effects of accidents. There are similar treatment centres elsewhere in Brittany, but they do not treat people who have suffered serious injuries with long-term effects.

**Spotcheck
B3**

Finistère

Things to do
Visit to a cannery
Tréboul water-sports centre
Harbour museum
Hillside walks

Within easy reach
*Quimper 14 miles (23 km) SE, p. 220,
Pont-l'Abbé 21 miles (33 km), p. 224,
Locronan 6 miles (10 km), p. 218.*

Tourist office
**Douarnenez:
☎ 02 98 92 13 35**

THE HILL PATHS
These paths offer an opportunity for several easy and pleasant rambles from Douarnenez. The Plomac'hs path, which starts east of the old port of Rosmeur, leads to the beach at Ris. The walk over the hillside takes just over an hour and there are wonderful views of Douarnenez. The Roches Blanches path (signposted in orange) also offers lovely views of the bay as it follows the coast for 3¼ miles (6 km) before reaching the Pointe du Leydé.

Audierne
and its bay
dunes, birds and surfboarding

Audierne is a small, busy port with traditional Breton houses and brightly coloured boats which come in and out with the tides of the Goyen estuary. Audierne is a real find, as its charms have yet to be discovered by mass tourism. Take time to explore the upper town with its narrow streets, tiny shops and old houses. Audierne is also an ideal stopping place for anyone wishing to explore the adjoining bay on sea or land.

(625 ha) of dunes, beaches and marshland belonging to the Conservatoire du Littoral, the coastline conservancy authority. The centre organises ornithological trips (more than 285 species of migrating bird has been recorded), evenings on the marshes, binocular hire (5 F), as well as guided tours with advance booking.

A trip to the Île de Sein

About 1½ miles (2.5 km) west of the town is the large Audierne beach which faces south, has a marina, a watersports club and the Sainte-Evette pier, from where there are sailings for the Île de Sein. The **Penn ar Bed** company (☎ 02 98 70 02 37) has daily sailings from September to June (9.30am) and three departures a day in July and August. The crossing takes an hour.

La Maison de la Baie

Saint-Vio, 29720 Tréguennec
☎ 02 98 82 61 76
Open 2–6pm off-peak; July–Aug., 11am–7pm.
Admission charge.
La Maison de la Baie Audierne is a centre that encourages research into the numerous natural treasures of the 1,550 acres

La Chaumière

Rue de l'Amiral-Guépratte
☎ 02 98 70 13 20
Open July–Aug., 10am–1pm and 2–7pm.
Admission charge.
This large thatched cottage on the road to the beach belongs to André Kersaudy, who has preserved the traditional 17th- and 18th-C. Breton furnishings and

household objects in their entirety in his home. He will explain the difference between the *penty* and the *ty braz* and how a *druestill*, a partition between the kitchen and living room, is used.

Les viviers d'Audierne

1, Rue du Môle, towards the beach
☎ 02 98 70 10 04
Sept.–June, 3–5pm;
July–Aug., 9am–noon and 3–6pm, except weekends

LES FRÈRES DOUIRIN

Impasse de la Poste, 29710 Plozévet
☎ 02 98 91 42 04
If you collect marine memorabilia you can do no better than to buy from the Dourin brothers. The quality is impeccable and no more than 1,000 copies are made of any item. The woods used are beech or sometimes cypress or pine and they make sure that the finish is perfect. The Douirin brothers make half-shells, lighthouses, figurines, models of interiors and workshops and tools, which are reproductions of traditional scenes of craftsmen at work. Their products can be bought here in the brothers' own workshop and retail outlet.

and public holidays.
Free admission; shop.
This is one of the few covered fish-farms in Europe. It consists of about 20 large tanks next to the sea, containing impressive specimens of crabs and other crustaceans – crayfish, lobsters, edible crabs, spider crabs and so on – all of which are very much alive. This is the perfect chance to prepare a dish of really fresh seafood.

Pointe de la Torche, centre of Breton surfboarding

The headland is worth a visit in itself. There is a path all the way around it. In the centre of this peninsula, which ends in the Rock of la Torche, there is a gigantic dolmen. It's galleries and side-chambers are unique. This headland is famous internationally for its huge breakers – be careful to obey the warning signs about bathing – and its surfing and funboard contests. It is no

Spotcheck
B3

Finistère

Things to do

Sea trip to the Île de Sein
Guided walks through the bay
Surfboarding,
fun-boarding and sand-karting

Within easy reach

Quimper 22 miles E (36 km), p. 220,
Pont-l'Abbé S-E 20 miles (32 km), p. 224,
Locronan 20 miles N-E (32 km), p. 218.

Tourist Office

Audierne : ☎ 02 98 70 12 20

accident, therefore, that the Brittany surfing school, which offers training courses (☎ 02 98 58 53 80), has its headquarters at this beach, which is a centre for surfboarders and sandkarters (Speed Evasion, ☎ 02 98 58 56 20).

The calvary of Notre-Dame-de-Tronoën

This is one of the oldest calvaries in Brittany. It was created between 1450 and 1470 and stands in splendid isolation in an austere landscape south of the bay on a hillock overlooking the sea.

Locronan
600,000 visitors a year

L ocronan is a small city built on the
heights of the Douarnenez bay, and it
has been remarkably well preserved
from the ravages of time and still has an
architectural unity that is unusual. There are
mansions and granite houses dating from the
17th and 18th C. surrounding the old well
in the main square, evidence of Locronan's
former prosperity, when a community of weavers
made the city wealthy. These sights are a great attraction,
and help the city derive the majority of its modern income from tourism.

Place de l'Église

Locronan's main square is
classified as an historic
monument, and it has also
become a place of pilgrimage.
Furthermore, it is a shopping
centre which is busy all year
round. In several of the
surrounding streets there are
indications of the wealth the
town enjoyed in
the 17th C.
There are

craftsmen's shop signs in
streets radiating from the
square, such as the **Rue Moal**,
which was once filled with
weavers. This lively street has
retained all its charm and
draws you irresistibly to the
chapel of Notre-Dame-de-
Bonne-Nouvelle, 200 yards
(200 m) further on.

The Saint-
Ronan church

This church, which was built
between 1420 and 1444, due
to donations from the dukes
of Brittany, is a masterpiece of
the Flamboyant style. Duke
Jean wanted a church that
looked like a cathedral, and
there is no doubt that the
porch was inspired by one of
the portals of the cathedral of

Quimper. The church tower is
only two storeys high, having
lost its spire when it was hit
by a thunderbolt in 1808. On
the right there is the chapel
of Pénity. The interior contains ancient statuary, a reredos and stained glass windows, which are marvels of
religious art.

À la Galette
Saint-Ronan

Place de l'Église
☎ 02 98 91 70 24
Open daily, 7am–7.30pm.
This bakery and pastry shop
was founded more than a
century and a half ago, and it
specialises in Breton cakes,
including *far*, *palets* and *kouign
aman*. Everything is made on

the premises using fresh Breton butter from the churn. A large portion of *kouign aman* costs 11 F; a box of *palets* costs 52 F.

La Maison des Artisans

Place de l'Eglise
☎ 02 98 91 70 11
Open daily all year round, 10am–12.30pm and 2.30–5.30pm.

Four authentic craftsmen have joined forces in this building, which is open on three levels. On the ground floor, there is a range of hand-woven table linen as well as towels and other linen at prices starting at 60 F. Beautiful glazed ceramics are also on display. On the next floor, a wood-carver's studio is open to the public from June to September. The top floor is occupied by a Celtic bookshop.

Locronan mountain

Locronan mountain lies in the direction of Châteaulin. It is really a hill – it is only 950 feet (289 m) high – and is about 1¼ miles (2 km) from the town.

STYVERTIN

S. RONAN BREIZH XOX ANIMAUX

Spotcheck

B3

Finistère

Things to do

La maison des Artisans
Locronan mountain

Within easy reach

Châteaulin 12 miles (19 km) NE, p 208, Douarnenez 6 miles (10 km) W, p. 214, Audierne 20 miles (32 km) SW, p. 216.

Tourist office

Locronan: ☎ 02 98 91 70 14

TROMÉNIES

These pilgrimages are unique to Locronan, and they keep on attracting bigger crowds of pilgrims and sightseers. The Petite Troménie is held on the second Sunday in July. The procession with banners and relics of the saints walks 2½ miles (4 km), stopping at three stations. The Grande Troménie walks a distance of 7½ miles (12 km) with the same number of stops in the Locronan countryside, but it is only held once every six years. There is one in 2001 so put the date in your diary!

Even if no pilgrimage is taking place at the time, it is worth the walk for the spectacular view of the whole range of the Montagnes Noires, the Monts d'Arrée, the bay of Douarnenez and the Crozon peninsula. The summit is topped with a recently built chapel (only completed in 1977), which replaced a building constructed in 1912.

Quimper
a city with a strong personality

Quimper is the obvious choice as the historic and economic capital of the part of Brittany known as Cornouaille. It lies at the confluence of the rivers Steir and Odet, which run through the town that is the administrative capital of Finistère. It has a handsome cathedral and narrow lanes, with perfectly preserved half-timbered houses. But it is not merely a repository of history. It has many high-tech industries and an important food-processing industry, and is known for its local pottery, which continues to delight visitors.

The cathedral of Saint-Corentin

This is one of the three oldest cathedrals in Brittany. Work on it began in 1239, but it was not completed until the 19th C., in the reign of Napoleon III. Its elegance seems to be summed up in its two 22 feet (7 m) high spires, one each side of an imposing porch. Inside there are 10 stained-glass windows in the 15th-C. Flamboyant style, and a choir that, strangely, is 15° off-centre in relation to the alignment of the nave.

Old Quimper

The old town has quaint place-names, such as Place au Beurre, Venelle du Pain-Cuit and Rue des Boucheries, all of which refer to the medieval food markets. Some of the half-timbered houses with their steep roofs date back to the 16th C. One of the most attractive stands on the corner of the Rue Kéréon

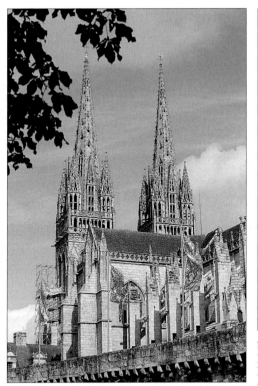

Spotcheck

B3

Finistère

Things to do

The Cornouaille festival
The Breton historical museum
Guided tour of a pottery

Within easy reach

*Montagnes Noires 22
miles (35 km.) NW,
p. 192,
Châteaulin 19 miles
(30 km) N, p 208,
Douarnenez 14 miles
(23 km) NW, p. 214,
Pont-Aven 19 miles
(30 km) SE, p. 232.*

Tourist Office

Quimper : ☎ **02 98 53 04 05**

('cobbler' in Breton) and the Rue des Boucheries. There are many tiny squares, alleys and passageways, behind

RUE DES BOUCHERIES

which there are more half-timbered, slate-roofed houses. Many are open to the public in the form of cafés, brasseries and restaurants.

Les halles

The building that houses the central market dates from only 1979. Before that a convent stood on the site, then a saltpetre factory and, finally, a clog-making factory. The market plays an important part in local life, since everyone comes here to stock up on fresh fruit, vegetables and other local produce. It also has a couple of excellent delicatessen

stalls, the **Buffet Campagnard** and the **Charcuterie Artisanale** (☎ 02 98 64 32 14), where the famous pork products of Brittany can be sampled at their best. Round the corner, at 29 Rue Saint-Mathieu, there is an excellent bakery and pastry shop, called the **Pâtisserie Legrand** (☎ 02 98 55 41 79), which is highly recommended for all the local sweets and cakes.

The river banks

The banks of the river Odet are always busy. The quaysides are lined with administrative offices, alternating with the terraces of cafés. The flower-lined footbridges across the river add to the charm of the delightful surroundings. The old city walls run alongside the Boulevard de Kerguelen. The tourist office is on the left bank of the river, at the foot of Mont Frugy, a 233 feet (71 m) high hill. This is a good place for a ramble, as there is an excellent view of Quimper from the top.

Musée des Beaux-Arts

40 Place Corentin
☎ 02 98 95 45 20
Open daily except Tues., July–Aug., 10am–7pm; the rest of the year, 10am–noon and 2–6pm.
Admission charge.
The fine arts museum has been completely renovated and is one of the largest in the whole of Brittany. It is also one of the most important. As well as 19th-C. Breton paintings, there are works by Fragonard, Boucher, the Dutch, Flemish and Italian old masters, and paintings from the school of Pont-Aven. A room is dedicated to the life and works of Max Jacob (1876–1944), a poet who came from Quimper.

Musée Départemental breton

Rue du Roi-Gradlon
☎ 02 98 95 21 60
Open daily except Mon. and Sun. 9am–noon and 2–5pm.
Admission charge.
This is the main historical and ethnographical museum of Finistère. It is housed in the former palace of the bishop, a building dating from the 16th C. On the ground floor there are various prehistoric objects and medieval relics. The first floor is devoted to embroidery, costume and traditional furniture, and the second floor contains a lovely collection of earthenware and pottery from the region.

Faïence

This is the local pottery, and the best way to learn about it is to visit the Musée de la Faïence (14 Rue Jean-Baptiste-Bousquet, ☎ 02 98 90 12 72; open mid-April–end Oct., Mon–Sat., 10am–6pm. Closed Sun. and public holidays; guided tours on Sat (admission charge). The techniques, development of styles and the work of various artists, who developed patterns, are on show, and there are many temporary exhibitions. Guided tours are available out of season for groups of 10 if booked in advance. After the theory comes the practical. The most famous

maker of faïence, H. B. Henriot, is in Rue Haute in the Locmaria district, where the whole faïence industry was born. The factory offers guided tours of the potteries (admission charge) from Monday to Friday (9.15–11am and 1.30–4.15pm). Groups should book in advance: (☎ 02 98 90 09 36). The Faïencerie

d'Art Breton, run by Pierre Henriot, at 50 Route de Locronan, organises free guided tours from Tuesday to Friday (9.30–11.30am), but only for groups and by prior arrangement (☎ 02 98 53 72 72).

The *kabig*
Novy Nick, 9 Rue du 19-mars-1962
☎ **02 98 52 29 28**
If you want to protect yourself against blustery winds, buy yourself a *kabig*. This heavy cape, which was inspired by the thick outer garments of seafarers, is the height of fashion and the decorative scallops are there to ensure tight fastening, so that rain cannot get in. A *kabig* costs from 450 F for a child's size and up to 1,100 F for a woman's model. They come in dark blue, red, blue and cream.

Just outside Quimper, the Odet runs through the Stangola gorges

Pont-l'Abbé
and the Pays Bigouden

The Pays Bigouden is a district of Cornouaille that is famous for its tall Breton headdresses. Pont-l'Abbé is the largest town in a district that extends from Plozevet in the west to the banks of the Odet in the east. The landscape is varied, but the inhabitants have a strong sense of local identity. Before the advent of tourism, the only industry was fishing.

Pont-l'Abbé and its river

The capital of the Pays Bigouden is a small town of 8,000 inhabitants. Built beside the estuary it owes its name to the bridge built by the abbots of Loctudy between the port and the lake. Pont-l'Abbé is famous for its embroidery and doll-making, and holds a festival of embroiderers, the Fête des Brodeuses, in the second week of July. The town also has boat-building yards. There is a 1¼ mile (2 km) towpath along the right bank of the river, which is a favourite place for birdwatchers, strollers and anglers. On the Île Tudy (a peninsula) there is a typical fishing village.

Le Minor, hand embroidery

5 Quai Saint-Laurent
☎ **02 98 87 07 22**
Open Mon-Sat., 9am–noon and 2–7pm.
Although it is possible to buy machine-embroidered items here, Le Minor is the only place where you can still buy items that are entirely hand embroidered. The shop sells tablecloths and table sets, and also local clothing, including *kabig* capes and sailors' jerseys.

Museum and Maison du Pays bigouden

Rue du Château
☎ **02 98 66 09 09**
Open 10am–noon and 2–6pm June–Sept.
Closed Sun. and public holidays. Off-peak closed at 5pm. *Admission charge.*
The museum is housed in an 8th-C. castle and is devoted to the Breton heritage in the form of furnishings, costumes, domestic artefacts and the like. The **Maison du Pays**

Bigouden is at the Kervazegan farm (☎ 02 98 87 35 63), 1¼ miles (2 km) from Pont-l'Abbé on the road to Loctudy. Here, the emphasis is on Bigouden crafts and artefacts, such as bunk beds, clocks, churns and apple presses.

Loctudy

Fishing and sailing

2½ miles (6 km) SE of Pont-l'Abbé
Fishing trips organised from the marina
☎ **02 98 87 40 14**
Special group rates.
Loctudy is the biggest crayfish fishing port in Brittany as well as a small seaside resort with sheltered beaches in sandy coves. From May to September, fishing trips are organised for tourists to show how crayfishing is done. You

can drop nets or put down lobster-pots, and there is also mackerel fishing with a line. Best of all, you are allowed to keep anything you catch!

Le Guilvinec
Inside a boatyard
7 miles (11 km) S from Pont-l'Abbé
Rue Saint-Jacques-de-Thézac, Le Guilvinec
☎ 02 98 58 11 38
Open Wed. and Fri., at 11am, 1 July–31 Aug.
Admission charge.
Le Guilvinec owes its prosperity to crayfish and lobsters, and it has remained an important fishing port, the fourth largest in France. The whole economy of the district, from fish auctions and canneries to naval dockyards, is dependent on the sea. A sight not to be missed is the return of the trawlers at about 4pm every day. Jacques Henaff – not be confused with Jean Hénaff (*see right*) – opens his boatyard to the public. This is an occasion to learn about the history of trawlers, how they are built, the various ways in which fishing boats catch fish and the rituals that accompany the launch of a vessel.

Penmarc'h
Penmarc'h and the Eckmühl lighthouse
10 miles (17 km) SW of Pont-l'Abbé
Penmarc'h ends at the reefs but also includes **Penmarc'h bourg**, **Kerity**, a little port for pleasure boats, and **Saint-Guénolé**, an important fishing village. You can attend the fish auction here (information at the tourist office ☎ 02 98 58 81 44, 15 June–15 Sept., admission charge). The auction takes place in the evening, and you will be able to board a trawler, watch a catch being unloaded, see it being sorted and attend the sale. This part of the coastline is littered with dangerous rocks and reefs. Consequently, at the Pointe de Penmarc'h there is a large lighthouse, the **Eckmühl lighthouse**, 214 feet (65 m) tall (guided tours all year round; free access; tips welcome; bookings ☎ 02 98 58 61 17).

Saint-Guénolé
The Penmarc'h cooperative
11 miles (17.5 km) SW of Pont-l'Abbé
☎ 02 98 58 66 24.
Open Mon.–Fri., 8am–noon, 2–6.30 pm; Sat., 8am–noon.
At this huge ships' chandlers skippers and sailors can buy anything they need for a sea voyage and for fishing, from a little sailing dinghy to the biggest factory ship. The cooperative stocks everything, including a wide range of sailing clothes, as well as barometers, side-lights, timepieces, navigation devices and marine paint. Authentic and fascinating.

Things to do
Visiting a boatyard
Fishing trip at sea

Within easy reach
Audierne 20 miles (32 km) NW, p. 216.

Tourist office
Pont-l'Abbé:
☎ 02 98 82 37 99

JEAN HÉNAFF, THE KING OF PÂTÉ
Pouldreuzic
14 miles (22 km) NW of Pont-l'Abbé
☎ 02 98 51 53 53
Open 15 June–15 Sept., Mon.–Fri., at 9am, by appointment.
Admission charge.
The *pâté du mataf,* as it was once called, was first created in 1914, and no Breton would put to sea without a good supply of the distinctive blue tins of this delicacy. The pure pork pâté is made from roast ham and loin of pork from the 250 pigs that are butchered daily at Pouldreuzic. The secret of the delicious recipe is jealously guarded, so do not try and extract it during your visit!

Bénodet and the banks of the Odet

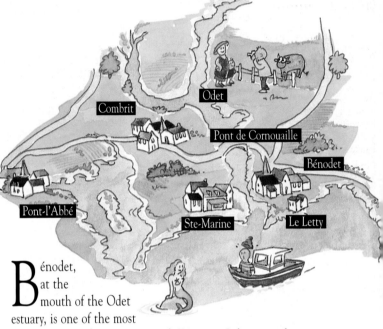

B énodet, at the mouth of the Odet estuary, is one of the most prestigious seaside resorts in south Finistère. It has a conference centre, a marina and three corniche roads: the Corniche de la Mer, the Corniche de la Plage and the Corniche de l'Estuaire, which give views of the sea, beach and estuary respectively. Your enjoyment will be enhanced here by the large, sandy beach edged with wooded dunes. Don't forget to try your luck at the casino, the focus of much of the nightlife.

The calm beauty of the Odet

The Odet is actually a landlocked *ria* (sea inlet), which the sea invaded several thousand years ago, following the folding of the granite landmass. Its steep banks are topped with opulent manor houses and châteaux set in thick woods. Because the Odet is heavily tidal, it is used by overwintering wading birds, such as woodcock, red-shanks, curlews and ducks. It is one of the few spots on the coast where the rare estuary horseradish grows. This is a plant that is partly terrestrial and partly aquatic and is now

protected. Cruises up the Odet are organised daily in season. They leave from the old port of Bénodet between May and September. For more information, contact **Vedettes de l'Odet** (☎ 02 98 57 00 58), which organises two to five sailings a day. The round trip lasts for about 2¼ hours. It is also possible to rent a former sailing barge – which was once used for carrying sand – with its crew

from the **Gouelia Company** ☎ 02 98 95 32 33). You can also make the trip on foot on the Bénodet bank, but you should wear sturdy hiking shoes and carry the guide that is available from the tourist office. It is more than 9 miles (15 km) along the coastal paths (☎ 02 98 57 00 14).

The casino
☎ 02 98 66 27 27
Free admission.

The Bénodet casino on the Avenue de la Plage is something of an institution. It's possible to have fun without losing your shirt, because the minimum bet is 2 F, whether you are playing boule, a cut-down version of roulette, or the one-arm bandits. And the staff do not insist on the dress code. The casino is open daily, all year round, from 11am to 3am; boule begins at 9pm. There is a room containing 66 slot machines, mostly for playing video-poker. The casino has a bar, restaurant and even a cinema.

The white sea
This huge lagoon is separated from the ocean by a 2½ mile (4 km) sandbar, on which nothing grows but a few tufts of marram grass. It

stretches from the Pointe de Bénodet to the Pointe de Mousterlin, and there is nothing else like it in Brittany. The little hamlet of **Letty** has a water-sports centre. There is a telescope and a map of the area at the Pointe Saint-Gilles, the entry to the lagoon.

❀ **Musée du Cidre**
☎ 02 98 51 90 84
Open daily except Sun., 15 May–15 Sept., 10am–noon and 2.30–7pm.
Admission charge.
The cider museum traces the history of the local apple varieties, through orchards, old cider presses and the fermentation of the apple juice into cider. At the end there is a distillery, where the cider is converted into apple brandy. The guided tour ends with demonstrations and a tasting, of course!

Sainte-Marine
½ mile (800 m) from Bénodet
Sainte-Marine is an important harbour for pleasure craft on the other side of the estuary. Since 1970 it has been reached by the Pont de Cornouaille, a bridge 2,000 feet (610 m) long, suspended 230 feet (70 m) in the air. The harbour contains a number of floating pontoons with moorings for yachts and sailing dinghies of all kinds. The neighbouring fishing harbour offers opportunities for a few moments of pleasant relaxation at one of the quayside cafés. There is also an attractive little chapel and a beautifully restored 'sailor's rest'.

Spotcheck
B3

Finistère

Things to do
Cruise on the Odet
Ramble along the coast
Visit the cider museum
Cornouaille botanical park

Within easy reach
Pont-Aven 22 miles (35 km) E, p. 232.

Tourist office
Bénodet : ☎ 02 98 57 00 14

CORNOUAILLE BOTANICAL PARK
Combrit, 2½ miles (4 km) NW of Bénodet
☎ 02 98 56 44 93
Combrit is a little commune set in the Cosquer woods beside an inlet of the sea that runs inland, through the heart of the countryside, for 1¾ miles (3 km). Combrit has lovely sandy beaches, which are quiet and secluded. It also benefits from an exceptionally mild microclimate, which is why the Cornouaille botanical park has been established here. This huge garden contains no fewer than 550 varieties of camellias, 85 types of magnolia and, above all, an amazing water garden covering 64,500 sq feet (6000 m²). Other attractions include a rose garden, an alpine garden and massive banks of hydrangeas. Plants are available for sale.

Concarneau
the prettiest walled city in southern Brittany

I ts architecture, its busy fishing village and its wave-swept corniche help to make Concarneau one of the loveliest towns on the coast of Brittany. It is situated in one of the most sheltered bays on the Atlantic coast, and is now the third largest French fishing port for fresh fish and the largest of all for tuna from the tropics, including all the related industries, especially canning. The Halle à Marée, in which the fish auction and market are held, is enormous, covering a surface of 150,700 sq feet (14,000 m²).

The fortified city

This little walled city was built in the 14th C., and it can only be reached by a drawbridge. The city itself is a gem, with its cobbled streets and tiny squares, which seem to have been forgotten by time. The ramparts can be visited (10am–7.30pm in summer; admission charge).

The fishing museum

3 Rue Vauban, in the walled city
☎ 02 98 97 10 20
Open 10am–noon and 2pm–6pm off-peak; 15 June–15 Sept., 9 30am–7.30pm. Closed in Jan.
Admission charge.

This is one of the most comprehensive fishing museums in the region. It contains a number of boats and covers the history of the town and port, fishing techniques for catching hake and tuna and trawling methods. There are aquaria filled with fish, both familiar and exotic. It takes at least an hour to go through the rooms and wander around the two trawlers in the dock.

À l'Assaut des Remparts

5 Impasse de Verdun
☎ 02 98 50 56 55
Open 10am–5pm.

This association organises guided tours for groups around the town on every day of the year, and from 15 June to 15 September there are tours for individuals. You can visit a semi-industrial trawler, the harbour, a small canning factory and the quayside fish auction. Nothing that matters to Concarneau is left out. The tours usually begin at 10am or at 10pm, because the catch is unloaded at the fish docks from midnight to 7am, and are reasonably priced.

Circuit of the corniche

This is a very pleasant walk, signposted in green, which will lead you to the **Marinarium**, at the entrance to the port, as well as to the beaches of **Cornouaille** and the west-facing **Sables-Blancs**. Walk down the Quay Nul, which consists of a row of cement barrels that were recovered from the shipwreck of a Russian ship in 1904, and you may find yourself tempted by one of the little beaches surrounded by rocks. Another coastal path leads to the Forêt-Fouesnant via the coves of Saint-Jean and de Saint-Laurent,

from where there is a magnificent view over the bay.

Rosporden, capital of the hinterland

Rosporden lies on the Brest-Nantes road and is now a peaceful little town that earns its living mainly from food-processing and farming. In the past, it attracted many painters, including Adolphe Leleux (1812–1891), who

produced a series entitled *Femmes de Rosporden* (Women of Rosporden). The town is also famous for its mead production and for the ponds, which are popular with anglers. Its local delicacies include seaweed. **Globe Export** (Z.I. de Dioulan, ☎ 02 98 66 90 84, open Mon.–Fri., 2pm–6pm by appointment; admission charge) sells fresh, canned and vacuum-packed seaweed and seaweed-flavoured condiments. The growing and packing techniques are explained, as well as the nutritional benefits of seaweed.

Sailings to the Glénan islands

There are two sailings a day on the **Vedettes Glenn** and the **Vedettes de l'Odet** (☎ 02 98 57 00 58) pleasure boats from May to mid-September All the boats leave the Îles des Glénan between 5pm and 6pm. This archipelago of seven islands is famous for its sailing school, as well as for its immaculate beaches and transparent waters.

Spotcheck
C3

Finistère

Things to do

Fishing museum
Guided tours of the town
Circuit of the corniche
Sailing to the Glénan islands
Festival of the blue nets

Within easy reach

Pont-Aven 9 miles (15 km)
L, p. 232.

Tourist office

Concarneau:
☎ 02 98 97 01 44

LA FÊTE DES FILETS BLEUS

The festival of the blue nets is one of the most important folk festivals in Brittany. It originated as a demonstration of solidarity with the families of the fishermen who were ruined when the sardine shoals disappeared from the inshore waters in the early 20th C. It is held on the second-last Sunday and is the occasion for folk music and dancing and the wearing of traditional costumes. (Information: ☎ 02 98 50 59 10).

Fouesnant and district
cider-making, fishing ports and sandy beaches

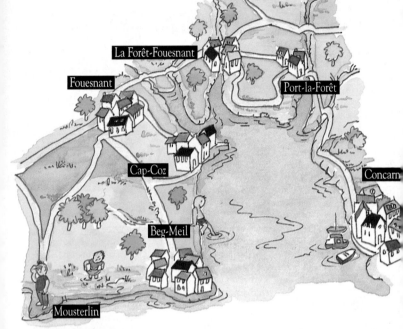

La Forêt-Fouesnant

Fouesnant

Port-la-Forêt

Cap-Coz

Concarn

Beg-Meil

Mousterlin

D eep in the heart of the woods and meadows, there lies a sandy beach. Fouesnant is sheltered from wind and storms and is a haven of peace and quiet, combining the plea-sures of the coast with those of the countryside, the sea and the land. The town is the cider-making capital of the area and is famous for the traditional headdresses, which are the most elaborate in Brittany. Fouesnant has long been an important tourist centre, but it now has a food-processing industry and has kept a population of about 150 fishermen, who unload their catch in one of the three small local ports.

The church of Saint-Pierre

Even visitors who are not interested in religious art will not fail to be moved by this building, a masterpiece of Romanesque art, which was constructed in the late 11th and early 12th C. Notice the double sloping roof and,

inside, the tall, sweeping arcaded nave, the arrow-slit windows and the capitals on the pillars in the transept.

The Menez-Brug cider factory

56 Hent-Carbon, on the road to Beg-Meil
☎ **02 98 94 94 50**

Guided tours organised 1 July–31 Aug., Mon. 10am–12.30pm and Wed. 9.30am–5pm. *Admission charge.*
There are dozens of cider-makers, but

the Menez-Brug cider factory offers tastings on every day of the week and sells a wide range of products based on apples, including AOC cider,

apple brandy (applejack), apple juice and pommeau (cider mixed with apple brandy). You can visit the cellars, see the cider-presses and learn how cider is made.

Cap-Coz
Seaside resort and fishing harbour

Cap-Coz is one of Fouesnant's three small fishing ports – the other two are **Beg-Meil** and **Mousterlin** – and it doubles as a seaside resort. The cape itself is a long sandbar, which extends out into the water. A coastal path, edged with camellias, azaleas and rhododendrons, hugs the bay of Le Forêt, right up to the **Roche-Percée**. From here there is a lovely view of Concarneau and the Pointe de Trévignon.

Beg-Meil
The Pointe du Moulin

Beg-Meil is a seaside resort known for its fine sandy beach edged with pines and cypresses. It has been spared the overdevelopment that has spoiled some of its sister resorts. As you approach the Pointe du

Mousterlin, you will notice huge stretches of deserted white sand, which are, for this very reason, popular with naturists.

Mousterlin
The marsh

After following wooded paths, you come to a landscape of ponds and woods extending as far as the eye can see and covering more than 370 acres (150 ha). Not far from the church, the Descente du Dourig path leads to the salt ponds of **Penfoulic** and the

Maison du Marais, an ecological centre that explains the flora and fauna of these lonely stretches of watery landscape (July–Aug., free admission). The Beg-Meil tourist office (☎ 02 98 94 97 47) organises tours into the marshes. The Fouesnant-les-Glénan tourist office also offers nature walks to explore these well-preserved areas of outstanding natural beauty and to watch the birds (☎ 02 98 56 00 93).

La Forêt-Fouesnant
A charming village

Lost in the middle of greenery at the back of a bay that bears its name, La Forêt-Fouesnant is a pleasant place to stop far from the crowd of tourists that invades the coast in high season. A little marina is

currently being developed here. Take a look at the calvary, the parish close and the church, whose porch is decorated with ancient statues. If you are feeling more adventurous, cruise down the Odet or take a sailing trip to the Îles de Glénan.

AT FULL SAIL

Port-la-Forêt
This marina has more than 700 moorings reserved for pleasure craft. CDK Technologie, which is based at the ports, is a small company specialising in building prototypes of racing yachts in composite materials. Its clients include leading French racing yachtsmen, such as Olivier de Kersauson and Loïc Peyron. A visit to the boatyard makes it easier to understand how the boats are constructed and what sort of materials are being used to build these craft, which are designed to break records and be sailed around the world single-handed. Free guided tour, by appointment (☎ 02 98 51 41 00).

Pont-Aven
and district
painters and biscuits

This is the land of flour-mills – '14 mills, 15 houses', goes the old adage. Pont-Aven used to be a centre of industry, and it is famous for its painters thanks to the school of painting that bears its name. The little town nestles in the hollow of an estuary that has been particularly favoured by history and nature. Today, it is full of art galleries and tries hard to remain quaint and unspoiled, while retaining its main economic activity, biscuit-making. Nearly two million boxes of Pont-Aven biscuits (*galettes de Pont-Aven*) are produced annually.

The Pont-Aven museum

Place de l'Hôtel-de-Ville
☎ 02 98 06 14 43
Open daily, except beginning Jan., 10am–12.30pm and 2–6.30pm; July–Aug., 10am–7pm.
Admission charge; children under 12 free.
You will not find paintings by Gauguin displayed in this museum as they cost too much. On the other hand, the Pont-Aven school is well-represented through temporary exhibitions and a permanent collection of the drawings and engravings of Maurice Denis and Émile Jourdan. Fascinating photographs and other material trace the history of the Pont-Aven school of painting.

The painters' road

Groupement Touristique de Cornouaille, 145 Avenue de Kéradennec, Quimper
☎ 02 98 90 75 05
There are seven tours, all of which begin at Pont-Aven, that explore the region through the eyes of its painters. A study of the paintings is an invitation to learn about the nature and traditions that they immortalised and the society and the way of life that created them. To follow the painters' road is like taking a walk between past and present.

Walking in the wood of love

After taking a look at Marie-Jeanne Gloanec's boarding-house in which Gauguin stayed, but which is now a

newspaper office, take the Xavier-Grall Promenade, which winds along the Aven. The river bed is littered with heaps of rocks, including the so-called Gargantua's Shoe. The route contains many footbridges and leads up to the heights of the **Bois d'Amour**, the wood of love, where in the 19th C. the

Symbolist painters came for inspiration. The walk also leads to the marina, once a fishing port, and a few of the preserved remains of local flour mills.

Port-Manech
At the mouth of the Aven

The resort of Port-Manech hugs the estuaries of the Aven and the Belon. It has a fine sandy beach, which first became popular at the turn of the 19th and 20th C. The bathing huts along the shore are reminders of this era. If you walk to the Pointe de Beg ar Vechen, you will have a magnificent view of the islands in the bay and the two neighbouring *rias* (sea inlets) of the Aven and the Belon.

Grand-Poulguen
Le Moulin
2 Quai Théodore-Botherel
☎ 02 98 06 02 67
Open 1 April–30 Nov., 11am–11pm.

The Grand-Poulguen mill is five centuries old and is the last witness, in working order, to Pont-Aven's past. Today it has been converted into a bar-*crêperie*, but all the old mechanisms are still there – mill-wheel, millstones and

brackets – to be admired by the eaters of *crêpes* and drinkers of cider. The owner also organises free tours with a running commentary and, when the place is not too crowded, impromptu demonstrations of the workings of the mill.

Nizon
Artists' colony
2 miles (3 km) NW of Pont-Aven

Nizon is best-known for its little 15th-C. church and its Romanesque calvary, which inspired one of Gauguin's paintings. The town of Nizon is much more modest and self-effacing than its flamboyant neighbour. In its *estaminets* (bars) the walls are embellished not with the works of old masters but the creations of the local inhabitants themselves, in a variety of media, based on the style of the American artist Andy Warhol.

Spotcheck
C4

Finistère

Things to do

The painters' road
Visit to a biscuit factory
Walking in the wood of love

Within easy reach

*Quimper 19 miles (30 km) NW, p. 220,
Concarneau 9 miles (15 km) W. p. 228.*

Tourist office

Pont-Aven:
☎ 02 98 06 04 70

LES DÉLICES DE PONT-AVEN

Z. A. de Kergazuel
☎ 02 98 06 05 87
Open July–Aug., Mon.–Thurs., at 10.30am; by appointment. The rest of the year, call for information.

By the time you get to the end of the guided tour you will know all there is to know about the famous biscuits called *galettes de Pont-Aven*. The biscuits in this factory have the distinction of being made with typical churned Brittany butter. The tens of thousands of biscuits made daily are sent to all parts of France and neighbouring Switzerland, and even as far afield as Japan, Hong Kong and the USA. There are tastings and a shop.

Quimperlé and district

The delightful city of Quimperlé stands at the point where the rivers Isole and Ellé merge to form the Laïta. Quimperlé is divided into two parts, the upper town, which is dominated by the church of Notre-Dame-de-l'Assomption, and the lower town, which surrounds the church of Croix. The city was founded 1,500 years ago and retains its cobbled streets and ancient dwellings, but it has entered the modern era with its thriving food-processing industry and the Mauduit paper mill. The district combines countryside and coastline.

Quimperlé

Forêt de Carnoët

Moëlan-sur-Mer

Laïta

Le Pouldu

Rue de Brémond-d'Ars

This was the street lived in by notables and the officers of the royal guard, so it has handsome, half-timbered mansions and other large residences. No. 15 has a double staircase with balustrade,

marking it as a courthouse. It was built in 1680 and is now used as the town museum. Another striking example of local architecture is the Hôtel Cosquer in the Rue Audran, which is typical of the style of building in the lower town in the 17th and 18th C.

Sainte-Croix church

This is the only circular Breton Romanesque church and, like the Temple de Lanleff in the Côtes-d'Armor, it is a copy of the church of the Holy Sepulchre in Jerusalem. It contains a

Renaissance reredos carved from local limestone. The 60 feet (18 m) rotunda is surrounded by the choir and the crypt on two levels. Three short naves lead off from the rotunda, the whole forming a cross. One of the two tomb figures is said to cure headaches.

The church of Saint-Michel

The church is best reached by the steep Rue Savary, a pedestrian shopping street, and is

easy to spot from a distance thanks to its huge, square tower. It was built in 13th-C. Gothic style but rebuilt in the 15th and 16th C. The portal and the north porch, which dates from 1450, are covered in beautiful carvings.

Le Pouldu
A house decorated by Gauguin

10 miles (16 km) S of Quimperlé.
Maison Marie-Henry, 10 Rue des Grands-Sables
☎ **02 98 39 98 51**
Open daily 1 June to 30 Sept., from 10.30am–12.30pm and 3–7pm.

The beaches of Le Pouldu first became popular in the late 19th C. Between 1889 and 1893 Paul Gauguin stayed in this delightful seaside resort. The Marie-Henry boarding house where he stayed is worth a visit – it is decorated from floor to ceiling by the painter and his friends' work.

Moëlan
Coastal walks

6 miles (10 km) SW of Quimperlé
Moëlan is a trading centre with an elegant 16th-C. chapel, the chapel of Saint-Philibert-Saint Roch, which has a 16th-C. calvary next to it. The Moëlan commune is one of the most extensive in Finistère, and it includes the little resort of Kerfany-les-Pins, which unfortunately lost the pines that are part of its name in the 1987 hurricane. The little port of Brigneau, with its tangle of picturesque, winding streets, is also part of the commune. There is a menhir on the road to Brigneau. Several signposted coastal paths running beside creeks and oyster-beds are very inviting, and hiking and rambling are the best

The beach at Le Pouldu, a favourite haunt of Gauguin

Spotcheck
C3

Finistère

Things to do
Walks along the Ellé
The beaches of Le Pouldu

Within easy reach
Hennebont 14 miles (23 km.) SE, p. 240.

Tourist office
Quimperlé :
☎ **02 98 96 04 32**

way of seeing this very hilly district with its lush, green valleys.

RAMBLING BESIDE THE ELLÉ

The tourist board and the rambling club organise walks every Wednesday in June, July and August, beginning at 2pm. They explore the banks of the Ellé or the beautiful national forest of Carnoët, in which the copses of oak and beech trees are traversed by the Laïta, a favourite river with anglers because of its stocks of trout and salmon. Ramblers can follow its course by taking the GR342, and themed walks are also possible. All walks are free and are accompanied by volunteer guides. They usually last for two to three hours over distances of 3¾ to 5 miles (6–8 km). Information at the tourist office, Rue Bourgneuf,
☎ **02 98 96 04 32**.

Lorient, the city of five ports

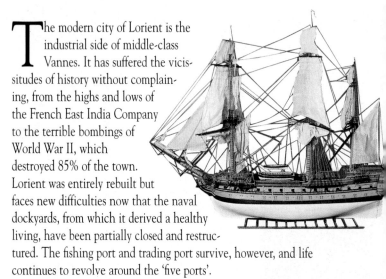

The modern city of Lorient is the industrial side of middle-class Vannes. It has suffered the vicissitudes of history without complaining, from the highs and lows of the French East India Company to the terrible bombings of World War II, which destroyed 85% of the town. Lorient was entirely rebuilt but faces new difficulties now that the naval dockyards, from which it derived a healthy living, have been partially closed and restructured. The fishing port and trading port survive, however, and life continues to revolve around the 'five ports'.

Fishing harbour

The massive Lorient-Keroman complex, built in 1927, has recently been brought up to date. It is now the biggest fishing port in France in terms of the value and diversity of the catch. The port combines industrial and factory fishing with semi-industrial and family-run fishing enterprises, and it provides a livelihood for thousands of people. Every Wednesday, at 8am, there is a guided tour organised by the tourist office (☎ 02 97 21 07 84), which will take you to the huge fish market, covering 5 acres (2 ha), where you can see the catch auctioned. On Saturday the fish are auctioned on the quayside among the fishermen themselves and wholesale fish merchants, but set your alarm clock because this exciting event takes place at 4.30am!

Visiting the seafront

July and Aug. daily, departures at 3.30pm and 4.30pm.
This guided tour of the town centre, which is organised by the tourist office, is very interesting as it takes you back to the rebuilding of Lorient after it had been ravaged by World War II.

Guérande butter

Guérande salt butter is a great delicacy, and it can be found in Lorient at the **Boutique de la Laiterie Kerguilett** (30 Halle Chanzy-Merville, ☎ 02 97 64 39 16).

Larmor-Plage
Water-sports
4 miles (6 km) S of Lorient
As its name suggests, this resort is concentrated along its fine sandy beach, with a busy water-sports centre, a favourite for surfboarding and sailing. There are pleasant beach-side cafés for less strenuous activity.

Port-Louis

Sea bathing
4 miles (6 km) S of Lorient

Port-Louis is an ancient fort at the entrance to the Lorient seafront, which was built in the heyday of the French East India Company. The Lohic promenade on the 17th-C. ramparts offers picturesque views of the little village of Gâvres and the

boats and dinghies that are beached at low tide. The Grands-Sables beach is a favourite with locals for bathing and water-sports.

Memories of the Compagnie des Indes
☎ 02 97 82 19 13.
Open daily except Tue., June–Sept., 10am–7pm; 1 Oct–30 Mar., 1.30–6pm; closed 1 Dec.–15 Jan. *Admission charge.*

The entrance ticket to this fort, built in the reign of Louis XIII, admits you to the parapet walk, the large pavilion of the Porte Royale, the Arsenal museum, containing models of the ships of the company, the museum of ships and the 15 rooms devoted to the history of the organisation.

Pont-Scorff

Village of crafts
4 miles (7 km) W of Lorient

Open daily 10am–noon and 2–7pm; 1 Sept.–30 June, daily except Tues.

Pont-Scorff is only ten minutes' drive from Lorient. It is a picturesque home for many craftspeople, including leather-workers, musical instrument makers, cabinet-makers, jewellers and the like. Inside a group of 17th-and 18th-C. houses is a courtyard called the Cour des Métiers d'Art (☎ 02 97 32 55 74), consisting of five workshops housing a glass-blower, makers of stained-glass, a rug-maker, a ceramics decorator and a potter. You are sure to find something here that you like the look of.

Spotcheck
C4

Morbihan

Things to do
Visit to the fishing port
Larmor-Plage water-sports
Citadel of Port-Louis
The Interceltic festival

Within easy reach
Hennebont 7 miles (12 km) NE, p. 240,
Auray 19 miles (30 km) E, p. 252.

Tourist office
Lorient : ☎ 02 97 21 07 84

INTERCELTIC FESTIVAL

Between 1 and 15 August, Celts flock to Lorient from all over the Celtic world for this festival, which brings the whole town to life. There are players of bagpipes and bombards, folk dancers, and performers of all kinds, combining live performances with *son et lumière*, fireworks, parades, *bagadou* competitions, concerts and, of course, the famous Breton *festou-noz* (feast nights), which last far into the evening. It is attended by several hundred thousand people, making it the largest festival of its kind in France and the highlight of the Lorient year. Information ☎ 02 97 21 24 29.

Île de Groix
miraculously preserved

The Îsle de Groix lies about 3¾ miles (6 km) off the coast of Lorient, between sheer cliffs and sandy beaches. The island is known familiarly as the island of *greks*, the local name for the large coffee-pots favoured by the islanders. Groix is a land of contrasts. In the early 20th C. it was the biggest tuna port in France, but it now relies on its wildlife and scientific heritage, and tourism accounts for much of its income. The giant rocks of Groix, its fields, valleys and scattered hamlets have all remained untouched and unspoiled in rare and precious authenticity.

How to get there

There are between four and eight sailings a day to the island, depending on the season. All are from Lorient with the **Compagnie Morbihanaise et Nantaise de Navigation** (☎ 02 97 64 77 64). The crossing takes about 45 minutes.

Rambles and hikes

This tiny island measures only 5 by 2 miles (8 by 3 km), so it offers lots of opportunities for pleasant walks and cycle rides. From **Port-Tudy**, which has a harbour for yachts and a fishing port, there are 15½ miles (25 km) of signposted footpaths encircling the island. It is a short walk to the beach of **Grands-Sables** via the hamlet of Mené. You could also walk to **Locmaria**, a delightful little fishing village with a maze of narrow lanes. Alternatively, you might prefer to discover the **Trou de l'Enfer** (the hell hole), a natural opening in the cliffs.

King tuna

Although tuna fishing has been the main occupation here for centuries, it is not what it once was. The fish, like many others, makes its mark everywhere on the island, even on the spire of the church of Saint-Tudy, where it has replaced the traditional cockerel as a weather-vane. The summer arrival of a few tuna boats at Port-Tudy is an occasion for celebration, during which the tuna are auctioned at the quayside for cooking fresh or canning for the winter.

THE GRANDS-SABLES BEACH

This is one of the finest beaches in Brittany and is the sole example of a convex beach in Europe. You could think that you were on a tropical isle, the water is so clear and the sand so white and fine. That is why this area is such a favourite for scuba-diving. You may be lucky enough to discover a garnet, of which there are deposits on the island. The beach of Sables-Rouges is a red, sandy beach, whose name derives from these stones. It is situated further along towards the Pointe des Chats (cats' point) and is well worth a visit.

Ecomusée
Port-Tudy
☎ 02 97 86 84 60
Open daily except Tues., 1 Oct.–14 April, 10am–12.30pm and 2–5pm; open daily 15 April–31 May, same opening hours; 1 June–30 Sept., 9.30am–12.30pm and 3–7pm.
Admission charge.
This fascinating museum, Écomusée, is housed in a former canning factory and takes a practical approach to the natural, historic and ethnographic heritage of the island. The ecomuseum also offers guided tours of Groix, using the signposted trails that begin nearby.

❀ The Francois Le Bail reserve
La Maison de la Réserve
☎ 02 97 86 55 97
Open daily except Sun., July–Aug., 9.30am–12.30pm and 5.30–7pm; June–Sept., open Tues. and Sat., 9am-noon. Off-peak, Sat. 9am–noon.
Admission charge.
The nature reserve of Pen Men, created in 1982 and covering 116 acres (47 ha), lies at the northwestern tip of the island. The marine nature reserve of the Pointe des Chats, at the other end of the island, is an excellent spot for birdwatching and also has interesting mineral deposits and flora. The **Maison de la Réserve** nature centre offers opportunities for learning about the crested cormorant and the properties of blue glaucophane, a local mineral.

Kerlard houses
Near to Port-Saint-Nicolas there is a sea inlet that cuts

Spotcheck
C4

Morbihan

Things to do
Walks around the island
The ecomuseum
The Francois Le Bail reserve
The Grands-Sables beach

Tourist office
Île de Groix:
☎ 02 97 86 53 08

into the cliffs until it reaches the village of Kerlard, where the low shale houses are very typical of the early 20th-C. homes of the island's 'peasant fishermen'. One of the houses dates from the 18th C. and is furnished in keeping with the period, as it is part of the ecomuseum and is open to the public in July and August from Wednesday to Sunday inclusive, from 2pm to 6pm.

Hennebont
a stronghold dominating the Blavet

The stones of Hennebont, a little town on the left bank of the river Blavet, are proof of its long and rich history. Its key geographical position, with access to the river and the sea, made it a trading crossroads and one of the most coveted strongholds in Brittany. The town suffered cruelly from air raids during World War II, and subsequently had to abandon its iron and steel industry in order to concentrate on trade and tourism.

The walled city

The walled city is entered through the 13th-C. **Broërec Gate**, which is flanked by two towers that have been used as guardrooms and prisons but are now a little museum. Immediately to the left, a staircase gives access to the ramparts and the circular path, which overlooks the French-style gardens and the valley of the river Blavet. Most of the houses in the walled city were destroyed

by incendiary bombs in 1944. However, a few still survive in the Rue des Lombards and the Grand-Rue which date from the 16th and 17th C. The best preserved of all is the house at **1, Rue de la Paix**.

Notre-Dame-du-Paradis

It took ten years to build the basilica of Notre-Dame-du-Paradis, which has stood in the Place du Maréchal-Foch since the 16th C. The square also has several 17th-C. houses and a wrought-iron covered well dating from 1623. Inside the church, look out for the stained-glass windows by Max Ingrand, which trace important events in the history of Hennebont.

The stud farm

Rue Victor-Hugo
☎ **02 97 36 20 27**
Guided visits 15 July–31 Aug., at 10am, 11am, 2.15pm, 3.15pm, 4.15pm.
Admission charge; children under 16 free.
The Hennebont national stud was first created in 1857 in a 60 acre (24 ha) park, which once belonged to the Cistercian monastery of Joie-Notre-Dame. Visitors are given

a guided tour of the stables, saddlery, tack room and the forge of the master blacksmith, and you will also see a beautiful collection of carriages. The stud farm holds national horse trials in late July, and between July and February it houses 75 stallions.

❀ The Hennebont forges

Z.I. des Forges, Inzinzac-Lochrist
☎ 02 97 36 98 21
Open all year round, Mon.–Fri. 10am–noon and 2–6pm, Sun. 2–6pm.
Admission charge.
The **Musée des Métallurgistes** stands on the right bank of the river Blavet, on the site of the ancient forge. It will take you back into the industrial history of what was the iron and steel capital of Brittany between 1860 and 1966. The museum has collections of tools, and includes audio-visual displays about the lives of the workers, the trades union movement and strikes. The visit takes in the water and hydraulics house, ¼ mile (400 m) away, which is devoted to the history of the Blavet canal.

The botanical park

Parc de Kerbihan in the city centre
Open all year round 9am–7pm.
Free admission.
The botanical park was laid out in the late 19th C. around a pond and stream with a series of waterfalls. There are between 350 and 400 species of trees and shrubs from five continents. The 22 acre (9 ha) park is designed to show the

Spotcheck
C4

Morbihan

Things to do

Visit to the stud farm
Learn to row
Metallurgists museum

Within easy reach

*Quimperlé 14 miles (23 km) NW, p. 234,
Lorient 7½ miles (12 km) SW, p. 236,
Auray 19 miles (30 km) SE, p. 252.*

Tourist office

Hennebont:
☎ 02 97 36 24 52

ROWING AT HENNEBONT

Rue du Port
☎ 02 97 36 43 71
Open daily all year round, except Mon. and Sun. afternoon, 9am–noon, 2–5pm.
Sculling through the water between the wild banks of the Blavet is not necessarily a gentle pastime. L'Aviron Hennebontais, the French school of rowing recognised by the Ministry of Youth and Sport, teaches rowing at all levels, including competitive rowing, and arranges trips and courses, under a state-qualified instructor, in a basin 6 miles (10 km) long. If you want to improve your rowing skills, this is the place.

visitor a partially cultivated garden of plants in surroundings as close to nature as possible, and one that changes radically with the seasons.

Baud and district
at the edge of the
Camors forest

Quistinic

Vénus de Quinipily

Baud

Forêt de Camors

Forêt de Floranges

Forêt de Lanvaux

aud stands at the edge of the Camors forest near the Lanvaux heath, and used to be a town of prosperous craftsmen. While wood-cutters and pit-sawyers were busy in the forest, clog-makers, carpenters and cabinet-makers worked in the workshops in the town. Today, the town lives mainly from the food-processing industry, but it has also developed as an enterprising tourist centre, which benefits from the woods, rivers, ponds and religious buildings of the district.

The Venus of Quinipily

Nothing is known of the origins of the majestic and enigmatic, larger-than-life statue except that it was once venerated by a cult that aroused the wrath of the local clergy. From her dress, she may be a Roman or even an Egyptian goddess. She is over 7 feet (2.1 m) tall and stands in a field on a hillside 1¼ miles (2 km) from Baud, on top of a monumental fountain.

Fishing in the Ével

Coarse fishermen flock to the Evel to fish for pike and perch. But trout and salmon fishermen can take heart because the region also has something to offer them. The Pays d'Acceuil de la Vallée du Blavet publishes a brochure, listing 28 fishing areas in the vicinity for all types of angling (☎ 02 97 51 09 37).

Camors

Camor clogs

2 miles (3.5 km) S of Baud.

Route d'Auray

☎ 02 97 39 28 64

Open daily except Sun., 9.30am–noon, 2–7pm. You will find every type of clog here, whether plain or with leather straps. Don't think that this traditional footwear is no longer in fashion. On the contrary, it is gaining more fans, especially among those who appreciate the practical nature of clogs for gardening or popping out to the shops. The shop has an exhibition about Camors clogs, since at one time there were 24 workshops employing over 100 clog-makers. You can stand on a platform and watch the makers at work.

The Camors forest

This state forest covers almost 150 acres (60 ha) and is extended to the east by the

forests of **Floranges** and **Lanvaux**. It is ideal for lengthy walks along its wide paths and is dominated in the centre at the Étoile, the circle where the paths meet, by an enormous oak tree, though the forest is predominantly beech. The forest contains two menhirs, **Bras** and **Bihan**, and near the **Motte Pond** there are the ruins of a château that belonged to a bloodthirsty killer called Conomor, a sort of early-day Bluebeard. Another pond, Petit-Bois, is a favourite with anglers and ramblers in the region.

Pont Augan
Ével-Blavet water-sports club
4 miles (7 km) W of Baud
☎ 02 97 51 10 83
Open July–Aug., 9.30am–6.30pm.
The Blavet rises in the Côtes-d'Armor and meanders through Morbihan from north to south. It can be explored by canoe or kayak, with or without an instructor. Experienced kayakers can rent a craft at the Club Nautique Ével-Blavet, while beginners can learn how to handle their craft so that they can enjoy their trip to the full.

Commune of Quistinic
The village of Poul Fétan
6 miles (10 km) NW of Baud
☎ 02 97 39 72 82
Open 6 June–20 Sept., 10am–7pm; 1 April–5 June and 21 Sept.–30 Oct., guided tour, 2–6pm, free weekend visits; the rest of the year, guided tours in the school holidays and at weekends.
Admission charge.
This hamlet contains only a dozen or so 15th-, 16th- and 17th-C. thatched cottages. It has been scrupulously restored by volunteers and is now inhabited by craftspeople. Leather and wood items are

Spotcheck
D3

Morbihan

Things to do

Visit to the Breton postcard collection
Fishing in the Ével
Canoeing on the Blavet

Within easy reach

Auray, p. 252, Sainte-Anne-d'Auray, p. 254.

Tourist office

Baud: ☎ 02 97 51 02 29

✿ POSTCARD COLLECTION
Rue d'Auray, Baud
☎ 02 97 51 15 14
Open daily, 1 June–30 Sept., 9.30am–12.30pm and 2–7pm; Oct.–May, open Wed.–Fri. and Sun. afternoon, *Admission charge.*
This postcard collection is unique in France. It contains nearly 20,000 old postcards, the oldest of which dates back to the invention of the illustrated card in 1889. All depict scenes from Breton life as it once was. A fascinating insight into the past.

on sale. There is a guided tour of an exhibition of local costumes and a video about women's work in the early 20th C. Tools and agricultural implements are also displayed.

Pontivy
the town with two faces

Pontivy is the capital of Brittany's interior and a regional cultural centre. It used to be known as Napoléonville – the canals and straight roads were laid out by Napoleon – but the little medieval town, with its half-timbered houses, was the fiefdom of the Rohan family. Pontivy is an important agricultural centre, thanks to the rich valley of the Blavet, whose right bank is typical of Breton farmland. The countryside is dotted with chapels, some of which are far out in the fields, such as the 16th-C. chapel of Saint-Nicodème.

The château
☎ 02 97 25 12 93
Open daily, 3 July–31 Aug.,10.30am–7pm; 10am–noon and 2–6pm in winter, except Mon. and Tues.

Admission charge.
This fortress is a remarkable example of 15th-C. military architecture. It is surrounded by deep moats and guarded by two large towers, which dominate the peaceful river Blavet. Before entering, note the pretty staircase with its wrought-iron balustrade in the courtyard. In one of the rooms a series of coats-of-arms decorates a massive fireplace taken from the manor house at Grandchamp. The castle chapel was one of the first Protestant places of worship in Brittany. Concerts and exhibitions are held here in the summer.

The medieval town and Napoléonville
The **Place du Martray**, the centre of old Pontivy, is extremely lively on Mondays, which is market day, as are the **Rue du Pont** and the **Rue du Fil**, which take their name from the weaving industry that made the town so prosperous in the 18th C. The winding lanes and cobbled squares of the medieval town have now been pedestrianised. The **basilica of Notre-Dame-de-Joie**, which was built in 1532, is the

frontier between the old town and the straight lines and right angles of the Imperial district, whose plans were commissioned by Napoleon Bonaparte as a reward for the town's declaration of allegiance to the new Empire.

Les Biscuiteries Joubard

Route de Lorient
☎ 02 97 25 45 61
Open Mon.–Sat., 9am–noon and 2–7pm.
The biscuit factory can be visited, but you can also watch the employees at work through a large window. The retail shop next door sells a wide range of biscuits, fruit cakes, pound cake, chocolate cake and other Breton pastries made with butter, in packets or tins. There are also gift boxes of all sizes, and a 10 oz

(300 g) gift box of little vanilla biscuits (*galets*) will cost about 27 F. Cake is also sold by weight. Group visits only to the factory, and by appointment.

Rustic charm
7 miles (12 km) S of Pontivy
This village on the left bank of the Blavet is built on a hillside. Its granite houses, some of which have thatched roofs, have great rustic charm. From its quayside, pleasure boats with guides sail down the river (☎ 02 97 51 92 93), which is a favourite with anglers. In the distance the spire of the **chapel of Saint-Nicodème** can be seen towering above the cornfields. It is worth visiting for its elaborate fountain. The strange **hermitage de Saint-Gildas**, which sits at the foot of a huge rock dominating the valley, was built in 570 and is also worth a detour.

Bienzy-les-Eaux
The Lezerhi Pottery
9 miles (15 km) S of Pontivy
☎ 02 97 27 74 59
Over the years M. Boivin has produced a large quantity of earthenware and porcelain, and he now offers courses in pottery-making and ceramics.

Spotcheck
D3

Morbihan

Things to do

Maison de la Pêche
Learning to make pottery
Trip on a tour boat

Within easy reach

Guerlédan 12 miles (20 km) N, p. 160,
Loudéac 14 miles (22 km) NE, p. 162,
Josselin 20 miles (32 km) SE, p. 270.

Tourist office

Pontivy : ☎ 02 97 25 04 10

LA MAISON DE LA PÊCHE
Île des Récollets
☎ 02 97 25 39 06
Open Thurs., 9am–noon and 1.30–5.30pm, and Sat. morning.
The river Blavet and the Nantes-Brest canal, both of which run through Pontivy, are full of fish. La Maison de la Pêche will tell you all you need to know about angling such as where to fish, when to fish, what it will cost etc. A fishing licence, including the stamp tax, will cost 50 F for a day and 125 F for a fortnight. If you intend to eat your catch, it is a good idea to go and tease out your roach, dace, pike or trout upstream of Pontivy. Ardent Pêche (Zone de Tréhonin, ☎ 02 97 25 36 56) is a fishing tackle shop that stocks everything that an angler could possibly need.

Quiberon and its peninsula
an authentic wild coast

Quiberon is a world apart, which is hardly surprising since it was once an island and is linked to the mainland only by a string of dunes called *tombolo*. Lovers of solitude and sightseers alike can lose themselves walking along the Côte Sauvage (wild coast), while the other side of the island offers an intimate, yet ever-growing, seaside resort, providing all the usual attractions and every type of water-sport.

Côte Sauvage
The coastline has been ravaged by the fury of the storms that hurl themselves against the rocks, creating bottomless whirlpools which echo to the sound of the pounding surf. The western side of the peninsula is exposed to the extremes of the elements. A tarmac road hugs the Côte Sauvage (wild coast), but you can also walk on the short grass that covers the clifftop. The rocks are interspersed with a few sandy coves, and there is a view along this lonely road of Beg er Goalennec and of the solitary castle of Turpeau, which is more dramatic than anything that Chateaubriand could have invented.

Boulevard Chanard
The Boulevard Chanard at Port-Maria is always busy because there are frequent sailings from here to Belle-Île, Houat and Hoëdic. The Boulevard is to Quiberon more or less what the Croisette is to Cannes. You should take a stroll along the Grande Plage, where you will meet a varied crowd.

The benefits of the sea
Thalassa Quiberon, Pointe de Goulvars, BP 170, 56170 Quiberon Cedex ☎ 02 97 50 20 00 Thalassotherapy is one of the healthiest of natural cures. Physiotherapy, seawater baths and massage have withstood

the tests of time and orthodox medicine. The Quiberon centre, which extends into the sea for 8¾ miles (14 km) at the southern tip of the peninsula, treats all types of rheumatic problems and has special re-habilitation courses for sports injuries.

Museum of the Chouan

☎ 02 97 52 31 31
Open daily, 1 April–30 Sept., 10am–noon and 2pm–6pm.
Admission charge; children under 13 free.
The museum is just off the road to Plouharnel, in an area that was a stronghold of the Chouans, the Breton royalists who opposed the French Revolutionaries and were soundly defeated. There are weapons, clothing, a guillotine and notices explaining the history of the movement. Nearby is a replica of an 18th-C. galleon, which houses a small museum.

Port-Haliguen

Fishing and pleasure-boating

2½ miles (4 km) E of Quiberon
Port-Haliguen is a former fishing village that has become an important marina in which about 900 boats are moored. In summer numerous regattas are held here, and the port also has a little beach, which is famous for its tranquillity and the fact that it is the warmest place in the bay of

Quiberon. The streets of the small hill that overlooks the port are a good place for a pleasant stroll.

NINICHES, A QUIBERON DELICACY
A *niniche* is a small cylindrical lollipop, which is also delicious as an ice-lolly. There are about 50 different flavours and they can be found all over the town and throughout the district. The name *niniche* is a registered trademark, indicating standard quality. If you like them so much that you want to know how they are made, a craft confectioner will let you watch him at work (Artisan Confiseur, Z.A. Plein Ouest, 56 170 Quiberon, ☎ 02 97 50 36 96).

Saint-Pierre-Quiberon

Sports and swimming

3 miles (5 km) N of Quiberon
This little resort just outside Quiberon is ideal for families as it has lovely sandy beaches. Since 1966 the National Sailing School, (École

Spotcheck
D4

Morbihan

Things to do
Excursion to the Côte Sauvage
Museum of the Chouans
Bathing and sand-karting

Within easy reach
Gulf of Morbihan, p. 256.

Tourist office
Quiberon: ☎ 02 97 50 07 84

Nationale de Voile), has had its headquarters at the Pointe de Beg-Rohu. It is one of the leading centres in Europe, and most of France's leading yachtsmen trained here. There is also a sand-karting club, the UCPA (☎ 02 97 52 39 90). South of the town, a group of menhirs arranged in a circle form the **Cromlec'h de Kerbourgnec**, which is completed by five lines of oblong stones.

Portivy

Gateway to the Côte Sauvage

5 miles (7.5 km) N of Quiberon
This picturesque and well-preserved little port, with its bistros that manage to withstand the summer invasions, is worth a detour. A few coastal fishermen tie up south of the town, which marks the start of the Côte Sauvage. Two bays, **Port-Maria** and **Port-Blanc**, are wonderful for surfing. The **chapel of Lotivy** is also worth seeing.

The beach at Saint-Pierre-Quiberon

Carnac
necropolis or temple of the sun?

With its beautifully sheltered beaches, particularly mild climate, stylish villas and seaside pines, Carnac is a foretaste of paradise for many summer holiday-makers. But this summer resort, which is divided between the town and the beach and is one of the most elegant in Brittany, is even better-known for its alignments of world-famous menhirs. In addition to its flourishing tourist industry, Carnac is also farming country, so it gains income from both sources and ensures that the landscape is well looked after.

Beneath the Saint-Michel tumulus are two funerary chambers containing stone axes and necklaces

❀ In the days of the megaliths
Musée de la Préhistoire, 10 Place de la Chapelle
☎ 02 97 52 22 04
Open daily July–Aug., 10am–6.30pm; rest of the year: 10am–noon and 2–5pm. Closed Tues.

Admission charge.
The two-storey museum boasts a collection of 6,500 items – ceramics, jewellery, tools, skeletons and so forth – covering every period from the Palaeolithic to the Middle Ages. The most complete collection is that of the Neolithic period, which includes many polished axeheads. There is a stimulating multimedia performance called the **Archéoscope**, which takes you right back to the time of the megaliths. Open mid-Feb. to mid-Nov. and during the Christmas holidays. For information ☎ 02 97 52 07 49.

The alignments
The lines of stones rise up from the moorland and scrub over a distance of about 2½ miles (4 km). There are

The church of Carnac, dedicated to St Cornély, who is reputed to be able to cure horned animals

THE BEACHES

The five Carnac beaches succeed each other over a 2 to 2½ mile (3 to 4 km) stretch from the Pô cove, which is closer to Plouharnel, up to the Beaumer cove, closer to La Trinité-sur-Mer. There is a coastal path and the coastline alternates between capes and sandy coves, much favoured by family holidaymakers. A seawater treatment centre has been established near the old salt marshes, (☎ 02 97 52 53 54) and surfboarding is an all-season sport here, since rough seas and breakers are almost unknown in the bay

three main henges and they are now protected by wire fencing. The **Kerlescan**, the smallest, consists of 240 standing menhirs. There is an observation post at the **Kermario**, from which the 982 standing stones can be admired. The most impressive menhirs are the **Ménec** stones, which cover about ¼ mile (1 km) and contain 1,170 menhirs arranged in 11 lines. Most of these megaliths are relatively modest in size, the largest being no taller than 13 feet (4 m). Everything points to the fact that there were far more of the stones originally and that they reached right to the river Crach, which means that they would have been up to 5 miles (8 km) long. A semi-circular cromlech precedes the Ménec and Kerlescan alignments, and the Kermario alignment is preceded by a dolmen. Like Stonehenge, all three are oriented precisely towards the sunrise at the summer solstice or the equinoxes.

The Saint-Michel tumulus

This tumulus on the road to Trinité-sur-Mer is 39 feet (12 m) high, 410 feet (125 m) long and 197 feet (60 m) wide. It is topped by a chapel, a little calvary and an explanatory notice detailing the huge panorama of the bay of Quiberon, Belle-Île, the Rhuys peninsula, the standing stones and the slate roofs of Carnac. Entry to the tumulus is through a very low corridor that opens into its southern aspect. It consists of two

funerary chambers and 20 or so stone boxes, which contained jewellery and various bones.

La Trinité-sur-Mer

Regattas and tall ships

3 miles (4.5 km) E of Carnac

La Trinité is the former port of

Carnac, and it has become world-famous as the yachting port of the champions. This is where Éric Tabarly and his successors experienced their moments of glory before they collected prizes around the world. The Trinité marina has berths for over 1,000 yachts and is always full. Races, regattas and parades of tall ships are held throughout the year, so it is not surprising that in season there is a major sale of maritime objects, new and old – scientific instruments, model ships, furniture and navigational aids. For information ☎ 02 97 47 26 32.

Locmariaquer, port of the Gulf of Morbihan

This important historical site, which contains the most impressive menhirs and dolmens of the region, is also a charming village, which faces Port-Navalo and controls the entrance to the gulf of Morbihan. The number of inhabitants of this little seaside resort, which out of season is mainly inhabited by farmers, market gardeners and oyster-farmers, grows tenfold in the summer. It is now at such a point that tourism is tending to take over from traditional local occupations.

The Mané Lud tumulus

When you arrive in Locmariaquer, look to your right and you will get an idea of the stones found in this area from the 260 foot (80 m) high tumulus, which contains two lines of menhirs.

When they were discovered, they were topped with horses' skulls and human bones were found at the end of a corridor leading to a sort of crypt. This imposing tumulus, terminating in a dolmen, is about 4,000 years old.

The Kerpenhir headland

If you follow the shoreline, you will reach the Pointe de Kerpenhir at the other end of the gulf of Morbihan. The granite statue of Notre-Dame-de-Kerdro was erected to protect sailors. From the narrows, there is a wonderful view of the gulf waters mixing with those of the Atlantic Ocean. From the Pointe de Kerpenhir to the mouth of the river Crac'h there is a succession of lovely sandy beaches, which are popular with water-sports enthusiasts and bathers.

Notre-Dame-de-Kerdro

This little 11th-C. granite structure near the new Locmariaquer town hall in the central square of the town has subsided several times. The nave and aisles were reconstructed in the 18th C., and the beautiful vaulted ceiling is now nearly 4 feet (1.2 m) lower than it was when the church was first built. The capitals of the columns are beautifully carved with foliage, rams' heads and other elegant motifs.

The Great Menhir and the Table des Marchands

These two great megaliths at the entrance to the town form part of the tumulus of **Er Grah**. The complex is open daily to the public in summer, 10am–7pm (in other months call for information ☎ 02 97 57 37 59). Admission charge. The **Great Menhir**, or broken menhir, is the largest in the world. It is about 65 feet (20 m) long and weighs 350 tonnes. Unfortunately, no one can tell with certainty whether it ever stood upright, and this large block of granite is now split into four and lies on the ground. The **Table des Marchands**, a dolmen with an interior passageway, is close to the Great Menhir and was built in about 3,000BC.

The tumulus of Mané-Er-Hroech

About ¾ mile (1 km) from Locmariaquer there is a strange mound, 39 feet (12 m) high. It is the tumulus of Mané-Er-Hroech, whose name means 'mound of the woman'. A flight of 23 steps provides access to the funerary chamber and the dry stones of which it consists. The top was drilled in 1863, and this revealed numerous artefacts, including a ring made of serpentine stone, pearls, pendants and at least 100 polished stone axes.

The vast dolmen is known as the Table des Marchands *from the name of the family who owned the land on which it stands.*

Spotcheck
D4

Morbihan

Things to do

Menhirs, dolmens and tumuli
Swimming and water sports

Within easy reach

*Morbihan Gulf, p. 256,
Vannes 17 miles (28 km)
NE, p. 258.*

Tourist office

Locmariaquer:
☎ 02 97 57 33 05

LA TRINITAINE

☎ 02 97 55 02 04
Open 9am–noon and 2–7pm; June–Aug. 9am–8pm.
La Trinitaine is based between Crac'h, home of the trans-atlantic oarsman, Gérard d'Aboville, and Locmariaquer. This company has its own retail outlet which offers a complete range of regional products – honey, jams, liqueurs, wines, pâtés and preserves, with the emphasis on cakes and biscuits, *galettes* and other sweets and deserts, which are sold in all types of packages.

Auray
from river to sea

Auray is an ancient town built on the steep-sided estuary of the Loch, which at this point is called the river Auray. It was the home of Georges Cadoudal (1771–1804), one of the leaders of the Chouans, the anti-Revolutionary movement. Auray's old town is intact, and its little harbour is miraculously preserved. It lives mainly on income from tourism and a flourishing retail trade, but it is also an important centre for small traders and craftsmen.

A walk in the town

The Saint-Goustan district is the area of Auray that has the most character. It is reached by crossing a 17th-C. stone bridge. The Place Saint-Sauveur, on the left bank of this old port, is used as a landing quay and is surrounded by handsome 15th-C. stone buildings. The Rue Saint-Sauveur, part of which is stepped, climbs the cliff to the church of Saint-Goustan, which was built in 1469. Another pleasant walk is from the Place de la République, from where the Rue du Père-Éternel leads to the **Loch Promenade**, a terraced riverside walk with a lovely view over the port and estuary.

Goélette-museum
Port de Saint-Goustan
☎ **02 97 56 63 38**
Open 28 Mar.–30 Sept., 10am–7pm.
Admission charge.
This old tuna-fishing boat, now converted into a schooner, is a museum dedicated to the story of the sailors and seafaring in the area. The port was very busy until the early 20th C., and Benjamin Franklin landed here in 1776, while fighting in the War of Independence, to ask for help from Louis XVI.

There are models and artefacts, and you can rent an audio tour.

The river Auray
You can explore the 3 miles (5 km) of estuary on a pleasure boat, sailing from Saint-Goustan on one of the **Navix** launches.

(☎ 02 97 46 60 00). There are various trips on offer (half-day, full day, trip to the gulf of Morbihan), at affordable prices. Sailings are from 17 May to 15 September. The banks of the Loch are lined with woods in which one can glimpse manor houses and other stately homes. These include the Château du Plessis-Kaer, built in the 16th C. to replace a medieval fortress. A detour to the neighbouring river Bono reveals another port.

The tide-mills

The tide-mills were a way of harnessing the powers of wind, fresh water and the sea, and they have been in use in Brittany since the Middle Ages. There are a few at the mouth of the Rance, but they are most numerous in the gulf of Morbihan, particularly around Auray. The space behind a dyke was filled with water while the tide was coming in and it was later released, turning the mill-wheels. Several of the remaining tide-mills are open to the public, includ-

ing one at Pont-Sal (near Pluméret) and another at Mériadec (near Baden).

Étel and its river

This large fishing village lies on an inlet and is very quiet except during the tourist season. The surrounding landscape is wild and magnificent, and Étel is

famous for the Étel sandbar, a long and dangerous reef that partially blocks the mouth of the river. The river Étel is only about 9 miles (15 km) from Auray. It is a lovely place to visit, and the marshes are home to rare birds and the charming bankside village of Saint-Cado. An enchanting trip in a motorboat lasts 1½ hours (☎ 02 97 55 23 80).

The Auray charterhouse

In 1482 Duke Jean IV built a chapel 1½ miles (2.5 km) north of Auray to celebrate his victory over Charles de Blois. The chapel and the nearby foundation became a charterhouse in the 17th C. and were subsequently restored in 1968.

Spotcheck
D4

Morbihan

Things to do

The schooner museum
Visit to the tide-mills
Excursion on the river Auray
Boat trip up the Étel

Within easy reach

Honnebont 19 miles
(30 km) NW, p. 240,
Golfe du Morbihan,
p. 256,
Vannes 10 miles (16 km) E,
p. 258.

Tourist office

Auray : ☎ 02 97 24 09 75

THE SMOKEHOUSE ON THE LOCH

Z. A. de Toul-Garros
☎ 02 97 50 78 80
Open Mon.–Sat.,
9am–noon and 3–7pm.
This is a little craft smokehouse, which uses green beechwood and local Guérande sea salt. The fish that are smoked include Irish and Scottish salmon, coley and Brittany mackerel. Prices start at 80 F for 2¼ lb (1 kg). Wild salmon may be available in summer as well as *rillettes* and salmon butter. The smoked fish are vacuum-packed and can be stored for about a month. For the best flavour, do not eat them until one or two weeks after purchase.

Sainte-Anne-d'Auray
Brittany's most important pilgrimage

Sainte-Anne-d'Auray confirmed its key position in the Christian world when Pope John Paul II visited the shrine on 20 September, 1996. On that day high mass was celebrated by tens of thousands of pilgrims, who came from all over western France and even further afield. The mother of the Virgin Mary is reputed to have appeared here in 1623 to a peasant named Yves Nicolazic. The shrine is now visited by 800,000 worshippers each year.

Anne retains a fragment of the original carving, burned down in 1796, inserted into the plinth. At least three masses a day are celebrated here at 9am, 11am and 6pm.

The treasury
☎ 02 97 57 68 80
Open daily,
7 March–7 Oct.,
10am–noon and
2.30–6pm. The
rest of the year, by
applying to the
Sacristy and on
Sundays after mass.
Admission charge.
The treasury is an
annex to the basilica
and contains magnificent votive objects,
including 17th-,
18th- and 19th-C.
paintings, jewellery
and weapons, the lace
scarf of the Empress
Marie-Louise and
even the yellow
jersey of Jean Robic,
winner of the Tour
de France in 1947.
This is a museum of
devotional objects.

The Carmelite convent

The basilica
This neo-Renaissance building was erected between 1866 and 1872 on the site of a former chapel. The basilica is linked to the old Carmelite convent, whose buildings surround a 17th-C. cloister. The stained-glass windows trace the life of St Anne and the story of Nicolazic. The altar to the Virgin has five 15th-C. alabaster panels. The present statue of St

Pilgrimage close
The miraculous fountain faces the basilica in the centre of the huge square. It consists of a basin and a column topped with the statue of St Anne. The **Scala Sancta**, the former entrance to the precinct, dates from 1872 and consists of an open-air chapel in which the most devout pilgrims climb the double staircase on their knees, chanting Hail Marys.

The Scala Sancta (1872) – devout pilgrims climb it on their knees

Spotcheck
D4

Morbihan

Things to do

The basilica and treasury
Breton costume museum

Within easy reach

*Baud 15 miles (24 km) N,
p. 242,
Gulf of Morbihan, p. 256,
Vannes 10 miles (16 km)
SE, p. 258.*

Tourist office

Sainte-Anne-d'Auray:
☎ 02 97 50 84 27

The close also contains a memorial to the 240,000 Bretons who fell in World

Votive offering in the basilica of Sainte-Anne-d'Auray

War I. It was erected by subscription from money collected throughout the region.

The home of Yves Nicolazic
Near the basilica
☎ 02 97 57 64 05
Open March–Oct.,
8am–7pm; by appointment the rest of the year.
Free access.

RELIGIOUS CALENDAR
The first pardon is held on 7 March. Then come the parish pilgrimages, which are held on Wednesdays and Sundays between Easter and 1 October, the day of the Rosary. The pardon of St Anne takes place on 26 July each year and is attended by about 20,000 people.

This is where the mother of the Virgin Mary appeared to a poor ploughman, asking him to erect a chapel in her honour. At the spot indicated, the peasant discovered a statue of the saint. Inside the house there are panels tracing the story, an oratory and old furniture from the Auray district, mostly dating from the 17th C.

Le Musée du Costume Breton
To the right of the memorial
☎ 02 97 57 68 80
Open daily, March–Oct., 10am–noon and 2–6pm.
Admission charge.
The museum contains a lovely collection of china dolls, dressed in traditional

Breton costumes. There are also two miniature ships, which were donated as votive offerings, and a number of the most diverse objects donated to the guardians of the shrine in order to thank the saints for having answered their prayers. A few items of antique furniture, processional banners and engravings of former pilgrimages complete this collection, which was started by the parishioners in 1920.

The home of Yves Nicolazic

Gulf of Morbihan
Brittany's 'little sea'

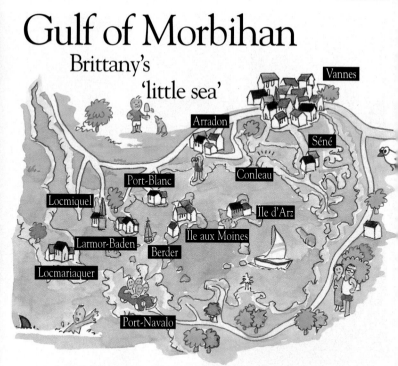

Vannes

Arradon

Séné

Port-Blanc

Conleau

Locmiquel

Ile d'Arz

Larmor-Baden

Ile aux Moines

Berder

Locmariaquer

Port-Navalo

I t is impossible to visit Morbihan, which means 'little sea' in Breton, without a tour of the gulf. It is almost enclosed by narrows, which leave a channel less than $\frac{1}{2}$ mile (1 km) wide that has dangerous currents and contains a host of islets and islands that constantly change their appearance, depending on the sky and the seasons. The ecological richness of the gulf, which has mudflats and marshes and is inhabited by nesting and migratory birds, makes the area even more attractive.

Exploring the gulf
From Larmor-Baden, Vedettes Blanches-Armor
☎ **02 97 57 15 27**
From the Pointe d'Arradon,
Le Blanc Marine, boat hire.
☎ **02 97 44 06 90**
There are several ways of seeing the gulf. The simplest is to take a **Vedettes Navix** motorboat from Auray, Vannes, Locmariaquer or Port-Navalo (☎ 02 97 46 60 00). These boats sail around the gulf and will stop at either the **Île d'Arz**

or the **Île aux Moines**. Alternatively, you can hire a private motorboat or a sailing dinghy (beware of the oyster-beds and the currents!) or

hire a yacht with its own skipper (An Avel ☎ 02 97 60 94 27; Woody Location, ☎ 02 97 47 10 30). The ultimate experience is to fly over the gulf in a light aircraft (Aéroclub de Vannes-Meucon ☎ 02 97 60 73 08).

Île aux Moines and Île d'Arz
The two largest islands in the gulf are very different from each other. The Île aux Moines contains pretty villas and is covered with sub-tropical vegetation – camellias, mimosas, orange trees – and woodlands

with poetic sounding names, while the Île d'Arz seems barren and unwelcoming at first sight. Both islands have fishing villages with quaint cottages and lanes, several megaliths and pleasant beaches from which to paddle or swim. The Île aux Moines (monks' island) is the larger and is easily accessible as there are sailings every 15 minutes in season from **Port-Blanc**. The Île d'Arz is linked to the mainland by ferry from **Conleau**.

The Gavrinis cairn
☎ 02 97 57 19 38
Open June–Sept., 10am–noon and 2–6pm: the rest of the year, call for information.
Admission charge; tickets sold at the harbour of Larmor-Baden.
The island, accessible from Larmor-Baden, contains one of the most impressive megaliths in Brittany. It is a cairn, about 165 feet (50 m) in diameter, containing a corridor 46 feet (14 m) long leading to an underground dolmen. It contains slabs covered with strange drawings, some of which are figurative and which were produced in about 4,000 BC.

Falguerec Nature Reserve
☎ 02 97 54 96 05
or ☎ 02 97 66 92 76
Open daily July–Aug., 10am–1pm, 2–7pm; April-June, weekends and public holidays.
A few years ago, the SEPNB (Société d'Étude et de Protection de la Nature en Bretagne), a Breton conservation association, restored 100 acres (40 ha) of the Séné salt marshes, which now contain a large number of birds and typical salt marsh plants. There is a visitors' centre, which provides explanations about the life cycle of the flora and fauna of the salt marsh.

La Plage des Sept-Îles
From the pretty Île Berder, which is accessible on foot from Larmor-Baden, walk along the beach at low tide to the Pointe de Locmiquel, and then to the Plage des Sept-Îles (beach of the seven islands), opposite Locmariaquer. It has a wonderful pale yellow sandbar, which you can enjoy in peace and seclusion.

❀ Louison Bobet Institute
Port du Crouesty, B.P. 53, 56640 Arzon
☎ 02 97 53 90 90
The Louison Bobet Institute chose to place its headquarters at the entrance to the gulf. It is built beside a salt-water lake next to the Fogeo beach and is in the shape of a ship. It is a health farm and treatment centre,

Spotcheck
D4

Morbihan

Things to do
A boat trip around the gulf
Falguerec nature reserve
Plage des Sept-Îles
Hiking or biking around the gulf

Within easy reach
*Quiberon, p. 246,
Carnac, p. 248,
Locmariaquer, p. 250,
Auray, p. 252.*

Tourist office
Vannes: ☎ 02 97 54 06 56

RAMBLING ROUND THE GULF
Leave from the Kerat parking area at Arradon and follow the red-and-white markers for the coastal path, then the yellow markers to return to Arradon via the interior. This is a walk of about 6 miles (10 km) over moorland and scrubland, via a tide-mill and a windmill. The path skirts an old quarry and woodland, and throughout there are magnificent views of the gulf. You can take the same route by bicycle.

where all your ills will be attended to. You may well encounter one of the numerous French celebrities who come here to slim and recover from their hectic life in Paris. Louison Bobet, the founder of the centre and an outstanding athlete, was a multiple winner of the Tour de France bicycle race in the 1950s.

Vannes, almost on the sea

Musée des Beaux-Arts

Cathédrale St-Pierre

Musée Archéologique

Tour du Connétable

Vieux Lavoirs

Porte St-Vincent

Place Gambetta

V annes is a city of shops and tourism, with hundreds of retail outlets and an old town that looks like an open-air museum. In recent years Vannes has experienced a revival, thanks to the many small- and medium-sized busi-nesses that have opened up here. Its trump cards, however, are its old build-ings which are particularly well preserved, its proximity to the sea and the gulf of Morbihan, and its strategic position on a coastline rich in historic and natural heritage.

A stroll through the old town

The walled city of Vannes is easily comparable to the other Breton cities with a rich medieval history such as Vitré and Dinan. Wander down the cobbled streets, discovering crossroads at which there is a 15th-C. half-timbered house or an 18th-C. mansion. The main market is held in the **Place des Lices** every Wednesday and Saturday. From here, a maze of streets will even-tually lead you to the

Place Valencia or the Place Saint-Pierre, in front of the cathedral, which is a particularly delightful part of the town.

Musée des Beaux-Arts and the *cohue*
La Cohue
☎ 02 97 47 35 86
Open daily, except Tues., Sun. morning and public holidays., 10am–noon and 2–6pm; June–Sept. 10am–6pm.
Admission charge.
In the heart of old Vannes, the market hall, the former *cohue*, is now a museum of fine arts, but the building is worth a visit in itself. Temporary exhibitions are held on the ground floor, but there is also a permanent exhibition devoted to old prints and the art of print-making. Upstairs, the centrepiece of the museum's exhibitions is the world-famous *Crucifixion* by Eugène Delacroix. There are also paintings by famous Breton artists, including Flavien Peslin, Jules Noël and Henri Moret, as well as sculptures and other objects of art.

The Conleau peninsula
Conleau is linked to the mainland by a short road lined with moorings for brightly coloured craft. It has a huge salt-water

Spotcheck
D4

Morbihan

Things to do
Promenade de la Rabine
Excursion in a shrimp-boat
The aquarium
The butterfly farm

Things to do with children
The museum of automata

Within easy reach
Auray, p. 252,
Sainte-Anne-d'Auray,
p. 254,
Rochefort-en-Terre,
p. 276.

Tourist office
Vannes : ☎ 02 97 54 06 56

BUTTERFLIES AND AUTOMATA
Parc du Golfe
Open daily, 10am–noon and 2–6pm; June–Aug. 10am–7pm. Butterfly house closed Nov.–March.
Admission charge.
There are two important attractions, which are very close to the Aquarium but in separate buildings. La Papillonneraie (butterfly house) (☎ 02 97 46 01 02), is a huge, tropical greenhouse inhabited by hundreds of butterflies of all colours. Le Palais des Automates (☎ 02 97 40 40 39) is a museum of automata, which date from the late 19th C. to more recent times. These moving dolls, which can even talk and perform tricks, such as smoking a cigarette, are quite enchanting.

swimming pool to which admission is free. From here, you can also take a trip to the

Île d'Arz. The key to this special place at the mouth of the gulf, which is covered in pine trees, lies in the magnificent view of **Port-Anna** and all the islets. You may even be lucky enough to catch a glimpse of a rare bird.

Promenade de la Rabine

This tree-lined avenue runs along beside the yacht harbour and leads to the Conlau peninsula, 2½

miles (4 km) away. On the way, there is a former **Carmelite convent**, which is now a conservatory of music. The avenue breaks off at **Pont-Vert**, a trading port with an embarkation pier for pleasure boat trips around the gulf. Boatyards and dockyards line the waterside, and the road continues along the coastal path beside the **Pointe des Émigrés** to Conleau.

The Aquarium

Parc du Golfe
☎ 02 97 40 67 40
Open daily, 9am–noon and 1.30–6pm; June–Sept. 9am–7pm.
Admission charge.
This oceanographic and tropical aquarium offers a voyage to the bottom of the sea through 50 or so pools and waterfalls inhabited by several hundred different species of fish. They include swordfish, electric eels and the sucker-fish, as well as piranhas, sharks and giant

turtles and there are even a few crocodiles. The scientific and technical aspects of underwater exploration are explained, and there is a laboratory and shops.

❋ Archaeological museum

**Château-Gaillard,
2, Rue Noé**
☎ 02 97 42 59 80
Open daily, except Sun. and public holidays, 9.30am–noon and 2–6pm; July–Aug. 9.30am–6pm.

Admission charge.
This private museum, which is housed in a 15th-C. manor house, displays various finds from the archaeological digs made at the various megalithic sites in the region. Of particular note are the very beautiful funerary axes made of

TRIP ON A SINAGOT

A *sinagot* was a sloop, which was used by fishermen to collect shrimps and oysters. Take a trip with the Amis du Sinagot (☎ 02 97 42 61 60) in one of these distinctive craft, which are recognisable by their scarlet sails. They sail from island to island around the gulf of Morbihan. Departures are from Vannes.

polished stone, and the necklaces made of variscite, a kind of turquoise, which look very modern. The collections range from the Bronze Age to the Renaissance. An Egyptian sarcophagus as well as a mummified cat and a hand are also on display.

The ramparts

Free access.
Take a short walk from the Saint-Patern gate along the fine city walls, which are

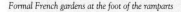
Formal French gardens at the foot of the ramparts

among the best-preserved in
France. Lovely formal gardens
and lawns have been laid out
beside the moat. Among the
sights to see are the interesting 18th-C. wash-houses in
front of the **Tour Poterne**
beside the river Marle, the
Tour du Connétable, whose
distinctive shape has made it
an emblem of the city, and
the 18th-C. **Château de
l'Hermine**, which is only
on the other side of the
gardens.

Place Gambetta

The district around the
marina extends as far as the
foot of the ramparts and is
always busy. It is pleasant to
watch the activities from one
of the south-facing pavement
cafés that cover the Place
Gambetta, the area in which
visitors to Vannes tend to
congregate. The site was
designed in the 19th C. in a
crescent shape, broken in the

Statue of St Paul by Fossatti (1776) in the cathedral of Saint-Pierre

centre by the **Porte Saint-
Vincent**, topped by a statue
of St Vincent Ferrier and
surrounded by elegant residences. Access to the old
town is through the gate.

The cathedral of Saint-Pierre

The cathedral of Saint-Pierre
underwent extensive restoration between the 13th and
19th C. and thus does not
present a particularly

homogenous architectural
style. Nevertheless, it contains some interesting
features. The entrance on
the **Rue des Chanoines** is
through a handsome
Flamboyant Gothic portal,

with 12 niches containing
Renaissance statues of the
apostles. Inside the chapel of
Saint-Sacrement, and in the
nave, there are altars, a reredos and statues dating from
the 17th and 18th C. Several
works of art are dedicated to
the life of St Vincent Ferrier,
a Spanish monk who died in
Vannes in 1419 and who was
canonised in 1455.

Biscuiterie de Kerlann

Z.A. de Kerlann, Rue
Théophraste-Renaudot
☎ 02 97 40 89 95
Daily except Sun. and
Mon. morning, 9am–
noon and 2–7pm.
The huge self-service shop is
650 sq. feet (200 m) long and
has space for 30 different
types of Breton cakes and
biscuits. The factory, behind
the shop, can be visited in a
group by prior arrangement.

Rhuys peninsula
Enclosing the gulf of Morbihan

The Rhuys peninsula, which encloses the gulf of Morbihan to the south, has two very different characters. On one side there are marshes and bays populated by the flora and fauna that are typical of the gulf, and on the other there are the wave-lashed, windswept beaches and cliffs, which benefit from their southern aspect and have an extraordinarily mild microclimate. In winter the peninsula is peaceful, interrupted only by the oyster-farming, but in summer the crowds are beginning to invade the Rhuys peninsula from Quiberon, disturbing its tranquillity.

Rambles on the peninsula

There are 50 miles (80 km) of signposted paths around the peninsula, which leave hikers and ramblers with almost too many routes to choose from. On the gulf side (leaving from **Saint-Armel**, at the entrance to the peninsula) walking is the best way of getting to see the thousands of migratory birds that overwinter in the marshes. Another route leads to the **Château de Kerlévenan**, a rather strange, Italianate building built out in the fields in the late 18th C. Maps and information are available from the tourist office, Place des Trinitaires, Sarzeau, ☎ 02 97 41 82 37.

Museum of crafts and trades

Manoir de Kerguet, between Suscinio and Sarzeau
☎ **02 97 41 75 36**
Open daily except Sun. morning, July–Aug., 10am–noon and 2–7pm; of-peak, daily, 2–7pm. *Admission charge.*

The rooms of this manor house have been turned into reconstructions of workshops and shops dating from the 17th C. to the 1950s. The shops are perhaps the most interesting aspect of the museum, and all of them are beautifully authentic. There is a barber shop, a grocer with thousands of boxes and a chemist with a machine for making suppositories.

Arzon and Port-Navalo
The handsomest vessels

Although Arzon has suffered from over-enthusiastic re-development, it has retained its magnificent beach, the dune-lined **Plage de Fogeo**,

which extends its long sand-bar southwards, facing the Atlantic. Those who love to watch yachts and pleasure craft should visit the Port du Crouesty, where there are berths for up to 1,200 craft. The harbour at Port-Navalo is smaller and more picturesque. The view of the narrows and its fierce currents is one you could never tire of. Find the time to walk around the Port-Navalo headland as it is a lovely place.

Kermoizan

Château de Suscinio

☎ 02 97 41 91 91
Open daily, April–May, 10am–noon and 2–7pm; June–Sept., 10am–7pm; 1 Oct.–31 March, Thurs., Sat., Sun. and public holidays, otherwise 10am–5pm, 2–5pm.
Admission charge.
The castle was once the hunting lodge of the dukes of Brittany. The 13th-C. fortress contains a huge inner courtyard, a chapel, curtain walls and towers edged with machicolations. You will be transported back into another era during your visit.

Saint-Gildas-de-Rhuys

Naturism

The **Plage de Kervert** is an extension of the Plage de Fogeo in the direction of Saint-Gildas. It is largely unspoiled and is edged with

dunes planted with marram grass. This idyllic area is now a naturist beach, but the prospect of all this nudity should not deter you from visiting the village of **Saint-Gildas**. It is the religious centre of the peninsula due to its famous abbey, which was

Suscinio: Brittany in the time of the English invaders

Spotcheck
D4

Morbihan

Things to do

Rambles around the peninsula
The Oyster Road
Museum of crafts and trades

Within easy reach

La Roche-Bernard 25 miles (40 km) E, p. 280.

Tourist office

Sarzeau: ☎ 02 97 41 82 37

founded in 530 by St Gildas. The theologian Peter Abelard stayed in the 1130s and wrote letters to Heloise from here.

THE OYSTER ROAD

Association L'Ostréane, Place de la Poste, Surzur
☎ 02 97 42 05 16
L'Ostréane is an association whose members include oyster-farmers, restaurateurs and communes from the Rhuys-Muzillac coast. Its aim is to promote all the activities connected with oyster-farming. You can visit an oyster-farm in the company of a professional guide and a farmer. Anyone who would like to try an oyster can taste one, with lemon, bread and butter and a glass of Muscadet. If you have a passion for oysters, don't forget the oyster bars, which are very close to the oyster-beds themselves. Oysters are available at any time of day and at any time of the year.

Belle-Île-en-Mer
so aptly named

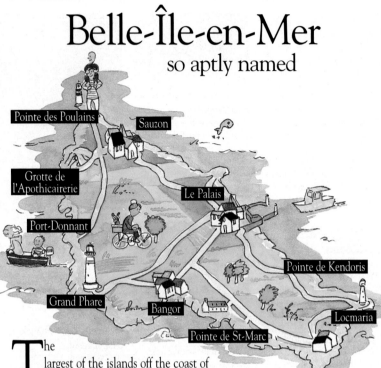

Pointe des Poulains

Sauzon

Grotte de l'Apothicairerie

Le Palais

Port-Donnant

Pointe de Kendoris

Grand Phare

Bangor

Locmaria

Pointe de St-Marc

The largest of the islands off the coast of Brittany, Belle-Île is 10½ miles (17 km) long and between 3 and 6 miles (5–10 km) wide, and it thoroughly deserves its name of 'beautiful island'. Everything here will put you under its spell – the green valleys, the moorland, the magnificent beaches surrounded by dark reefs and the tiny villages with their quaint little houses. All these attractions have brought floods of tourists to the island, whose economy is derived mostly from this source. The island has, however, retained all its original charm.

At the tip of the island: the headland and the Poulains lighthouse

Le Palais

The most striking features as you approach Belle-Île are the massive ramparts and walls of the citadel, which proudly guard against the waves. As soon as you set foot on the quay you will feel that life goes on at a different pace – everything seems to be slower and calmer. Le Palais, the main town on the island, is redolent of this tranquillity.

The Quai Jacques-le-Blanc is lined with a succession of bars and cafés, and the road leads to the Porte Vauban. The sea has cut into the coast, creating a good spot for fishing and a natural harbour. Le Palais combines countryside and ocean views in a way that is typical of the island.

The citadel

Le Palais
☎ 02 97 31 84 17
Open daily, 9.30am–6pm (7pm in summer).
Admission charge.
After crossing the footbridge over the lock and going through the Porte du Bourg, walk beside the large moat to

Spotcheck
D5

Morbihan ○

Things to do

Go round the island on foot or bike.
Visit the Grands-Sables beach
Visit the Grand Phare

Tourist office

Le Palais : ☎ 02 97 31 81 93

the castle keep. A signposted tour takes you to the various parts of the citadel, on which work began in 1549. It was later extended by Vauban, before being abandoned, then sold by the French army in 1960, and it is now in private hands. The visit includes the museum, the round powder magazine, the armoury with its fine timbering, and the

block-houses. From the Bastion du Gouverneur there is a wonderful view of Le Palais and the coastline.

The museum

Open daily, 9.30am–6pm. *Admission charge.* The museum is housed in the blockhouses. Beneath the handsome Louis XIII vaulted ceiling, the history of Belle-Île and its famous visitors can be traced

through dozens of documents. The actresses Sarah Bernhardt and Arletty and the composer Albert Roussel were frequent visitors. Claude Monet is said to have painted the Needles of Port-Coton 38 times.

Sauzon

The village is at the western tip of the island. It stands on the banks of an estuary ³/₄ mile (1.2 km) deep and looks like something out of a picture postcard. At the entrance to the little fishing

harbour, where the quays are piled high with boxes of shellfish, there is also a small lighthouse. The rainbow of the pastel pinks, blues and greens of the doors and windows harmonises with the brighter colours of the boats which are moored just below the houses.

Pointe des Poulains

The Pointe des Poulains in the northwest of the island is one of the most magnificent of the sights Belle-Île has to offer. The ragged reefs, islets and isthmuses are partially submerged by the raging surf – it may even be as wild as the Côte Sauvage! It is here, at this isolated and majestic spot, close to the fort that bears her name and whose ruins can still be seen, that the great actress Sarah Bernhardt (1844–1923) chose to live in 1893.

Work on the citadel began in 1549, but it was Vauban, more than a century later, who built the wall and gate around the fortress

Grotte de l'Apothicairerie

This is another extraordinary sight. The cave is called 'the apothecary's shop' because the cormorants' nests are lined up on the cliff above it just like bottles in an old-fashioned chemist's shop. The cave is reached by a little path that runs along the cliff top, from where slippery steps lead down to it. Inside, you can hear the waves pounding on the rock. The cave is too dangerous to visit in bad weather although the cliff top view is dramatic. When the sea is calm, the water is a magnificent turquoise blue.

Barnacle collection is strictly controlled and is permitted only in December and January. Although not eaten much in France, goose barnacles are popular in Spain, and exports fetch high prices.

pleasure boats leave from Vannes and Port-Navalo, and the **Le Garcie-Ferrande** company (☎ 02 40 23 34 10) has boats leaving from La Turballe and Le Croisic.

Port-Donnant beach

This is the most beautiful beach on Belle-Île. It is shaped like a trapezium,

Barnacle collecting

Belle-Île is known for a rare crustacean, which enjoys being pounded by the surf. The French name, *pouce pied*, comes from the fact that it is said to resemble a thumb (*pouce*). In English it is called a goose barnacle because it resembles a goose-neck. Like all barnacles, it clings to inaccessible rocks and can be detached only with difficulty.

How to get there

In season the **Compagnie Morbihanaise et Nantaise de Navigation** (☎ 02 97 50 06 90) has 13 daily departures from Quiberon. Out of season there are fewer sailings (8 to 10), but the crossing time is the same – 45 minutes. Between April and September the **Vedettes Navix** (☎ 02 97 46 60 00)

LE GRAND PHARE

Commune de Bangor
☎ **02 97 31 82 08**
Open daily 1 July–15 Sept., 10.30am–noon and 2–5pm.
Free access.
The lighthouse tower is 154 ft (47 m) tall and was built between 1824 and 1835. It stands at 302 ft (92 m) above sea level. After climbing its 256 steps and if the weather is clear, you should be able to see the whole of the coastline from Lorient to Le Croisic. This is one of the most powerful French lighthouses, with a range of 70 miles (110 km).

deserted by fishermen. It has a fine sandy beach.

Grands-Sables beach

This, the largest beach on the island, is 1¼ miles (2 km) long. It is also one of the nicest and most sheltered beaches since it is located on what on Belle-Île is called the 'inside coast' (*en dedans*), meaning that it faces north towards Quiberon and the mainland.

This side of the island is less subject to storms and has lush green valleys. The Grands-Sables are separated from the road by a string of sand dunes and retain important remnants of the fortifications erected in the 17th C. to protect the island from the English invaders.

wider at the back than the front, and is surrounded by a lattice of cliffs. It is swept by gigantic breakers, especially in bad weather, so bathing is dangerous. There are other beaches where the rocks act as breakwaters and where it is safe to swim. One of the best of these is the **Herlin** beach, located within the little commune of Bangor, between the Grand-Village headland and the Saint-Marc headland. Since these beaches are less accessible, they are quieter in high season.

Locmaria

This quaint little village in the southeast corner of the island has tiny, white-painted houses and a parish church which dates from 1714 and is dedicated to Notre-Dame de Boistord. Inside, there is a handsome votive offering of a frigate with two rows of cannon. A road below Locmaria, which is said to be the home of wizards, leads to Port-Maria, once the port of the commune but now

TOURING THE ISLAND ON FOOT OR BY BIKE

The best way to see the island is by bicycle. It is easy to rent one on the quayside in Le Palais (facing the landing stage). There are lots of signposted routes, which avoid the main roads and allow easy access to each of the four villages on the island in turn. The tourist office also sells a guide in which all the hiking, rambling and biking routes are marked (☎ 02 97 31 81 93).

The little church of Locmaria

Houat and Hoëdic
duck and duckling

The islet of Er Yoc'h, near Houat

B elle-Île's two neighbouring islands, Houat and Hoëdic, are havens of peace and quiet. No cars, or very few, are allowed here. There is only the wind, the moor, the sand, the cliffs and a few low houses huddled together against the elements. The combined population of these twin islands, which are 3 miles and 1½ miles (5 and 2.5 km) long respectively, amounts to barely 530 inhabitants, but they cling to their way of life, deriving their income mainly from fishing and tourism.

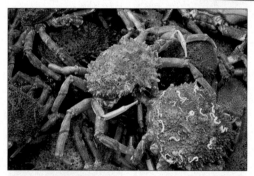

How to get there

From Quiberon, the **Compagnie Morbihanaise et Nantaise de Navigation** (☎ 02 97 50 06 90) has from three to five sailings daily out of season, and six or seven sailings in the summer for the island of Houat (about half the boats serve the island of Hoëdic). The trip takes about 45 minutes, but the timetables vary considerably with the tides and the seasons. There are also sailings from Vannes, with the **Vedettes Navix** (☎ 02 97 46 60 00) and from Port-Navalo, with the **Vedettes Thalassa** (☎ 02 97 53 70 25, only in

season). Other more southerly points are Le Croisic and La Turballe, on the *Garcie-Ferrande* (☎ 02 40 23 34 10) or the *Sirius* (☎ 02 40 62 94 43).

Houat

Port and village

Port-Saint-Gildas is the centre of the island. About 40 multicoloured boats are moored in a V-shape, the

pleasure boats being relegated to the centre of the dock. The quayside is always littered with mountains of lobster-pots and crab-pots. A tiny, sloping street climbs to the village, where limewashed houses huddle together in delightful winding lanes around the church of Saint-Gildas, which was built in 1766.

The Treac'h-er-Goured beach

This beautiful long, sandy beach, which faces southeast, is one of the most sheltered spots on the island, mainly thanks to the string of dunes planted with marram grass and tamarisk, which protects it from the prevailing winds. The beach extends right along to the little port of Er-Beg and beyond in a series of inlets to the beach of **Treac'h-Salus**, which is closest to the ruins of Fort Vauban. In the opposite direction the **Treac'h-Er-Venigued** beach has ragged

The Beg-Lagad beach on Hoëdic

Spotcheck
D5

Morbihan

Things to do

Beaches and footpaths
The Houat ecomuseum

Tourist office

Quiberon: ☎ 02 97 50 07 84

cliffs behind it, which are criss-crossed with paths, making it easy to walk round the island. There are some great views, so don't forget your camera!

BOTANISTS' PARADISE

The landscape of the interior of Houat and Hoëdic is a fragrant moorland which covers four-fifths of the two islands and conceals botanical treasures and rarities. The east coast of Hoëdic is a little paradise in which wild carnations, sea lilies and other wild flowers abound. The dunes of Houat are carpeted with yellow everlasting flowers, wild oats, jasmine and spikenard, which is a plant found only on Houat, in the Algarve and in Galilee. It is mentioned in the Bible as a rare perfume and ointment.

✤ The Ecomusée

☎ 02 97 30 68 19
Open April, May, June and Sept., 10am–noon and 2–5pm; July–Aug., 10am–6pm.
Admission charge.
The Ecomusée is about ½ mile (1 km) outside the village. It is divided into three parts, covering the history of Houat, microscopic organisms and cultivating plankton. You will soon know all there is to know about microscopic seaweeds.

Beg-er-Vachif

The grey granite Beg-er-Vachif rock glistens with flakes of mica and is topped with an old battery. It turns red in the setting sun when it is lit from a certain angle.

From this part of the island you can see the Quiberon peninsula, the islets which extend beyond Houat – Guric, Glazic, Valhuec and Seniz – and further away, the Île aux Chevaux.

Hoëdic
The duckling's charter

Hoëdic is similar in shape to Houat but smaller, which is why it is called 'duckling' in Breton, as opposed to Houat, whose name means 'duck'. It is an independent commune and gave its name to a charter drawn up in 1822, which granted the local rector or curate administrative and judicial responsibility for both islands. The only settlement on the island today consists of a few rows of houses, the presbytery, the school, the post office and the church of Saint-Goustan, which has an attractive 19th-C. interior.

Josselin
the waterway from Nantes to Brest

An astonishingly well-preserved medieval town, Josselin is centered on its basilica and the imposing castle. The winding lanes are lined with 15th-, 16th- and 17th-C. houses. The town stands on a hillside and runs down to the river Oust at the bottom. It is in a region of beautiful countryside, which has many religious monuments and earns as much

of its living from tourism as it does from agriculture and the small-scale food-processing industry it has developed.

The château of the Rohans

☎ 02 97 22 36 45
Open daily July–Aug., 10am–6pm; June–Sept., 2–6pm; April–May and Oct., Wed., public holidays, weekends and school holidays, 2–6pm. *Admission charge.*
This château has belonged to the Rohan family since the 15th C., before which it belonged to Olivier de Clisson. The three-towered fortress beside the Oust is one of the most impressive castles in Brittany, but although the exterior is austere and forbidding, the interior is richly ornamented. The stables now house a doll museum.

Basilica of Notre Dame-du-Roncier

The original building dates from the 11th C. but has been rebuilt and extended many times, and the current basilica is mainly in the Flamboyant Gothic style. It was founded after the discovery of a miraculous statue in a bramble bush (*ronce*). A pardon is held on 8 September, in honour of the cult of Notre-Dame-du-Roncier, who is reputed to be able to cure epileptics.

Canal boating

At Josselin the river Oust becomes part of the Nantes–Brest canal. If you want to explore the 130 miles (211 km) of the canal or sail to Pontivy, **Le Ray Loisirs** hires boats (Rue Caradec, ☎ 02 97 75 60 98).

Lizio

The treasure village

6 miles (10 km) S of Josselin
There is so much to see and do in this beautifully restored village. Several signposted paths offer delightful rambles in verdant, hilly countryside. If you prefer the

shops, there are some excellent local products on sale. In July and August only you can visit the **Cidrerie du Terroir**, on the

road to Ploërmel (☎ 02 97 74 95 34), and the **Ferme des Sangliers** (☎ 02 97 74 86 45), a wild boar farm. The **Écomusée de la Ferme et des**

Vieux Métiers (☎ 02 97 74 93 01) is a farming and craft museum. Every second Sunday in August there is a local crafts fair.

Rohan

The abbey of Timadeuc
7 miles (12 km) NW of Josselin
☎ **02 97 51 50 29**
Open Mon.–Sat., 9am–7pm (except during mass).

This community of trappist monks, founded during the 19th C., earns its livelihood from farming. It sells delicious cheese stamped 'Trappe de Timadeuc', as well as biscuits and fruit preserves made by the monks. Because the monks are trappists, casual visitors are not allowed inside the abbey, but the monks run a retreat for those who wish to taste the contemplative life.

Lanouée

A walk in the forest
3 miles (5 km) N of Josselin
With its 8,890 acres (3,600 ha) of oaks, conifers and chestnuts, the forest of Lanouée is one of the biggest and most

The tall furnace at Les Forges

magnificent in Brittany. The forest also has iron deposits and was once a centre of industrial activity. The village of Les Forges still has a tall shale furnace and the house of the master blacksmith, remnants of the iron and steel industry which made canons for the French navy in the 18th C. The Lié is a stream whose waters once provided steam for the forges but which now provides the energy for a small hydroelectric power station. The forest is criss-crossed with many roads and paths and is a wonderful place for a ramble.

Spotcheck
E3

Morbihan

Things to do
The Oust Canal by boat
Walk in the forest of Lanouée
Crafts and traditions at Lizio

Within easy reach
Loudéac 21 miles N
(34 km), p. 162,
Baud 20 miles (32 km) W,
p. 242.
Pontivy 20 miles (32 km)
NW, p. 244.

Tourist office
Josselin: ☎ 02 97 22 36 43

OBÉLIX'S FAVOURITE DRINK
Servant-sur-Oust,
3 miles (5 km)
S of Josselin
The character of Obélix in the Asterix the Gaul comic has a passion for *cervoise,* **the primitive ale of the Gauls.** *Cervoise* **is still made in Brittany. It is a mixture of hops, honey and water, which has a powerful taste and is an amber colour. To find out more visit the largest** *cervoise* **brewery in Brittany at the manor house of Guermahia, Servant-sur-Oust, a few miles south of Josselin, (☎ 02 97 73 04 75) (open weekdays, 9am–noon and 2–6pm).**

Ploërmel
the heart of Brittany

This town is in an area called Gallo, between Rennes and Lorient, Saint-Malo and Vannes. Ploërmel has expanded rapidly in recent years, thanks to the introduction of new enterprises, in particular food processing and ready-to-wear clothing. Ploërmel stands at the edge of the forest of Brocéliande; this fact and its strategic position on major transport arteries has enabled it to develop tourism and trade.

Place Lamennais

Facing the square, at No. 1 Boulevard Foch, is the entrance to the family home of the Brothers of Ploërmel (☎ 02 97 74 06 67, open daily all year round, by appointment). There is free admission to an exhibition tracing the history of the order, a small **natural history** museum and the

The astronomical clock

extraordinary astronomical clock, which was built between 1850 and 1855 by Brother Bernardin. At 7 Rue Beaumanoir, there is the famous **Maison des Marmousets**, whose 15th-C. wooden façade is decorated with strange wooden caryatids. The 16th-C. church of Saint-Armel is in both Renaissance and Gothic styles.

Excursions in the district

Ploërmel is the centre of a large and very interesting district. For instance, north of

the town at Loyat there is the **Château aux Cent Fenêtres** (castle of 100 windows), which, according to tradition, is inhabited by wizards. Further afield, the villages of **Néant-sur-Yvel** and **Mauron**, at the edge of the forest of Brocéliande, are also worth visiting. South of Ploërmel, the town of **Malestroit**, which is more than 1,000 years old, should not be missed. It has retained a number of delightful buildings in the Gothic and Renaissance styles and has many bridges spanning the Oust.

The 18th-C. Château de Loyat, 5 miles (8 km) from Ploërmel

Spotcheck

E3

Morbihan

Things to do

Hiking and water sports
Museum of the Resistance

Within easy reach

*Vannes 28 miles (45 km)
SW, p. 258.*

Tourist office

Ploërmel : ☎ 02 97 74 02 70

The duke's pond

This large lake is set in lovely countryside about 1¼ miles (2 km) from Ploërmel. It is one of the largest lakes in Brittany and is the ideal place for walking or indulging in water-sports such as canoeing and kayaking, surfboarding or water-skiing. (Information at the **Club les Belles-Rives**, open from Mon. to Fri. and Sat. afternoon from 1 Feb. to 31 Oct.; ☎ 02 97 74 14 51.) There is a 2½ mile (4 km) path around the lake. The lake is very popular with anglers who fish for perch, pike and carp.

Musée de la Résistance

Near the village of Saint-Marcel
☎ **02 97 75 16 90**
Open daily, June–Sept., 10am–7pm; off-peak 10am–noon and 2–6pm, closed Tues.
Admission charge.
The Saint-Marcel resistance cell (*maquis*) is one of the most famous in France. The museum reconstructs various scenes and displays documents and artefacts, such as weapons and vehicles, and retraces the period of resistance against the German invaders. In July and August, a trip in a half-track vehicle

of the period is offered through the undergrowth (*maquis*), in which the resistance fighters hid and from which they got their nickname.

Porcaro

Curates and Hell's Angels

6 miles (10 km) SE of Ploërmel
This is definitely the most unusual of the Breton pardons. During the long weekend of 15 August, bikers from all the regions of France converge on Porcaro in order to participate in the only pardon held especially for bikers (town hall ☎ 02 97 22 06 38). There are usually around 6,000 of them, and they travel to the village every year. The Abbé Prévoteau created this pardon in the late 1970s. Because this pardon is unique, Porcaro is worth a detour, especially as the bikers hold a celebration afterwards, the Fête des Motards, to express their devotion to 'their' priest.

TAKEAWAY PANCAKES
Istace Isabelle, 3 Rue de l'Église, Ploërmel
☎ **02 97 73 33 23**
Open Mon.–Fri., all year round, 8.30am–12.30 pm and 2.30–6.30pm.
This is a wonderful place to buy buckwheat pancakes, which are absolutely fresh and cooked in the pure Breton tradition. They cost 2.50 F each or 26 F for a dozen. You can eat them as they are, still warm, or with just-melted butter, a sausage or a piece of home-cured ham. Another good place for take-away buckwheat pancakes is in Mauron at Andrée Quelleuc, 19 Place de l'Èglise. Here also the pancakes are cooked for you while you wait (☎ 02 97 22 79 85).

Paimpont forest
land of Merlin the magician

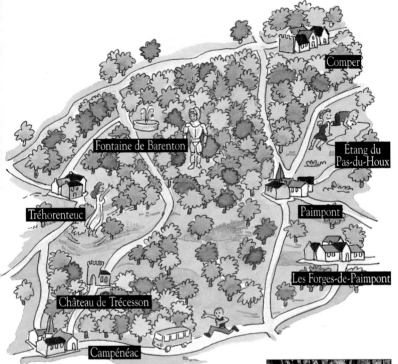

Comper

Fontaine de Barenton

Étang du Pas-du-Houx

Tréhorenteuc

Paimpont

Les Forges-de-Paimpont

Château de Trécesson

Campénéac

This is the land of legend and magic, the heart of Brocéliande, the land of the fairy Viviane and of Merlin the magician in his Breton incarnation. Do not expect to see any strange sights or apparitions, but you may suddenly come across a brilliant lake reflecting the clouds or a mysterious castle, surrounded by ancient oaks. The soil and the district are poor, with scattered grazing land, little villages and heathland. Wander through it at will, taking narrow country lanes, and rambling through the enchanting undergrowth.

Around Paimpont

The village of Paimpont in the heart of the forest is worth a visit. It has a beautiful lake beside which stands a 17th-C. abbey surrounded by thick woodland. The village itself consists of one long street, lined with granite, and is entered through a massive gateway. A few miles further on the **Forges-de-Paimpont** get their name from the forges founded in 1633, of which only ruins now remain

The abbey of Paimpont

squeezed between two lakes.
The site is very picturesque,
as are the **château** and the
lake of the **Pas-du-Houx**,
north of Paimpont.

Château de Trécesson

This 14th-C. château
between Paimpont and
Campénéac is built of local
shale. It looks almost unreal
but is perfectly intact. It is
privately owned and not open

to the public but deserves to
be seen from the outside.
Continuing along the same
road, you pass beside the
Coëtquidan army camp
(where French officer cadets
are trained) and reach a group
of buildings comprising the
chapel of Saint-Jean and
some abandoned farm buildings, which are surrounded by
an outcrop of rock.

Tréhorenteuc

The village of Tréhorenteuc,
near Barenton, is best known
for its church, which may be
one of the most unusual in
Brittany. It was built in the
17th C. but restored in the
1950s in a rather strange way.
The Way of the Cross com-
bines the figures of Christ's
calvary with characters taken
from Arthurian legend,
against a background of local
views. In the village you will

find a story-teller and guide
who will take you to the legendary places in the forest
(☎ 02 97 93 05 12).

❋ The Arthurian legend centre
Comper
☎ 02 97 22 79 96
Open daily, except Tues.,
10am–7pm; entertain-
ments in July and Aug.
on Sun.
Admission charge.
The magical setting for the
centre is a lake which is often
bathed in mist, dominated by
a shale castle, which was
rebuilt after the Revolution.
The centre recreates all the
myths and legends of the
Knights of the Round Table;
King Arthur, Sir Lancelot and
their companions. It also
organises guided tours of the
forest of Brocéliande. The
highlight of the year is
Arthurian Week, which takes
place in July. There are conferences, lectures, rambles,
exhibitions, markets and a
medieval feast, as well as
story-tellers and musicians.
Everything is designed to take
you back to the days of
Merlin, Viviane and le Fay.

The fountain of Barenton and Merlin's platform

This legendary spot lies deep in
the forest and can be discovered only after a good 30 minutes' walk through the trees.
Cars must be left at the

THE VALE OF NO RETURN

Taking the footpaths
marked in yellow,
white and red from
Tréhorenteuc, it is easy
to tour the site, which is
dotted with pointed red-
dish rocks surrounding a
little pond called the
Miroir aux Fées (fairy
mirror). It is here that
Morgan le Fay held back
the unfaithful knights by
weaving spells. Near the
pond there is the Arbre
d'Or (golden tree), a dead
tree covered in golden
leaves, erected in memory
of the terrible fires that
raged through here in the
summer of 1990.

strangely named village of
Folle-Pensée (mad thought),
and from there the route is
signposted. The fountain itself
is a mere spring, which wells up
at the foot of a large block of
sandstone known as Merlin's
platform (*perron de Merlin*).
The little clearing in which it
stands seems to exude an air of
mystery. Allegedly, if one drop
of water falls on the 'platform',
terrible storms are unleashed.

Rochefort-en-Terre
a fairy tale setting

T he little village of Rochefort-en-Terre is utterly enchanting. For a start, the sight of the houses huddled on top of a spur of shale overlooking a luxuriant green landscape seems to have come straight out of a fairy story.

When you visit the village it is no disappointment, as there is not a television aerial or an electricity pole in sight. Rochefort-en-Terre is remarkably homogeneous architecturally and seems to come from another age. Furthermore, its granite walls are brightened with huge banks of multi-coloured flowers in boxes and baskets.

The 13th- and 14th-C. Château de Rochefort-en-Terre

The château
☎ 02 97 43 31 56
Open daily 1 July–
31 Aug., 10am–7pm;
June and Sept., 10am–
noon and 2–7pm; April,
May, Oct. open after-
noons, weekends, public
and school holidays.
Admission charge.
Most of the original château
has now disappeared. The
present house consists of
18th-C. buildings turned into
a manor house after it was
bought by an American
painter, Alfred Klots, who
used several parts of the
Château de Keralio, near
Muzillac. Four rooms are open

to the public, and they are
filled with *objets d'art* and
furniture collected by the
painter. A little **regional
museum** displays items from
local village life. Behind the
château there is a wonderful
view of the valley and the
shale plateau of Grées.

Antiques from the Rochefort district
**Au Bon Vieux Temps
Route de Malansac**
☎ 02 97 43 32 73

Open daily except Sun.,
10am–noon and 1.30–
7.30pm.
The owner, an enthusiastic
collector, has assembled every
type of local artefact and furnishing into a huge space of
10,765 sq feet (1,000 m²), of
which 2,150 sq feet (200 m²)
are accessible to the public.
There is
Malansac
pottery, tools,
implements
and utensils
of every
type, from
a simple
flail to
measuring
jugs, and
everything for every
taste and every budget.
For example, a little bottle
of tooth powder from de
Ploërmel, dating from 1906,
costs only 10 F.

The upper town
There are some wonderful
buildings in these narrow,
winding streets, although they
may give you a crick in the

Spotcheck
E4

Morbihan

Things to do

Rochefort antiques
Walking through the Grées
Magpie Island

Within easy reach

Vannes 21 miles (34 km)
W, p. 258.

Tourist office

Rochefort-en-Terre:
☎ **02 97 43 33 57**

ÎLE AUX PIES

Magpie Island is quite near Rochefort and Saint-Vincent-sur-Oust. It is a miraculously preserved example of nature. There are many signposted rambles, but you can also ride through the island on horseback (there are two livery stables nearby), or take a mountainbike or even a kayak. On the island there are some exceptional granite rocks, which have resisted erosion and are an irresistible challenge for rock-climbers, who come from near and far. If you don't like climbing, you can sit back and watch the agility of the climbers as they clamber over the rock face (information at the Redon tourist office, ☎ 02 99 71 06 04). The island is also an excellent place to have a picnic *(see right)*.

neck. The Grand-Rue is lined with 15th-, 16th-, 17th- and 18th-C. houses, with carved granite window frames and corner turrets. In the **Place des Halles**, the former *cohue* (market hall) contains the town hall and exhibitions. In the **Place du Puits**, the doorway of the former court house is surmounted with a pair of scales. The church of **Notre-Dame-de-la-Tronchaye**, which dates mainly from the 16th and 17th C., is set slightly apart from the town on the hillside.

The Grées plateau

From the parking area, a path marked in yellow and blue takes you around Rochefort-en-Terre. Those with stamina can walk the 6 miles (10 km) to the slate quarries of Malansac, which now contains the **Parc de la Préhistoire** (☎ 02 97 43 34 17). The walk takes you beside a stream and shale cliffs, across moors and through woods of oak and chestnut with magnificent views of the Grées, the rocky hills around Rochefort and the village itself.

Redon and the Vilaine district

Redon's arms declare it a 'small town, great renown'. It is here that Celtic Brittany was born, in an alliance between two princes, Conwoïon and Nominoë. Their alliance gave

Brittany great power and made Nominoë the first king of Brittany, putting the French king, Charles the Bald, to flight in 845. The abbey of Saint-Sauveur, with its fine Romanesque towers, witnessed the rout of the French armies. Redon was born of an alliance, but it is also the site of a happy marriage, between land and water. The opening of the Nantes to Brest canal made it an important home for barges and bargees, to which a museum is dedicated.

Musée de la Batellerie
Quai Jean-Bart
☎ 02 99 72 30 95
Open daily, 10am–noon and 3–6pm, 15 June–15 Sept.; off-peak, open Mon., Wed. and weekend. *Admission charge.*
This canal museum contains a small collection of models and photographs from the great days of the river barges.

The Oust and Vilaine rivers
Redon stands at the confluence of two pretty rivers, the Vilaine and the Oust. Boat and canal trips are available from Redon, and they make it possible to explore the countryside, the Oust lock,

with a stop-over at Glénac, a fishing village, and the Corbinière lock. A gastronomic cruise is also available for romantics and revellers (**Vedettes Jaunes**, Arzal, ☎ 02 97 45 02 81).

Capital of the chestnut
The Redon chestnut can be eaten as it is, roasted, used as stuffing or in a terrine. There are a thousand ways to cook chestnuts, and they are all delicious. There is even a national chestnut terrine competition. Every year in late October, the famous **Foire aux Marrons** (chestnut fair) is held, which brings together food producers and enthusiastic buyers and tasters. At the **Ferme-Auberge de La Morinais** (Route de la Gacilly, ☎ 02 99 72 12 17), just outside the town, you can order chestnuts cooked with

local roast pork, and the whole dish cost less than 100 F.

Tours and detours in the streets
There is a delightful district of half-timbered houses clustered around the abbey. Its narrow passageways lead to the Cours Clemenceau, a square at which players of *boules* gather at pastis-drinking time to show their cousins

LOCAL DAIRY PRODUCE

At Saint-Jacut-les-Pins, Vincent Thébault continues to produce full-fat milk from the local black and white cattle, called *pie noire*. The rich, creamy milk is especially delicious with hot buckwheat pancakes or on cereal for breakfast (☎ 02 99 91 27 12).

from Marseille a thing or two. A walk down to the Vilaine follows the line of the 14th-C. city walls. You find yourself in the old port with its houses belonging to boat-owners, whose ground floors were used for storage, as in Bordeaux. The canal makes it possible for pleasure boats to sail up the Vilaine, which is why the port is so busy in high season.

La Gacilly
The home of Yves Rocher

9 miles (15 km) N of Redon
☎ 02 99 08 35 84
Admission charge
At the entrance to the little town of La Gacilly a local man opened one of the first cosmetics factories in France. Yves Rocher opens the doors of its domain with an exhibition about the background and work of the company. You can also tour the premises and watch the cosmetics and beauty preparations being produced. Look out for the Végétarium, an area of 10,765 sq ft (1,000 m²) that is reserved for

The Végétarium

the plant kingdom, in which there is a reconstruction of a tropical forest and a desert. Naturally, there is a shop where you can buy anything in the Yves Rocher range. La Gacilly is a very pretty little village in which several traditional craftsmen still ply their trades, including glass-blowers, potters and ceramicists. The village is also a good place from which to take a canoe or kayak trip down the river to the Aff valley (information at the tourist office).

Spotcheck
E4

Ille-et-Vilaine

Things to do
Trips by boat or kayak
Visit to the Yves Rocher factory

Within easy reach
Blain 20 miles (33 km) SE, p. 302.

Tourist office
Redon: ☎ 02 99 71 06 04

La Roche-Bernard
and the Vilaine estuary

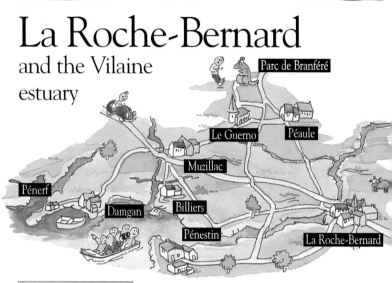

Place du Bouffay

The quaint little town of La Roche-Bernard clings to the rocky cliff face overlooking the Vilaine estuary. A visit to its narrow streets, which are lined with old houses, should be followed by a stop at the Maison du Canon, the town hall, which will soon give you an idea of the town's attractions. The town has a small marina with 300 berths, and it is the perfect place to use as a base for exploring the various attractions of the region.

Streets in the medieval district

Musée de la Vilaine Maritime

Château des Basses-Fosses
☎ 02 99 90 83 47
Open 15 June–
15 Sept., 10.30am–
6.30pm; open
weekends the rest
of the year.
Admission charge.
This museum in a château shows what life in the past was like in the Vilaine estuary through models, reconstructions and a very informative diorama. La Roche-Bernard was an important river trading and boat-building centre, and there was fishing, inshore navigation and shellfish cultivation.

Mine d'Or

This large beach on the left bank of the mouth of the Vilaine belongs to the commune of **Pénestin** and is called the **Mine d'Or** (the gold mine) because of its east-facing cliff, which turns to gold with the setting sun. Pénestin is an important mussel cultivation area and

Cliff at the Mine d'Or beach

also has a water-sports centre (☎ 02 99 90 32 50), open from March to November, for beginners and experienced sailors alike to learn or practise yachting.

Arzal
The dam
3 miles (5 km) SW of La Roche-Bernard
Arzal lies a few miles southwest of La Roche-Bernard and has a dam that closes off the mouth of the river Vilaine. A fish ladder has been created, which is open to visitors (for information: ☎ 02 99 90 88 44).

Muzillac
7½ miles (12 km) W of La Roche-Bernard
The paper mill
Domaine de Pen-Mur
☎ 02 97 41 43 79
Open daily 1 April–30 Sept., 10am–12.30pm and 2–6.30pm; the rest of the year weekends only and daily during school holidays.
Admission charge.
The mill, which stands amid woods, makes hand-made paper using age-old techniques. Visitors are shown every step of the production process, from the pulp to the final drying stage. The shop sells souvenirs and, of course, all the mill products are on sale, from a

plain sheet of paper to paper containing the most beautiful patterns.

Damgan
Beside the ria
12 miles (20 km) W of La Roche-Bernard
Damgan is a popular seaside resort, thanks to its 2½-mile (4 km) beach running from the **Pointe de Kervoyal** to Govet, which attracts thousands of holiday-makers throughout the summer. Nearby, the little port of Pénerf, which has a quaint chapel and stands on a *ria* (sea inlet), is much quieter and is surrounded by lovely countryside. On the way back to Muzillac, it is worth stopping at the port of **Billiers** and the **Pointe de Penlan**.

Péaule
Foie gras
5 miles (8 km) NW of La Roche-Bernard
Doyennée de Lanvaux Moulin neuf
☎ 02 97 42 91 00
Open daily except weekends and public holidays, 8am–noon and 1.30–5pm.

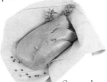

Strangely, Morbihan has now become an important centre for foie gras production, normally associated with southwestern France. The shop is near the factory and sells delicious duck products, such as smoked breast of duck, terrines, pâtés, liver mousse and fresh foie gras. The quality is excellent, and the prices are reasonable.

Spotcheck
E4

Morbihan

Things to do

Visit to a fish ladder
Swimming and sailing
Visit to a paper mill

Things to do with children

Parc de Branféré zoo

Within easy reach

Guérande, p. 284,
La Baule, p. 286,
La Brière, p. 288.

Tourist office

La Roche-Bernard :
☎ 02 99 90 67 98

❀ PARC DE BRANFÉRÉ
Le Guerno
☎ 02 97 42 94 66
Open daily, 1 March–30 Sept., 9am–6.30pm;
1 Oct.–end Feb., 1.30–6.30pm.
Admission charge.
This 86-acre (35-ha) zoo has many original features. Its 1,500 animals (120 species of birds and mammals) are allowed to roam freely here. Apart from the pleasures of getting to know the amusing gibbons or elegant storks without having to watch them through the iron bars of a cage, the grounds are a huge botanical garden and are a delightful place in which to stroll.

Croisic peninsula

The port of Croisic still has an important fleet of shellfish boats, in particular shrimp boats, and it has retained all its authenticity. Now that crabs and lobsters are becoming rarer, this little town, which is still known for its shellfish, is tending to rely more and more on income from tourism. It is conveniently situated for some very pleasant beaches, for Batz-sur-Mer, for the salt marshes and for the beautiful countryside of the Côte Sauvage.

Walk in the town

Le Croisic is the main town on the peninsula and is full of 16th-, 17th- and 18th-C. houses with half-timbering and corbels. Most are huddled around the church or in the harbour area.

The Côte Sauvage

The rugged cliffs, rocky inlets, crevasses and the little bays along the coast offer a great variety of landscapes. After the **menhir of Pierre-Longue** and the bay of Sables-Menus, there is a 22-acre (9-ha) park, the Parc de Pen-Avel, which is planted with evergreen oaks. The beach at Port-Lin, over-

looked by 19th-C. and early 20th-C. villas, which form the beach and resort area of Le Croisic, is well worth seeing, as are the beaches of Saint-Valentin and Saint-Michel, an oasis of calm beside the town of Batz. The Côte Sauvage continues from the Pointe de Croisic past Batz-sur-Mer and Le Pouliguen to the Pointe de Penchâteau. This part of the coast contains many caves, of which the largest and best-known is the cave of Korrigan. A round trip of the Côte Sauvage by car will take about two hours.

Craftsmen at the fish market

For the past decade or so, a craft fair has been held in August in the fish market (La Criée) at Le Croisic. There are puppet-makers, jewellers, wrought-iron makers, glass-blowers and crafts to suit every taste. To find out the exact date of the next one, ☎ 02 41 88 06 27.

Océarium

Avenue de Saint-Goustan, Le Croisic
☎ **02 40 23 02 44**

Open daily, Sept.–May, 10am–noon and 2–6pm; June, 10am–7pm; July–Aug., 10am–9pm. Closed in Jan. *Admission charge.* From the tiniest sardine to the largest denizens of the Atlantic Ocean, more than 1,000 species of underwater wildlife live in this huge marine information centre, which also has displays of marine flora. You can walk through a clear tunnel under the water for about 30 feet (10 m). Feeding time, when the fish are fed by hand by a scuba-diver, is a sight not to be missed.

Batz-sur-Mer

City of Salt

6 miles (10 km) S of Croisic
Batz-sur-Mer, which was built between the ocean and the salt marshes, owes its prosperity to salt. Some of the salt-worker villages, such as Kervalet or Roffiat, have remained typical of the region. Batz is dominated by the

LE MUSÉE DES MARAIS SALANTS

29b Rue Pasteur, Batz-sur-Mer
☎ 02 40 23 82 79
Open daily, 1 June–30 Sept. and school holidays, 10am–noon and 3–7pm. The rest of the year, open Sat.–Sun., 3–7pm. *Admission charge.*
The salt marsh museum was founded in 1887, and is one of the oldest folklore museums.

The history of the salt-pan worker is told through their clothes and wooden tools, the furniture from their

houses and other artefacts from the region. There are models showing how the salt marshes worked and video films showing the techniques for collecting salt and about the wildlife of the marshes.

unusually shaped, pepperpot tower of the 15th- and 16th-C. church of Saint-Guénolé. From the top of the 200 feet (60 m) tower, there is a panorama of the whole Guérande peninsula and the Atlantic, from Belle-Île to

Spotcheck
E5

Loire-Atlantique

Things to do
Salt marsh museum
The house of clogs
Craft fair
The Océarium aquarium

Within easy reach
Saint-Nazaire 16 miles (25 km) E, p. 290.

Tourist office
Le Croisic: ☎ 02 40 23 00 70

Noirmoutier.

La Maison du Sabot (clogs)

5 Rue des Étaux
☎ 02 40 23 90 62
Open daily all year round except in Jan., 8.30am–12.30pm and 2–7.30pm. Closed Sun. off-peak.
The shop has been selling clogs for decades. It has every style, shape and colour, whether in plain wood or decorated with leather. The least expensive costs 200 F. The company also has Breton mules for wearing indoors from 169 F., which would make a good gift.

Guérande peninsula
the salt of the earth

Piriac-sur-Mer

Pointe du Castelli

La Turballe

Guérande

Château de Careil

Salt marshes

The magnificent medieval town of Guérande, whose city walls overlook the sparkling chequerboard of the salt marshes, used to be the economic and administrative capital of the region. On the seaward side of the walls there is the Brière National Park (see pp. 288–9). The city has grown rich from farming, vine-growing and salt, but today much of its income derives from tourism. In addition to its own attractions, it is close to several resorts such as La Turballe and Piriac-sur-Mer. The latter is a *Station Voile* (see pp. 18–19) and has an excellent water-sports centre.

The ramparts

This handsome city wall, built in the 14th C., is completely intact, and you can walk among the flowerbeds of the grounds for about a mile (1.5 km). The local tourist office and a **regional art museum**, whose exhibits include local furniture and costumes, are inside the Porte Saint-Michel. (Open 1 April–31 Oct. ☎ 02 40 42 96 52. Admission charge.)

The walled city and its shops

The fine granite collegiate church of Saint-Aubin is surrounded by a maze of winding, cobbled streets inside the walled city. The collegiate church has long been used for famous organ concerts, which are held on Friday evenings in July. Inside the walled city a market is held every Wednesday and Saturday. This is an ideal opportunity for stocking up on the famous salt or on *sali-cornes* (seaweed used as a condiment). Take advantage of the opportunity to visit the galleries that display local arts and crafts, pottery and paintings. The ground floors of the old houses are now largely occupied by souvenir shops and those selling Breton plates and tableware as well as many decorative items with a nautical theme.

Château de Careil

Between la Baule and Guérande
☎ 02 40 60 22 99
Open 10.30am–noon and 12.30–7pm, 1 June–31 Aug. Candlelit guided tour Wed. and Sat., at 9.30pm, July–Aug. Out of season, by arrange-

A lousse or lasse is a type of rake without teeth, which is used to 'pick' the salt from the surface of the pools. Salt gathered from the edge of the marsh is then made into small heaps with the help of a boyette, a wooden or metal shovel. The wheelbarrow is used to collect the piles of salt, which form large heaps.

Spotcheck
E5

Loire-Atlantique

Things to do

Concerts and markets
Visit to a sardine port
Visit to the salt pans

Within easy reach

La Roche-Bernard 16 miles (25 km) N, p. 280, Saint-Nazaire 9 miles (15 km) SE, p. 290.

Tourist office

Guérande:
☎ 02 40 42 96 52

ment. *Admission charge.* This impressive monument, whose exterior façade dates from the 14th C., has been remarkably well preserved. One façade, with its decorated diamond-paned windows, is typical of 16th-C. Breton Renaissance architecture. The guardroom and reception room contain interesting items of furniture.

La Turballe
Fishing harbour
4 miles (7 km) NW of Guérande
La Turballe is France's major Atlantic sardine port, and it

has a modern fleet. Early risers should visit the port to see the catch being landed. Guided tours are possible, and you can visit the fish auction and market (☎ 02 40 23 31 52). The fish auction has its own small exhibition about the history of fishing (☎ 02 40 62 80 40). South of the town, the fine sandy beach of **Plage de la Grande-Falaise** extends over 3 miles (5 km) between the

salt marshes and the ocean. The sea is very popular with windsurfers, and the beach is a favourite with naturists, who congregate around the **Pointe de Pen-Bron**.

Piriac-sur-Mer
A trip along the coast
8 miles (13 km) NW of Guérande
Piriac is a delightful resort with an old quarter of ancient streets winding around a small, 18th-C. granite church. The little harbour is still used by the local fishermen and has retained its traditional charm. Nearby, there are cliffs and sandy coves all along the coast. The drive from the headland at the **Pointe du Castelli** towards La Turballe is a pleasant excursion.

LAND OF SALT

In this timeless land, everything is still done by hand. The principle behind the salt pans is to ensure that the shallowest covering of seawater circulates over the largest possible surface, in order to facilitate evaporation. The Maison du Sel (Village de Pradel, Guérande, ☎ 02 40 62 08 80) organises talks by salt pan workers (daily, April–Sept., at 10am) or excursions into the salt marshes to look at the wildlife. It is important to wear walking shoes for the visit to the salt pans. At the Maison des Paludiers there is an explanation of how a salt pan works, and you can visit one (18 Rue des Prés-Garnier, ☎ 02 40 62 21 96, open daily, unless it rains, July–Aug., at 4.30pm; Écomusée open daily 1 March–30 Oct., 10am–noon and 2–6pm).

La Baule and its coast
Five miles of fine sand

It is hard to imagine what La Baule was like in the mid-19th C., when all that was there was an expanse of sand dunes. Although it is one of the most famous French seaside resorts on the Atlantic coast, La Baule is a relatively new town, being founded at the end of the 19th C. when tourism was just beginning to take off in a big way. Today, this stretch of coast, which includes La Baule, Pornichet and Le Pouliguen, forms an almost uninterrupted stretch of seafront, consisting of large buildings and smart hotels, some 9 miles (15 km) long.

La Baule railway station, which was built in the 1930s

La Baule

Luxury hotels, a casino and magnificent villas are lined up behind a concrete wall that dominates 4 miles (7 km) of the resort's long, white, sandy beach. The Avenue du Général-de-Gaulle is the town's main shopping centre. Few of the handsome villas are left there, although there are some among the pines of the Benoît district. The SNCF (French railway) station through which the first holiday-makers discovered La Baule is now classified as an historic monument and is worth a visit.

La Baule-les-Pins

The area east of La Baule has retained the original sand dunes and the woodland behind them, which has its own **salt-water treatment centre**. The salt-water pools are open to the public all year round, from 10.30am to 1pm and from 4pm to 8pm (☎ 02 40 11 33 11; admission charge). After a dip, take the Allée Cavalière to the **Bois d'Escoublac**, the nearby

THE BEAUTIFUL BEACH
The main beach of the Côte d'Amour, as the La Baule district is called, is the headquarters for sailing and leisure clubs for children. The tide goes out a long way all along the seafront, exposing a huge area of firm sand that is ideal as a playground. You can walk or ride from Pornichet to Pouliguen along the promenade. Beach huts can be rented in the summer and the new pleasure boat harbour at Pornichet, La Baule Nautique rents sailing dinghies and motorboats from 900 F a day (☎ 02 40 61 03 78, open daily, 8.30am–12.30pm and 2–7.30pm). This huge stretch of sand is also a wonderful place for cantering on horseback. There are several local equestrian centres (Centre Équestre de La Baule, ☎ 02 40 60 39 29; Centre Équestre Les Grands Parcs, ☎ 02 40 61 31 62). The Treveday riding centre (Centre Équestre Les Rosières, ☎ 02 40 62 12 56) offers a special rate for a one-hour ride on the beach.

wood, which has been well conserved. Near the Place des Palmiers, the **Parc des Dryades** is planted with numerous rare trees, and there are many flowerbeds.

Le Pouliguen

La Baule's marina and a former fishing harbour, Le Pouliguen is still a busy port, and it has retained many of its original narrow, winding streets. The resort is full of handsome hotels with classical façades and is famous for its shady 15-acre (6-ha) park,

the **Bois d'Amour** (the wood of love), a favourite for walking and playing various games, including *boules*. It is very popular with children. On Tuesdays, Fridays and Sundays there is a lively market in the Halles and in the square, which spills over into the neighbouring streets.

The Penchâteau headland

After visiting the resort of Penchâteau, it is a good idea to take a rest before driving to the headland and the chapel of Sainte-Anne-et-Saint-Julien. This 16th-C. building has a handsome granite calvary in front of it. There are also traces of ancient fortifications on the headland from where high cliffs overlook the bay of Pouliguen and La Baule.

Spotcheck
E5

Loire-Atlantique

Things to do

Swimming in salt-water pools
Dinghy rental
Horse riding

Things to do with children

Parc du Bois d'Amour

Within easy reach

La Roche-Bernard, 18¹/₂ miles (30 km) N, p. 280, Saint-Nazaire, 9 miles (15 km) E, p. 290.

Tourist Office

La Baule : ☎ 02 40 24 34 44

Pornichet

The seaside resort of Pornichet is older than La Baule, and it was once the home of salt workers. Pornichet has retained its old neighbourhood, but, like its neighbour, it is best-known for its hotels, villas and bathing beaches. The new district of Pornichet is a carbon copy of La Baule-les-Pins. At **Bonne-Source**, east of the resort, there is a long, beautiful beach, which runs between the headlands of Le Bec and Congrigoux. Pornichet has a famous racecourse built on reclaimed marshland, a great attraction for all the neighbouring resorts.

Brière National Park
reeds, canals and birds

The Brière is a huge national park covering 49,000 acres (20,000 ha), the largest marshland area in France after the Camargue. The Grande Brière occupies 16,550 acres (6,700 ha) of it, covering 21 communes. In this area of reeds, peat-bogs, wild geese and ducks, all the traditional occupations by which the local people once earned their livelihoods – peat extraction, animal husbandry, reed-cutting and fishing – have almost disappeared. The region is nevertheless unique, thanks to the habitat and the landscapes which change with the seasons.

St-Lyphard

Morgat

Ile de Fédrun

Kerhinet

Parc animalier

Chaussée-Neuve

Trignac

La Briere's thatched cottages

The park of Grande Brière contains the largest number of thatched cottages in Europe – more than 1,000 of them. The preservation of this original habitat is almost entirely due to the enthusiasm of the residents, who have rediscovered the art of thatching. The roofs are thatched with a mixture of local reeds and peat, and they are regularly patched to make sure that they remain water-tight. They may be as much as 27–31 inches (70–80 cm) thick. The cottages are extremely simple in design. There are two gable-ends, a door, a window and a south-facing attic window – that's all.

Nature reserve
½ mile (800 m) from Rosé, along the canal
☎ 02 40 91 17 80
Open daily, 1 June–30 Sept., 9am–7pm
Admission charge.
Binoculars can be rented.

The Parc Animalier is a large and important nature reserve containing ducks, songbirds, herons and birds of prey. There is a 1 mile (1.5 km) long path, running between the meadows, reeds, mudflats and stretches of water, from which one can see the birds from various hides. A visit should last about two hours, and bird-watching is best done in the morning. Close by is the **Maison de l'Éclusier** (lock-keeper's house), which has two floors displaying the history and occupations of the marsh.

Saint-Lyphard
The bell-tower
☎ 02 40 91 41 34
Open daily April–Sept.,
10am–noon and 1.30–
5pm; the rest of the year
Wed., Fri. and Sat.,
11am–noon and 2–5pm.
Admission charge.
After stopping at the
Chapelle-des-Marais (tourist
office, ☎ 02 40 66 85 01),
you cross a mosaic of canals
and *piardes*, expanses of
water, until you reach
Saint-Lyphard. If you climb
the bell-tower you will have
a wonderful view over the
marshes, which will give
you a good idea of this
watery region.

Île de Fédrun
La maison
de la Mariée
130, Île de Fédrun
☎ 02 40 91 65 91
Open daily except Tues.,
1 April–31 Oct.,
10am–12.30pm and
2–7pm.
*Admission
charge*
Fédrun is an
island set amid
the reed-
beds and is
the most
interesting
of such
islands in
Brière. Although it
had been developed, the site

BOATING IN THE PARK
There is nothing quite
like a boat trip in a
chaland, a barge for
discovering the natural
wonders of the Brière
National Park. Some
trips combine a car-
riage ride with the
boat trip. Between land
and marsh, cottages
and little gardens, the
landscape is always
enchanting. Allow 30 to
40 F per person for a
guided tour or 80 to
100 F for hiring a
rowing-boat or a punt
if you know how to han-
dle one. It is best to
book in advance. On
the Île de Fédrun:
☎ 02 40 91 61 28
(Gisèle Aoustin);
☎ 02 40 88 50 73
(André Moyon). At
Saint-Lyphard ;
☎ 02 40 91 32 02
(Yannick Thual);
☎ 02 40 91 46 48
(Nicolas Legal). At La
Chaussée-Neuve;
☎ 02 40 01 21 46
(Anthony Mahé);
☎ 02 40 01 24 64
(Michel Crusson).

retained much of its charm
and is now protected. The
Maison de la Mariée at No.
130 contains a **collection of
wedding apparel**, and No.
308 is the restored interior
of a Brière thatched cottage.

Spotcheck
E5

Loire-Atlantique

Things to do
La maison de la Mariée
Kerhinet and its museum
The nature reserve
Boating in the park

Within easy reach
*La Roche-Bernard 9 miles
(15 km) N, p. 280,
Saint-Nazaire 6 miles
(10 km) S, p. 290.*

Tourist office
Chapelle-des-Marais:
☎ 02 40 66 85 01

Kerhinet
Open-air museum
This tiny village with its
restored thatched cottages
is a living museum, and no
cars are allowed in. At the
museum (open 1 June–
30 Sept., 10am–12.30pm
and 2–6.30pm) there are
displays of traditional
costumes and work imple-
ments. There is also a
permanent exhibition
at the **Maison des Artisans**
(Brière tourist office,
☎ 02 40 66 85 01), at
which craft items are sold,
including pottery, sculptures,
wood carvings and items of
furniture. The **Kerbourg
dolmen** stands not far from
the village, near the main
road.

Saint-Nazaire
birthplace of the floating palaces

Around the port and along its grid-patterned avenues, the atmosphere in Saint-Nazaire is that of an industrial town with the unusual attribute of having pleasant beaches along its seafront. The town is situated on the north bank of the Loire estuary, and 80% of it was destroyed by Allied bombing during World War II. The port became world famous for building the flagships of France's transatlantic liner fleet, such as the *France* and the *Normandie*. Its boat-yards continue to build ships, but the floating palaces produced no longer sail under the French flag.

The Normandie, *launched from the Bassin de Penhoët in 1935*

The Écomusée and the *Espadon*
☎ 02 40 22 35 33
Open daily 1 June–7 Sept., 9.30am–6.30pm. Closed Tues. and from noon–2pm the rest of the year.
Admission charge.
The Écomusée (ecological museum), in the heart of the port district, is housed in a distinctive building. It traces the history of the region and the port of Saint-Nazaire through a series of displays and gives access to the *Espadon*, the only French working submarine that admits visitors. After finding out what life is like beneath the waves in this impressive

The submarine Espadon

vessel, climb up to the blockhouse, as there is an exceptional view from the terrace of the estuary, the port and the various dock-yards and shipyards.

Atlantic shipyards
☎ 02 40 22 40 65
Individual visits July–Aug., Tues. and Fri. at 4.30pm, booking necessary; off-peak, one visit each month.
Admission charge.
The Saint-Nazaire shipyards are still the world's best and biggest builders of ocean

liners, as well as being signifi-cant builders of warships and the largest oil-tankers on

Spotcheck
E5

Loire-Atlantique

Things to do

The Écomusée and
the *Espadon*
Night-time at the docks
Visit the Atlantic shipyards
A drive around the coast

Within easy reach

*Guérande 9 miles (15 km)
NW, p. 284,
La Baule 9 miles (15 km.)
W, p. 286,
La Brière 6 miles (10 km)
N, p. 288.*

Tourist office

Saint-Nazaire :
☎ 02 40 22 40 65

earth. A coach trip around
the dockyards lasts for about
two hours. The tour includes
shipyards covering an area of
321 acres (130 ha), with
gigantic dock gates and massive cranes. An altogether
fascinating experience.

The creeks of Chémoulin

The streets running along the
seafront turn into a coast road.
At the Fort of Villes-Martin a
little footpath begins, a former
customs officers' path, which
hugs the coast to the Pointe
de Chémoulin. This gives
access to the beautiful, fine,
sandy beach of **Saint-Marc-
sur-Mer**, a peaceful small seaside resort, which was used as
the location for the famous
comedy by Jacques Tati,
Monsieur Hulot's Holiday.
It then goes to **Sainte-
Marguerite**, a resort that is
popular with the people of
Saint-Nazaire. Between these
two points there are a number
of creeks, where sandy, secluded beaches cut into the cliffs.

The harbour

After visiting the Saint-
Nazaire seafront, the Petit-
Traict beach and the promenade, you will notice that,
behind the motorboats and
fishing boats in the small port,
there are a few 19th-C. boats
that managed to escape the
bombing in World War II.
The **Pont Basculant de l'É-
cluse** (bascule bridge of the
lock) leading to the dockyards
will take you to the Petit-

NIGHTTIME IN THE DOCKS

**Since 1991 the port
of Saint-Nazaire has
been lit up at night in
a wonderful green, blue
or red glow. The port
buildings, its cranes,
the submarine base
and the silos are trans-
formed into a fantastic
landscape through the
work of the Breton
artist Yann Kersalé. If
you drive around the
port after dark, you will
feel as if you have been
plunged into a totally
different dimension.
Look out for the three
panels reproducing
scenes from *Sept
boules de cristal* ('The
Seven Crystal Balls'),
an adventure of the
cartoon detective,
Tintin, which is set in
Saint-Nazaire.**

Maroc district, which is the
site of the original village of
Saint-Nazaire. Unfortunately,
it was also flattened by the
bombings. The windlasses of
the fisheries standing on
either side of the old harbour,
beside the Quai des Marées,
are typical of the region.

Saint-Nazaire bridge

The bridge has the distinctive
shape of an extended S and
is 11,000 feet (3,356 m)
long. The Saint-Nazaire
bridge over the Loire, where
the river water mingles with
that of the Atlantic, is the
longest bridge in France and
perhaps the most elegant. It
was opened in 1975, and
stands 200 feet (60 m) above
the highest tides, so that
ships bound for
Donges or
Montoir can
pass under-
neath it.

Pornic
and the Jade Coast

The Jade Coast (*Côte de Jade*) is the name given to a series of attractive little resorts, strung out like pearls along this verdant coast of coves, headlands and megaliths, which has continued to develop as a tourist destination since it was first 'discovered' in the mid-19th C. Pornic, which also includes Clion and the lovely villas of Sainte-Marie-sur-Mer, is its 'capital', and there are many hotels, a deep-water marina and a sea-water treatment centre.

The old town and the beach

Any walk through the old town should begin at the old harbour, the heart of the town, which is dominated by the outline of the château. It was owned by Gilles de Rais and founded in the 11th C., although it has been rebuilt several times since then. Fishing boats still use the old harbour close to the walled city with its maze of little streets. Pornic's main beach, a huge crescent of sand outlined by the evergreen of the Jardin des Plantes (botanical garden), is beyond the marina and can be reached from the coast by a footpath.

The Côte Sauvage and the Pointe Saint-Gildas

From Sainte-Marie to the family resort of Préfailles, popular for its rock pools and beach, there is a coastal footpath leading to the wild and rugged Côte Sauvage. In the Grande Rue de Préfailles,

there is an unique **collection of kites**, dating from between 1900 and 1925, which are attached to the ceiling of the Grand Bazar. The headland of the Pointe Saint-Gildas offers a wonderful view of the Loire estuary, the Croisic peninsula, the bay of Bourgneuf and the island of Noirmoutier.

❋ Le Musée de la Marine

Fort de Mindin
Place de la Marine
☎ 02 40 27 00 64
Open daily, 13 June–
6 Sept., 3–7pm.
Admission charge.
The ancient fortress of Mindin, which stands opposite Saint-Nazaire, played an important role in the maritime history of the estuary. In 1983 it was turned into a museum and contains many models of ships, paintings of naval scenes and various navigational instruments.

Saint-Michel-Chef-Chef

Les Délices de Saint-Michel

Rue Chevecier
☎ 02 51 74 75 44
Open Tues.–Sat., 9.30–noon and 3–7.30pm. June–Sept.; also open Mon. and Sun. morning.
Saint-Michel-Chef-Chef is a village famous for its menhirs, its long beach and, in particular, for its famous butter biscuits (*galettes*). The biscuit factories are not

open to the public, but the shop stocks the whole range of local cakes and biscuits. They include the *galettes sablées*, *roudors* (thicker round biscuits), *michelettes* and *cigarettes dentelles* (rolled biscuits), which are sold in packets or metal boxes. A big 4¼lb box (1.6 kg) costs 60 F. A packet of 20 biscuits costs 4 F. You can taste them before you buy.

LE CURÉ NANTAIS

Le Port-Chéri
☎ 02 40 82 28 08
Visit and shop.
Although this curate is called *nantais* (from Nantes), he is actually found in Pornic. In fact, this is the name of a cheese, one of the oldest in Brittany. The dairy uses 5,280 pints (3,000 litres) of milk daily to make this large, round, soft cheese, which is a favourite with cheese connoisseurs.

The fisheries

The Jade Coast is dotted with strange, solitary wooden huts on stilts. These are called 'fisheries' (*pêcheries*) and contain a large, square net at the end of a hoist,

which are waiting for the right moment to be plunged into the water. The nets are used to scoop up a variety of small fish, which are then fried and eaten as whitebait. These makeshift 'fisheries' are particularly common at Tharon-plage, a vast expanse of fine sand near **Saint Michel-Chef-Chef.**

Spotcheck
E5

Loire-Atlantique

Things to do

Rambling along the Côte Sauvage
Maritime museum
Water-sports at Saint-Brévin

Within easy reach

La Baule 24 miles (38 km) NW, p. 286,
La Brière 22 miles (35 km) N, p. 288.

Tourist office

Pornic: ☎ 02 40 82 04 40

Saint-Brévin

All types of leisure activity

10 miles (16 km) N of Pornic
Saint-Brévin is a seaside resort with nearly 5 miles (7 km) of dunes and sandy beaches. Behind the beaches there are woods of pine, oak and acacia. The resort is a favourite for families with small children and the older generation. Saint-Brévin also has good water-sports facilities for surfboarding, catamaraning and sand-karting, as well as children's water-sports.

Grand-Lieu lake
and the Retz

The Grand-Lieu lake is actually a mixture of marshland and expanses of water, and it is a wonderful nature reserve whose area varies, depending upon the season, from 8,600 to 17,300 acres (3,500 to 7,000 ha). Similar landscapes, typical of the Retz district, are to be found around Machecoul and Bourgneuf-en-Retz. Between excursions to explore this watery region, which has

several châteaux that are worth visiting, you can also take advantage of sheltered beaches along the Atlantic coast, all of which have a lifeguard on duty.

View from the church of Saint-Lumine-de-Coutais

Inside the bell-tower of the church of Saint-Léobin
☎ 02 40 02 90 25

The bell-tower of the church of Saint-Léobin; the view over the Grand-Lieu is worth climbing the 173 steps for!

Open daily 8am–noon and 2–6pm.
Admission charge.
Once you have taken the trouble to climb the 173 steps you will have a magnificent view of the Grand-Lieu lake.

❀ Observatory and Fisherman's House

☎ 02 40 31 36 46
Open daily 10am–noon and 3–6.30pm.
Admission charge.
The Maison du Pêcheur at Passay displays fishing tackle used for angling on the lake. There are aquaria full of lake fish and photographs illustrating the lives of the fishermen over the centuries. The Observatory transmits images from a camera inside the nature reserve.

How to get to the lake

Unfortunately, the Grand-Lieu lake itself is not open to the public. However, there are footpaths and two observation posts. On 15 August only, the day of the Passay **Fisherman's Festival**, boating is allowed on the lake, and is an occasion not to be missed.

Footpaths

Signposted footpaths, 6–9 miles (10–15 km) long, lead to the lake from most of the surrounding communes. There is also a three-day hike around the lake's 45 mile (72 km)

The 9th-C. abbey-church of Saint-Philbert-de-Grand-Lieu

length. Information from the Association Culturelle du Pays de Grand-Lieu, Saint-Lumine-de-Coutais, ☎ 02 40 02 93 92.

La Maison du Lac
Le Prieuré, Saint-Philbert-de-Grand-Lieu
☎ 02 40 78 73 88
Open daily 1 May–30 Sept., 10am–12.30pm and 2.30–6.30pm; closed the rest of the year Mon., Tues., and Sun. morning.

RETZ AND THE LOCAL AREA IN A MICROLIGHT
Rand Kar
☎ 02 40 64 21 66
Training and introductory flights are offered by Rand Kar. If you are a pilot, or with an instructor, you can take to the air to discover the Retz district and the Loire estuary.

The museum is close to the abbey-church of Saint-Philbert, a 9th-C. Carolingian structure. The museum displays the wildlife in and around the lake, particularly the birdlife, of which there are 225 species, including various species of duck, egrets and herons. There is a slide-show of wildlife on the lake.

Machecoul
The ruined **Château de Machecoul** was the scene of many bloody episodes in the history of the Retz district, including the bitter battles between the Republicans and the people of the Vendée who opposed the Revolution in 1793, as well as the atrocities committed by the notorious Gilles de Rais (1404–40). Another local attraction is the **Seguin Distillery**, which specialises in *fine de Bretagne*, a brandy distilled on the slopes of the Loire (tours and tastings at 10 Boulevard Saint-Rémy, ☎ 02 40 31 40 50). After all this excitement, rest under the plane trees on the road to Nantes or beside the marshes.

Bourgneuf-en-Retz
Le Musée du Pays de Retz
6 Rue des Moines
☎ 02 40 21 40 83
Open daily except Mon., 10.30am–1pm and 2–6.30pm in July and Aug; off-peak call for information.
Admission charge.
In addition to the interiors and ancient crafts, this folk museum contains a remarkable collection of costumes and headdresses. There is also an exhibit about the local environment and landscape.

Spotcheck
F5

Loire-Atlantique

Things to do
Hiking round the lake
The lake museum
Canoeing through the Retz district
First flight in a microlight

Tourist office
Saint-Philbert :
☎ 02 40 78 73 88

Canoeing on the rivers
Canoeing on the Tenu and Acheneau rivers makes for a delightful excursion. It is suitable for all ages, since the canoes are perfectly stable and the waterways are calm and easy to navigate.

Nantes
the Loire district in Brittany

Musée des Beaux-Arts

Cathédrale St-Pierre

Jardin des Plantes

Château des Ducs

Cours des Cinquante-Otages

Palais de la Bourse

Nantes was the capital of Brittany in the Middle Ages and is, therefore, rich in history. With half a million inhabitants it is still the largest town in western France, is an important university city, and also has thriving high-tech industries. Nantes is situated at the point where the Loire, the Sèvre and the Erdre meet. It was a major slave-trading port in the 18th C., but most of the port activity has been moved downstream to Saint-Nazaire and the mouth of the Loire estuary, which together now constitute the fourth largest French port. Nantes is a pleasant town that in 1985, like many French cities, re-introduced trams. It is gaining an increasing amount of its income from industries such as aeronautics, mechanical construction and electronics.

Old Nantes

Between the Cours Saint-Pierre and the Cours des Cinquante-Otages, the two main arteries of the city of the dukes of Brittany, there is a maze of alleyways. These were once the heart of the city and include the Place du Bouffay and the huddle of houses around the church of Sainte-Croix. Today, these medieval streets have been pedestrianised. The 15th- and 16th-C. half-timbered houses are worth visiting. The most picturesque streets are the **Rue de la Juiverie** and the **Rue Sainte-Croix**, and there is the **Place de la Psalette**, a delightful little garden near the cathedral. It took 12 years to make the 5,400 sq feet (500 m²) of modern stained-glass windows that illuminate the choir of this Gothic building. The cathedral's greatest treasure is the tomb

Spotcheck
F5

Loire-Atlantique

Things to do

The Jules Verne Museum
The Planetarium
Festivals and events
Boat trips on the Erdre
Visit the Nantes biscuit
actories

Within easy reach

*Blain 20 miles (32 km)
NW, p. 302.*

Tourist office

Nantes: ☎ 02 40 20 60 00

of Duke François II of Brittany, decorated with four statues sculpted by Michel Colombe in the 16th C.

Castle of the dukes of Brittany
☎ 02 40 41 56 56
Open daily, 10am–7pm in July–Aug.; the rest of the year 10am–noon and 2–6pm, closed Tues. *Guided tours available; admission charge.*
This forbidding fortress was rebuilt in the 15th C. and is surrounded by deep moats and earthworks; the latter of which have been transformed into lovely gardens. The castle also contains a museum of the history of Nantes and its district. Major temporary exhibitions are held in the 18th-C. tack room which was completely restored in 1997.

Musée des Beaux-Arts
10 Rue Georges-Clemenceau
☎ 02 40 41 67 90

Open daily except Sat. and public holidays, 10am–6pm; Fri., 10am–9pm and Sun.,11am–6pm. *Free admission on Sunday.* This is one of the most important fine arts museums in the whole of France, containing paintings from the 12th C. to modern times. The museum's treasures include some of the *Waterlily* paintings by Claude Monet.

Île Feydeau
This island, which was where the rich merchants and ship-owners lived in the 18th C. when Nantes was a prosperous port, has long since ceased to be an island. It contains some

Detail of lintel carving, Rue Kervégan

handsome mansions with strangely carved representations of pirates and animals on the façades, particularly in the **Rue Kervégan**, one of the crookedest streets in Nantes.

The **Quai de la Fosse**, an extension of the Île Feydeau, was once the red-light district and contains ship-owner's residences, which are worth visiting.

The shopping district

The **Place Graslin** and its surrounding streets are the nerve centre of the modern city and are busy every hour of the day. **La Cigale**, a magnificent restaurant built in 1895, whose interior is a riot of mosaics and mirrors, is at no. 4 Place Graslin and should not be missed. After wandering down the **Rue Crébillon**, which is lined with elegant boutiques, visit the famous **Passage Pommeraye**, a 19th-C. three-storey shopping arcade. The **Place du Commerce** is also very busy, due to the large number of cafés there. The **Palais de la Bourse,** the stock exchange building which was erected in the early 19th C., is on the square, but has now been turned into a bookshop.

Musée Jules-Verne
3 Rue de l'Hermitage
☎ 02 40 69 72 52
Open daily except Tues., public holidays and Sun. morning, 10am–noon and 2–5pm. *Admission charge except on Sunday.*
The museum, which is housed in an opulent 19th-C. private residence, presents the life and work of the world-famous science fiction writer, who was born in 1828 on the Île Feydeau and who died in 1905. Twelve rooms are devoted to the life of this son of Nantes, includ-ing reconstructions of scenes from his works, posters, photographs, games and contemporary documents, accompanied by a collection of artefacts and objects. If you walk up to the top of the Butte Sainte-Anne you will have a magnificent view over the town, its port and the banks of the river Loire.

Jardin des Plantes
This delightful, English-style botanical garden has been open to the public since the 18th C. Its attractions include no less than 300 species of camellias. A path about $1\frac{1}{4}$ miles (2 km) long runs through this haven of

greenery, which is close to the railway station. The garden also contains the oldest *Magnolia grandiflora* trees in Europe, a huge cork-oak, magnificent, winding, tree-lined avenues, ponds, banks of flowers, a waterfall, a menagerie and a greenhouse of cacti and succulents. In the spring it is quite magical.

Boating on the Erdre

**Les Bateaux Nantais,
Quai de la Motte-Rouge
☎ 02 40 14 51 14**
Office open daily,
9am–7pm.
This company organises boat trips up the river Erdre, whose banks are lined with several châteaux and manor houses.

Departures are at 3pm daily in June, July and August, and the boats travel up river as far as the 16th-C. Château de la Gascherie. In July and August there are evening trips on Saturdays, starting at 9pm, to see the spectacle of the illuminated châteaux. You can also take a lunch cruise or a dinner cruise if you book in advance.

Vertou

Visit to the Biscuiteries Nantaises

*1¼ miles (2 km)
S of Nantes*
**Route du
Mortier-Vannerie
☎ 02 40 34 06 55**
Open Mon.–Fri., during school holidays, 2–3.30pm; booking required.
Guided tour and biscuit tasting. Admission charge.

NANTES CELEBRATES

The International Summer Festival, which, is held in early July, is dedicated to music, song and dance from all over the world. Artists congregate around the castle for several days. In September the Rendezvous on the Erdre is a three-day event to celebrate boats and the river. In November the Festival of the Three Continents is devoted to film and cinema.

The biscuits that are made in Nantes, such as Choco BN and the Petits-Beurres LU, are known and exported all over the world. Nowadays, they are

manufactured in a gigantic factory a mile or so outside Nantes. You can see the flour bins, the mixing machines, the cutters and the huge ovens. The whole production process is now automated, and you can follow an assembly line through all

the manufacturing stages of the biscuits right up to the packaging plant. Each visitor receives a complimentary packet of biscuits as they leave.

La Haie-Fouassière

Maison des Vins

*12 miles (20 km)
SE of Nantes*
**Bellevue
☎ 02 40 36 90 10**
Open Mon.–Fri., 8.30am–12.30pm and 2–5.45pm.
Free admission.
This wine cellar a few miles from Nantes offers a selection of about 200 estate-bottled wines chosen from the various vineyards in the Nantes region. The Maison des Vins operates as a local outlet for vineyards and wine-makers of Nantes, and specialises in Muscadet, Gros-plant and Coteaux d'Ancenis wines. There is also a tasting room, and prices are very reasonable. This is an excellent opportunity to sample the light Loire wines and buy a few bottles to take home.

Île de Versailles

This is an island in the middle of the Erdre, very close to the modern city centre. It is covered by a magnificent Japanese garden of waterfalls, fountains and little pebble beaches. There are also aquaria, a moss garden and a lively play area for children. The **Maison de L'Erdre**, which is also on the island, is an ecomuseum that explains the ecosystems of the river and the work done by the barges that used to ply up and down the river in its heyday as an artery and trading route. (☎ 02 40 41 64 16. Open daily 2–6pm, except Tuesdays. Free admission.)

Clisson
an Italian air

Clisson is a city of art and history, commerce and industry: it seems to have every advantage. It is impossible not to be won over by the romantic charm of the town, although the forces of the French Revolution were not impressed, since they set fire to Clisson in 1793. It was almost completely rebuilt in an Italianate style by the Caccault brothers and the sculptor Frédéric Lemot. After having experienced prosperity from the cloth and paper industries in the early 19th C., it lost none of its economic dynamism, and now has a thriving clothing industry, a foodstuffs industry and even uranium extraction!

The château
☎ 02 40 54 02 22
Open daily except Tue., 9.30am–noon and 2–6pm.
Admission charge.
Perched on the rocky peak dominating the valleys of the Sèvre and the Moine, this ruined fortress, built in the 13th and 16th C., is an imposing sight (*photo below*). Between the large tower and the castle keep there are a chapel, kitchens and the remains of the lord's private apartments. From the park there is a panoramic view of the lower town, the confluence of the two rivers and the Garenne-Lemot estate.

From the halles to the Saint-Antoine Bridge
The steep streets of the old town of Clisson, its bridges and flights of steps are a constant delight. When you are tired, you can rest in the shade of a cypress tree. One of the many places of interest

is the **Rue Tire-Jarrets**, which runs down to the Sèvre and has a 15th-C. market hall with oak and chestnut beams where a market is still held every Friday.

The Garenne-Lemot estate
☎ 02 40 54 75 85
Park open daily April–Sept. 9am–8pm (6.30pm the rest of the year).

Gardener's house open daily, except Mon., 1 Apr.–30 Sept., 9.30am–12.30pm and 2–7pm (5.30pm the rest of the year). *Free admission.*

The Temple of Vesta in the park of the Garenne-Lemot estate

This is a very special place. The 32-acre (13-ha) park beside the Sèvre is sprinkled with lovely little buildings, such as the **temple of Vesta** and the **Rousseau** and **Delille rocks**, in the Italianate style,

Loire-Atlantique

Spotcheck
F5

Things to do

The Garenne-Lemot estate
Canoeing
The museum of French
song

Within easy reach

Ancenis (36 km) N,
p. 306.

Tourist office

Clisson:
☎ 02 40 54 02 95

LE CAVEAU DES VIGNERONS

Place du Minage, Clisson
☎ 02 40 54 39 56
Open daily, 10am–12.30pm and 2.30–7pm.
In premises they shared with the tourist office, 30 or so local wine-makers have joined forces to sell and to offer tastings of their wines. These are mainly Muscadet (25 F a bottle) and Gros-plant. A number of the wine-makers also allow visits to their cellars, by appointment, except during the grape harvest, which is generally from mid-September to early October.

typical of Clisson in the 19th C. In the gardener's house, which is built in Tuscan style,

there is a permanent exhibition explaining how 'medieval Clisson became Italian'. The **Villa Lemot** is lavishly appointed and is also open to the public for temporary exhibitions. It has a tea-room, which has the same opening hours.

Industrial antiques

All along the Sèvre, upstream from Clisson, a strange row of Italianate buildings line the banks, evidence of the intense industrial activity in the region between the late 18th and early 19th C. There are brick-and-tile spinning-mills, old flour mills, tanneries, leather factories and paper-mills. The buildings are set in green surroundings and can be accessed from little winding riverside paths. There are two **leisure centres**, at the Moulin Plessard (Plessard mill) (☎ 02 40 54 04 82) and at Terbin (☎ 02 40 54 04 82), which offer canoeing and kayaking excursions on the river.

La Planche

The museum of French song

10½ miles (17 km)
SW of Clisson
8 Rue Paul Joyau
☎ 02 40 26 52 15
Open 1 May–30 Sept., Sat. and Sun., 2.30–6pm.
If you love French song and French singers you will adore the **Musée de la Chanson Française**, which contains a lot of unknown material about the great French singers, such as Georges Brassens, Jacques Brel, Léo Ferré and many more. The museum also contains old musical instruments in working order. Naturally, there will be a musical accompaniment throughout your tour.

Blain
and district

B lain is an important commercial crossroads, situated between Redon, Nantes and the Anjou. The surrounding district is known as the Pays Blinois, or Pays des Trois-Rivières (land of the three rivers: the Don, the Brivet and the Isac). The countryside is extremely beautiful, especially the nearby forest of Gâvre. The little port on the Nantes to Brest canal is used by small fishing boats and yachts, and is a good place to start a ramble. Blain is a small industrial town with some handsome 19th-C. houses, typical of the region, with carved and sculpted whitestone trim.

Le Château de la Groulais
Towards Saint-Nazaire, first road on the left after the canal bridge.
☎ 02 40 79 07 81
Daily except Mon., April–Oct, 10am–noon and 2.30–6.30pm.
Admission charge.
The imposing ruins of this medieval castle consist of two enclosures. You first encounter the austere Tour du Connétable (earl marshall's tower), the king's apartments, a handsome Renaissance façade adorned with gargoyles and high dormer windows. Then there is the Tour du Pont-levis (drawbridge tower), whose steeply pointed roof overlooks the moat.

Exhibitions are held in the castle in the summer.

❀ Maison Benoist
Grand-Rue, Le Gâvre
☎ 02 40 51 25 14
Every day from July–Sept., 2.30–6.30pm.
Admission charge.
At the beginning of the century, almost all the men in the village worked as **clog-makers**. The Maison Benoist is a handsome, 17th-C. bourgeois residence in the upper town, in which the Office National des Forêts holds many temporary and permanent exhibitions to revive interest in this local custom. The locals were not only clog-makers, they were woodcutters, knife-grinders and acorn gatherers. The exhibitions are reminders of the former way of life and also explain the flora and fauna of the forest

(wild boar, red deer, fallow deer and small game).

❊ Le Musée des Arts et Traditions Populaires

2 Place Jean-Guihard
☎ 02 40 79 98 51
Daily except Mon.,
2–6pm.
Admission charge.
This museum of popular culture is on two floors of the former residence of the dukes of Rohan. Among the notable exhibits are 100 Christmas cribs from many countries. In the next room,

there is a collection of 10,000 beans! The second floor is devoted to the daily life of the district in the early 20th C. There are several shops – a hairdresser,

The Gâvre forest

This forest is an extension of the ancient forest of Brocéliande, about which there are many legends. The Gâvre forest covers 11,120 acres (4,500 ha) and is popular for all sorts of activities. In the autumn it is invaded by mushroom pickers, and its 12½ miles (20 km) of paths are used throughout the year by hikers, horsemen and cyclists. The main paths meet in the centre at the **Grand Rond-point de l'Étoile,** from which ten avenues radiate into the woodland. There is a list there explaining the various routes to be taken – short or long rambles, nature walks, strenuous walks etc. There are even bungalows and a picnic site at this central point.

Valley of the Don

This green valley can be followed from **Guémené-Penfao** to **Marsac-sur-Don** by taking the D125. It is a scenic route running between the shale peaks of the district. There are many beauty spots, and the area is dotted with little villages, whose houses are built of the local shale. You may also come across the remains of a Roman

a chemist, a tobacconist and a cobbler – reconstructed around a village square.

Spotcheck
F4

Loire-Atlantique

Things to do

Learn to paint a fresco
Maison Benoist
Walking in the Gâvre
Forest

Within easy reach

*Redon 21 miles (33 km)
NW, p. 278,
Nantes 20 miles (32 km)
SE, p. 296.*

Tourist Office

Blain : ☎ 02 40 87 15 11

THE FRESCO CENTRE

This centre, which is based in the château, aims to revive frescoes (the art of painting on fresh plaster), which was such a common medium in the Middle Ages and the Renaissance. It adopts an original approach. A team of artists present mural painting techniques and organise courses for hands-on experience. You will learn how to handle fresh plaster and pigments and then all you have to do is let your imagination run wild. Information from the Blain tourist office ☎ 02 40 87 15 11.

causeway, which is now used mainly as a hiking footpath. It ends by the lake known as Étang de la Roche, near Marsac-sur-Don, where you will encounter plenty of anglers and hikers. The Don valley is a good place for camping.

Châteaubriant
and the Mée district

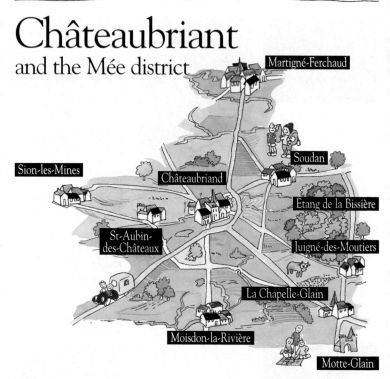

Martigné-Ferchaud

Soudan

Sion-les-Mines

Châteaubriand

Étang de la Bissière

St-Aubin-des-Châteaux

Juigné-des-Moutiers

La Chapelle-Glain

Moisdon-la-Rivière

Motte-Glain

etween the wars Châteaubriant was called 'the European capital of the plough', and it has not lost its agricultural heart. Every Wednesday it holds an important cattle market, and the Huard factory still exports ploughs through its outlets all over the world. Châteaubriant has beautiful houses and a famous château, and it is set in a region of lakes, rivers and forests, famous for being an ancient centre of industry and perfect for interesting walks, rambles and hikes.

The château and the old town
☎ 02 40 28 20 90
Open daily except Tue. and Sun. morning, 15 June–15 Sept., 10.30am–noon and 2–5pm.
Admission charge.
The huge grounds contain a medieval castle and a Renaissance château. There is a castle keep, a small castle, an entrance and a chapel, as well as rooms that are decorated with wood panelling and huge fireplaces, although most are fairly recent. At the foot of the château, in the old city, there are some fine 16th-C.

houses, mainly around the **Grand-Rue**, of which the Hôtel de la Houssaye (1769) is particularly notable.

Cattle markets
Whenever gourmets hear the word 'châteaubriant' they think of a large piece of fillet

The 16th-C. Château de Châteaubriant looks like the châteaux of the Loire valley

steak. That is hardly surprising because the town is the second largest beef producer in France. The famous cattle market, *foirail*, is held on Wednesday mornings. You will have to get up early to watch the proceedings, which have not changed for centuries. Information at the tourist office.

The iron way

Châteaubriant was once the centre of the iron and steel industry, and there are still many traces of the industry in Sion-les-Mines, Moisdon-la-Rivière and Martigné-Ferchaud. At Sion-les-Mines the ruins of the Hunaudière ironworks, founded in 1630, and the workmen's cottages can still be seen. The Etang de la Blisière, near Juigné-des-Moutiers, is a privately owned lake, like many that are close to former ironworks. Bathing is forbidden, but the lakeside is very pleasant and is open to the public.

La Forge-Neuve
An industrial past

12½ miles (20 km) S of Châteaubriant, near Moisdon-La-Rivière
There is little to be seen of this ironworks, which was built in 1668, except marks on the ground where its upper furnace, its refining forge and foundry stood. But several of the adjoining buildings can still be seen, such as the coal bunkers, the workers' cottages and two foremen's houses. The largest coal-bunker contains an exhibition tracing the history of the ironworks in the region (open Wed. am and Sat.–Sun., 10am–noon and 2–6pm, 5 July–31 August, ☎ 02 40 07 22 44).

La Chapelle-Glain
Château de la Motte-Glain

11¼ miles (18 km) SE of Châteaubriant
☎ 02 40 55 52 01
Open daily except Tue., 15 June–15 Sept., 2.30–6.30pm.
Admission charge.
This late 15th-C. château stands on a private estate dotted with several ponds. It was built by Pierre de Rohan, Marshall of Gyé. Inside the fortress, an unusual **Musée de la Chasse** (hunting museum) displays various African hunting trophies.

Saint-Aubin-des-Châteaux
Parc du Plessis

6 miles (9.5 km) E of Châteaubriant
☎ 02 40 28 40 05
(telephone beforehand)
Open Sat. and Sun. from 3pm.
Admission charge.
This park, which contains shrubbery, woodland and gardens, covers an area of 110 acres (45 ha). Jean-Pierre Prime organizes several types of guided tour. In the flower garden there is a **croquet lawn** on which visitors can play; and on the estate there is an old castle that can also be visited. The owner suggests rambles of 3¾–4¼ miles (6–7 km) in the surrounding countryside, starting from the Hunaudière ironworks.

Spotcheck
F4

Loire-Atlantique

Things to do
Cattle market
The iron way
Parc du Plessis

Within easy reach
Rennes 34 miles (55 km) NW, p. 196.

Tourist office
Châteaubriant:
☎ 02 40 28 20 90

L'OCCASION
SOUDANAISE
Route de Laval, Soudan 3¾ miles (6 km) E. of Châteaubriant
☎ 02 40 28 65 96
Open daily except Sun., 2pm–8pm.
This antiques shop specialises in local furniture and small items, especially glasses and carafes. There are examples of old Javardan glassware from Fercé, which was one of the largest glassworks in western France in the late 18th C. There are also chests, tables, chests of drawers and wardrobes, typical in their simplicity of the Mée district. Be prepared to pay between 2,000 and 6,000 F for an item of furniture.

Ancenis

Cabernet wine, pike in white butter sauce and châteaux on the Loire

Ancenis stands on the banks of the Loire, on a shale hill that was once an island in the river, midway between Nantes and Angers. Its position made it an important staging-post, and it retains many vestiges of its past. It has an ancient tradition of fishing and of creating delicious dishes. Be sure to taste the pike in white butter sauce, accompanied by a glass of Malvoisie (malmsey wine). Ancenis has an industrial estate, a thriving industry in electrical goods for the building industry and produces agricultural machinery.

La Toile à Beurre restaurant, Ancenis

Fishing and fine food

The vineyards and the Loire, a river particularly rich in fish, are responsible for the high culinary reputation of the region. Pike, perch and eels have pride of place on the tables of Ancenis, where white butter sauce was invented. This is a savoury mixture of melted butter, vinegar and shallots. **La Toile à Beurre** (82 Rue Saint-Pierre, ☎ 02 40 98 89 64, closed Sun. evening) is a delightful restaurant (menus from 95 to 185 F), where you can taste these local dishes, accompanied by wines from the region.

Tour d'Oudon
☎ 02 40 83 80 04
Open daily, 15 June–20 Sept., 10am–noon and 2.30–6.30pm; 1 May–15 June, open weekends and holidays. *Admission charge.*

This 14th-C. octagonal stronghold, which overlooks the Loire a few miles south-west of Ancenis, is the last vestige of a fortress that itself replaced a very ancient castle. A stone staircase cut into the thick walls enables you to climb to the top of the tower, from which there is an incredible view of the Ancenis district.

A stroll in town

Near the former château, of which only the 15th C. twin towers and a few ramparts and a Renaissance building survive, there is a street known as the **Rue des Tonneliers,** named after the barrel-makers who worked in the ancient cellars, which can still be seen there. The barrels were used for transporting wine, grain and salt. The street is lined with 18th-C. merchants' mansions, with grand entrances and interior courtyards. The **halles**, built in the reign of Napoleon III, is a good place for a rest and has a fountain. A lively market is held every Thursday in the Place de **l'Église Saint-Pierre-et-Paul**. The church was built in the 15th and 16th C.

The church of Saint-Pierre-et-Saint-Paul

Spotcheck

G5

Loire-Atlantique

Things to do

The châteaux of the Loire
Visit the wine-making cellars

Within easy reach

Clisson, p. 300.

Tourist office

Ancenis: ☎ 02 40 83 07 44

Iron gate, Rue des Tonneliers

The châteaux of the Loire

Anyone touring the region by car or walking along the footpaths beside the Loire will be able to view a number of châteaux. Unfortunately, most are privately owned and cannot be visited, but you can stop and admire the superb façade of the 17th-C. **Château de Clermont** not far from Nantes, where Louis de Funès died in 1983, or the **Château de Vair**, in the direction of Angers. Not far away, at Varades, the **Palais Briau**, a handsome residence built in 1864 near the ruins of a medieval château, can be visited on Saturday and Sunday from 10am to noon and from 2pm to 6pm

(☎ 02 40 83 45 00, admission charge). The park is open daily at the same times.

❀ CELLARS AND OLD WINES
Établissements Guindon, Boulevard des Airènes, Saint-Géréon
☎ 02 40 83 18 96
Daily except Sunday and public holidays, 9am–noon and 2–6pm.
Visit to the cellars and tastings.
Jacques Guindon is a passionate wine-maker who will guide you round his cellars and let you into the secrets of his trade. He produces a Muscadet on the slopes of the Loire, a Gros-plant of the Nantes district, a Cabernet and Malvoisie (malmsey), the smooth wine from pinot gris rootstock that is exclusive to the Ancenis region.
Light or fruity, red or white, the wines of Ancenis are an excellent accompaniment to the local hors d'œuvres, cold meats and fresh-water fish. A bottle of Cabernet Rouge will cost around 30 F.

The Château de Clermont belonged to the family of Louis de Funès

This guide was written by PIERRE-HENRI ALLAIN, OLIVIER GOUJON and CLAIRE ROUYER, with additional help from JACKIE BALDWIN, MARIE BARBELET, DENIS HILL, MURIEL LUCAS, FRÉDÉRIC OLIVIER, FRANÇOISE PICON and IRÈNE TSUJI.

The authors wish to thank MARIE-LOUISE CLAVIER.

Illustrations: FRANÇOIS LACHÉZE (P. 134 ARMEL BONNERON)

Illustrated maps: STÉPHANIE HUMBERT-BASSET

Cartography: © IDÉ-INFOGRAPHIE (THOMAS GROLLIER)

Translation and adaptation: CHANTERELLE TRANSLATIONS, LONDON (JOSEPHINE BACON)

Additional design and editorial assistance: CHRISTINE BELL, LYDIA DARBYSHIRE, MALCOLM COUCH AND CLAIRE WEDDERBURN-MAXWELL

Project manager: LIZ COGHILL

We have done our best to ensure the accuracy of the information contained in this guide. However, addresses, telephone numbers, opening times etc. inevitably do change from time to time, so if you find a discrepancy please do let us know. You can contact us at: hachetteuk@orionbooks.co.uk or write to us at Hachette UK, address below.

Hachette UK guides provide independent advice. The authors and compilers do not accept any remuneration for the inclusion of any addresses in these guides.

Please note that we cannot accept any responsibility for any loss, injury or inconvenience sustained by anyone as a result of any information or advice contained in this guide.

Hachette UK, Cassell & Co., The Orion Publishing Group, Wellington House, 125 Strand, London WC2R 0BB

Printed in Spain by Graficas Estella